TRAVELERS' TALES BOOKS

Country and Regional Guides
America, Australia, Brazil, Central America, China, Cuba, France,
Greece, India, Ireland, Italy, Japan, Mexico, Nepal, Spain, Thailand,
Tibet, Turkey; Alaska, American Southwest, Grand Canyon,
Hawai'i, Hong Kong, Paris, Provence, San Francisco, Tuscany

Women's Travel
A Woman's Europe, Her Fork in the Road, A Woman's Path,
A Woman's Passion for Travel, A Woman's World, Women in the Wild,
A Mother's World, Safety and Security for Women
Who Travel, Gutsy Women, Gutsy Mamas

Body & Soul
The Spiritual Gifts of Travel, The Road Within,
Love & Romance, Food, The Fearless Diner, The Adventure
of Food, The Ultimate Journey, Pilgrimage

Special Interest
Not So Funny When It Happened,
The Gift of Rivers, Shitting Pretty, Testosterone Planet,
Danger!, The Fearless Shopper, The Penny Pincher's
Passport to Luxury Travel, The Gift of Birds, Family Travel,
A Dog's World, There's No Toilet Paper on the Road
Less Traveled, The Gift of Travel, 365 Travel,
Adventures in Wine, Sand in My Bra and Other Misadventures,
Hyenas Laughed at Me and Now I Know Why

Footsteps
Kite Strings of the Southern Cross, The Sword of Heaven,
Storm, Take Me With You, Last Trout in Venice, The Way of
the Wanderer, One Year Off, The Fire Never Dies

Classics
The Royal Road to Romance,
Unbeaten Tracks in Japan, The Rivers Ran East,
Coast to Coast, Trader Horn

CHINA

TRUE STORIES

T R A V E L E R S ' T A L E S

CHINA

TRUE STORIES

Edited by

SEAN O'REILLY, JAMES O'REILLY
AND LARRY HABEGGER

TRAVELERS' TALES
SAN FRANCISCO

Art direction: Stefan Gutermuth
Interior design: Kathryn Heflin and Susan Bailey
Cover photograph: Edward J. Kazmirski. Cormorant fisherman.
Page layout: Cynthia Lamb, using the font Bembo

Distributed by: Publishers Group West, 1700 Fourth Street, Berkeley, California 94710.

Library of Congress Cataloguing-in-Publication Data

Travelers' tales China : true stories / edited by Sean O'Reilly, James O'Reilly and Larry Habegger.
    p. cm.
    ISBN 1-932361-07-3 (pbk.)
    1. China—Description and travel. I. O'Reilly, Sean II. O'Reilly, James, 1953–
III. Habegger, Larry.
  DS712.T725 2004
  915.104'6—dc22

2004004101

First Edition
Printed in the United States
10 9 8 7 6 5 4 3

For the Reverend James X. O'Reilly (1919-1999),
an Irishman and Columban priest who lived and worked
in China and was imprisoned during Chairman Mao's
reign of terror.

But I will walk the road however hard it is, because only on the road can you see that yesterday lies behind you and tomorrow waits on the path ahead.

—MA JIAN,
Red Dust: A Path Through China

Table of Contents

Part Four
THE SHADOWS

Part Five
THE LAST WORD

China: An Introduction

by Ji-li Jiang

A friend recently sent me a group of pictures via e-mail, titled "What can the Chinese do?" Curious, I opened one immediately.

A man was watching his child playing in a neighborhood street. Even from the back, I could see that he was well dressed: a light blue shirt, and clean white socks in shining shoes. But unfortunately there were no chairs, benches, or tree trunks nearby on which he could sit. What did he do? He turned two empty plastic bottles upside down, and squatted on their flat bottoms.

I looked at another one. A donkey was walking in the rain, pulling a cart as donkeys have pulled carts for thousands of years. However, this cart was enhanced by the cab of a modern blue truck. The driver, probably a farmer, was sitting inside this comfortable blue "truck," enjoying the modernization.

The sheer ingenuity exhibited in these and the other pictures was impressive. But there was something more, something deeper. As I stared at them, I realized that, to me, those pictures exemplified the spirit of the Chinese people and the essence of Chinese culture. The Chinese can endure enormous hardship and live with very limited resources. Instead of complaining, they use their ingenuity and determination to find ways to improve their circumstances, and to enjoy their lives to the fullest. That, the positive and productive approach toward life, is one of the most fascinating aspects of Chinese culture.

When I was growing up in Shanghai in the 1960s and 1970s, housing was very crowded. It was not unusual for a family of five or six people—perhaps three generations—to share one twelve-foot-by-twelve-foot room. Buildings that once had housed a single family now were shared by several. However, in a little kitchen shared by several families and crowded with several stoves, you would be amazed to see how many hours the inhabitants spent joyfully preparing each meal. They endured the heat and the smoke and the crowding to make sure that each dish had the elements—the color and the aroma and the taste—required of Chinese cuisine. To decorate their tiny rooms, they would spend hundreds of hours of their evenings and weekends, painstakingly sawing, nailing, sanding, and polishing, making furniture they could not afford to buy. The enthusiasm, the love, and the pride invested in their tiny rooms were testimony to their dedication and their unquenchable optimism. Like blades of grass, bursting out of the ground, squeezing between the hard rocks, they not only survived, they prospered.

That is the Chinese spirit: perseverance. That is how the Chinese managed to maintain their rich culture even through extremely difficult times of poverty and suffering.

In *Travelers' Tales China*, you will find ample evidence of this. As Mark Stevens notes in "The Walls Come Tumbling Down," during the SARS epidemic of 2003, Beijing became a forbidden city (the government literally closed the gate and stopped people from coming in and going out), but people adapted and "began to cultivate various internal gardens." They read books or listened to music instead of panicking or growing restless. In "Where Harmony Sings," Yinjie Qian tells her story of traveling to Lijiang, a small town 7,000 feet above sea level in Yunnan Province. She asked her taxi driver, a member of a minority without much education, when the rain would stop. The driver replied with a smile, "No one can predict. It's nature's blessing whether rain or shine." From Xuan Ke, a musician who was put in jail for twenty years, to the story of Guon Yen, a young lady working at a bar in Shanghai who knew nearly every pop and rock song from the '70s and '80s, the ordinary people described in these stories all *demonstrate* somehow that incredible balance. In this book, each traveler's personal experience in China is unique and fascinating, and at the same time illuminates the astonishing character and adaptability of the Chinese people.

In the last fifteen years, China has been changing with blinding speed. When I return to Shanghai after a six-month absence, I often get lost in my old neighborhood because of the new buildings and stores. When the computer was still a novelty in China, my friends were impressed by my little 386 laptop, but in less than two years, they skipped 286, 386, 486, and jumped into Pentium, generations ahead of mine. People who never had telephones at home are suddenly using the most advanced cellular technology. What's next? Men on Mars? The cure for AIDS? Anything is possible. Nothing that happens in the world's most populous country, a place with an average annual economic growth rate of 8 percent over the last twenty-five years, should surprise anyone.

However, there is a darker side. These exciting advances come with some very worrisome problems: the rapidly increasing gap between the rich and the poor, rampant government corruption, and a frightening unemployment rate, to name a few. These problems are serious enough that they could not only halt the progress, but also destabilize the nation.

At a recent conference, a teacher asked me to predict what China would be like in twenty-five years. Will China's growth continue? Will it turn out like Singapore? Or America? Will China become completely capitalist, while keeping only the name of the Chinese Communist Party? Or will it become a democratic country with a socialist system controlled by the Chinese Communist Party?

"I don't know," I said. I told him I couldn't possibly predict the outcome of this reform, because what China is doing is new, without a model to follow. Many predictions made by experts ten years ago were wrong. In the end, China might well turn out not like Singapore, nor America, but something different, something uniquely Chinese. "But," I said confidently, "I know that the Chinese spirit will endure, and that, no matter what, China will always be China."

China has "a heavy load, with a long road ahead," as the old saying goes. But as long as this spirit of perseverance and dedication persists, there is cause for hope. *Travelers' Tales China* is a breath of fresh air in the quest to understand a nation that is at the crossroads of all of our futures.

Ms. Ji-li Jiang was born in Shanghai, China, and came to the United States in 1984. She published her first book, Red Scarf Girl: A Memoir of the Cultural Revolution, *in 1997 and* The Magical Monkey King: Mischief in Heaven, *her retelling of the classic Chinese fairy tale, in 2002. She travels around the country to talk to students and teachers about China, and runs her company, East West Exchange, to promote cultural exchange between China and Western countries.*

PART ONE

ESSENCE OF CHINA

✳ ✳ ✳

Running

*A Peace Corps teacher becomes a student
of the dragon that is China.*

IN THE MORNINGS I OFTEN RAN TO THE SUMMIT OF RAISE the Flag Mountain. As I ran, I studied the propaganda signs along the route, although at the beginning there wasn't much about them that was recognizable. There were three signs on the road out to the mountain, and to me they looked like this:

建设精神 Culture, 更新生育观念

控 制 People Mouth 增长，促进社会进步

教育 Is 立 Country 基础

I finished my runs back in the center of campus, not far from the teaching building, where a stone wall served as a backdrop for an inscription of three-foot-high characters:

教书育 People, 管理育 People, 服务育 People,

环境育 People

That was how Chinese appeared in my first few months. I arrived in Fuling able to recognize about forty characters, all of them simple: people, middle, country, above, below, long, man, woman. There hadn't been time for more; the Peace Corps had given us an intensive course during our two months of training in Chengdu, but the emphasis was on learning enough spoken Mandarin to function. We had to study written Chinese on our own, and until I got to Fuling I simply hadn't had enough time.

I came to Sichuan because I wanted to teach, but I also had two other motivations: I thought the experience would make me a better writer, and I wanted to learn Chinese. These were very clear goals, but the way to achieve them was much less obvious. I hoped the writing would take care of itself—I would keep my eyes open and take notes, and eventually, when I felt I was ready, I would start to write. But Chinese was a different matter altogether and I had never undertaken something like that before.

That was one reason I had decided to come to China with the Peace Corps, because I knew they would try to teach me the language. Their Chengdu training course had been excellent: the classes were small and the teachers experienced, and it had been easy to make progress. In Fuling, though, language study was my own affair. The Peace Corps would pay for tutors, but I had to find them myself, and I had to decide which textbooks I would use and how I would structure my studies. It was a daunting task—essentially, I had to figure out how to learn Chinese.

For the first few weeks, Dean Fu searched for tutors who could help Adam [a fellow teacher] and me. He was as lost as we were— he had never known a foreigner who was trying to learn the language, and I suspected that secretly he felt the project was hopeless. *Waiguoren* (foreigners) couldn't learn Chinese—everybody in Fuling knew that. Our students found it hilarious that we even tried. They would ask me to speak a little Chinese, or write a character or two, and then they would laugh at my efforts. At first this didn't bother me, but quickly it became annoying. They thought I was dabbling in the language when in fact I was serious: I knew that studying Chinese was one of the most important things I could do in Fuling. So much depended on knowing the language—my friendships, my ability to function in the city, my understanding of the place.

I also wanted to learn Chinese out of stubbornness, because as a *waiguoren* you weren't expected to do that. Such low expectations had a long tradition; even as late as the early 1800s it had been illegal for a Chinese to teach the language to foreigners, and a number of Chinese were imprisoned and even executed for tutoring young Englishmen. This bit of history fascinated me: How many languages had been sacred and forbidden to outsiders? Certainly, those laws had been changed more than a century ago, but China was still at the heart of this issue. In good conscience I could not live there for two years and not learn to speak Chinese. To me, this was as important as fulfilling my obligations as a teacher.

But this need wasn't nearly as obvious to everybody else. Dean Fu took a long time finding tutors, and perhaps he was hoping that we'd forget about it. We didn't need Chinese to teach, after all, and

Frank Li, one of my new friends in Shanghai, shared an analogy about the differences Chinese people perceive in foreigners who come to China. "Birds" move only within the "cage" of what is familiar from Western culture. They could just as easily be living in New York. "Chickens" peck around and explore, but never venture too far beyond what Chinese friends help make accessible for them. "Pigeons" take a deep breath and immerse themselves in the world that is China. They inevitably learn Mandarin or other Chinese dialects, because their adventure would be awfully difficult otherwise.
  —Phyllis Edgerly Ring, "When West Meets East: A Chicken"

we already knew enough to buy groceries and eat at local restaurants. That should be adequate, people figured. In some respects, we were seen as English-teaching machines, or perhaps farm animals—expensive and skittish draft horses that taught literature and culture. We were given cadres' apartments, and we had our own Changhong-brand color televisions with remote. Our bedrooms were air-conditioned. Each of us had a good kitchen and two beautiful balconies. Our students were obedient and respectful. It didn't matter that, even as we were given all of these things, the leaders also gave quiet instructions to our colleagues and students that they should avoid associating with us outside of class. *Waiguoren* were risky, especially with regard to politics, and in any case we didn't need close friends in the college. We could teach during the day and return to our comfortable cages at night, and, if we needed friendship, we always had each other. They even gave us telephones so we could call Peace Corps volunteers who lived in other parts of Sichuan.

Some of the more insightful students sensed that this did not make a full life. In his journal, Soddy wrote me a short note, politely addressed in the third person:

> Pete and Adam come to our college to teach our English without pay. We are thankful for this behavior. But we are worried about Pete and Adam's lives. For example: Pete and Adam know little Chinese, so they can't watch Chinese TV programs. I think your lives are difficult. I want to know how you spend your spare time.

It was a good question. My teaching and preparation time rarely took much more than thirty hours a week. I ran in the mornings, and sometimes I went for walks in the hills. Adam and I played basketball and threw the Frisbee. I wrote on my computer. I planned other diversions for the future—subjects I wanted to cover in class, possible travel destinations. Mostly, though, I knew that there was plenty of exploring to be done in the city, but at the beginning this was the hardest place of all to open up.

Downtown Fuling looked good from my balcony. Often I'd gaze across the Wu River at the maze of streets and stairways, listening to the distant hum of daily life, and I'd think about the mysteries that were hidden in the river town. I wanted to investigate all of it—I wanted to go down to the docks and watch the boats; I wanted to talk with the soldiers; I wanted to explore the network of tangled staircases that ran through the old part of town. I longed to figure out how the city worked and what the people thought, especially since no foreigner had done this before. It wasn't like living in

Beijing or Shanghai, where there were plenty of *waiguoren* who had discovered what the city had to offer. As far as foreigners were concerned, Fuling was our city—or it would be once we figured it out.

But once I got there it didn't look so good. Partly this was because of the dirt and noise; the main city of Fuling was an unbelievably loud and polluted place. There wasn't as much heavy industry as in other parts of China, but there were a few good-sized factories that spewed smoke and dust into the air. The power plant on the banks of the Wu River burned coal, as did all of the countless small restaurants that lined the city's streets, and automobile emissions were poorly regulated. In winter the air was particularly dirty, but even in summer it was bad. If I went to town and blew my nose, the tissue was streaked with black grease. This made me think about how the air was affecting my lungs, and for a while I wondered what could be done about this. Finally I decided to stop looking at tissues after I blew my nose.

Noise was even more impressive. Most of it came from car horns, and it is difficult to explain how constant this sound was. I can start by saying: Drivers in Fuling honked a lot. There weren't a great number of cars, but there were enough, and they were always passing each other in a mad rush to get to wherever they were going. Most of them were cabs, and virtually every cabby in Fuling had rewired his horn so it was triggered by a contact point at the tip of the gearshift. They did this for convenience; because of the hills, drivers shifted gears frequently, and with their hand on the stick it was possible to touch the contact point ever so slightly and the horn would sound. They honked at other cars, and they honked at pedestrians. They honked whenever they passed somebody, or whenever they were being passed themselves. They honked when nobody was passing but somebody might be considering it, or when the road was empty and there was nobody to pass but the thought of passing or being passed had just passed through the driver's mind. Just like that, an unthinking reflex: the driver honked. They did it so often that they didn't even feel the contact point beneath their fingers, and the other drivers and pedestrians were so familiar with the sound that they essentially didn't hear it. Nobody reacted to horns anymore; they served no purpose. A honk in Fuling was like the tree falling in the forest—for all intents and purposes it was silent.

But at the beginning Adam and I heard it. For the first few weeks we often complained about the honking and the noise, the same way we complained about blowing our noses and seeing the tissue turn black. But the simple truth was that you could do nothing about either the noise or the pollution, which meant that they could either become very important and very annoying, or they could become not important at all. For sanity's sake we took the second option, like the locals, and soon we learned to talk about other things.

> When one is in China one is compelled to think about her, with compassion always, with despair sometimes, and with discrimination and understanding, very rarely. For one either loves or hates China.... If one comes to China, one feels engulfed, and soon stops thinking. One merely feels that she is there, a tremendous existence somewhat too big for the human mind to encompass, a seemingly inconsequential chaos obeying its own laws of existence.
>
> —Lin Yutang, *My Country and My People* (1936)

I realized this in early November, when a college friend of mine named Scott Kramer came to visit. For five years he had lived in Manhattan, and yet the noise in Fuling absolutely stunned him; he heard every horn, every shout, every blurted announcement from every loudspeaker. When he left, we took a cab from the college to the docks, and Kramer, who worked on Wall Street and had a mathematical turn of mind, counted the honks as our driver sped through the city. It was a fifteen-minute ride and the driver touched his contact point 566 times. It came to thirty-eight honks per minute.

If Kramer hadn't been counting, I wouldn't have noticed, and I realized that I had stopped hearing the horns long ago, just like everybody else in town. In fact, Kramer was the only person in the whole city who heard them, which explained why he was so overwhelmed. The entire city had been honking at him for a week.

For me it wasn't the same, and after a month or so the discomforts of Fuling weren't important enough to deter me from going into town. Despite the noise and the pollution, it was still a fascinating place, and I still wanted to explore its corners and learn its secrets. But the language was an enormous problem, and in the beginning it made the city frustrating and even frightening.

Mandarin Chinese has a reputation as a difficult language—some experts say it takes four times as long to learn as Spanish or French—and its characters and tones are particularly challenging to a Westerner, because they are completely different from the way our languages are structured. In Sichuan, things are further complicated by the provincial dialect, which is distinct enough that a Chinese outsider has trouble understanding the locals in a place like Fuling. The variations between Mandarin and Sichuanese are significant: in addition to some differences in vocabulary, Sichuanese slurs the Mandarin reflexive sounds—*sh* becomes *s*, *zh* becomes *z*—and certain consonants are reversed, so that the average person in Sichuan confuses *n* and *l*, and *h* and *f*. A word like "Hunan" becomes "Fulan." The Sichuanese tonal range is also shorter, and most significant, two of the four Mandarin tones are reversed in Sichuan. If Mandarin is your starting point, it seems that the entire language has been flattened and turned upside down.

In addition, Sichuan is an enormous province where lack of development, particularly with regard to road and rail links, has resulted in vast regional differences. The Chengdu dialect is distinct from that of Chongqing, which is also different from that of Leshan, and so on. The town of Fengdu is less than thirty miles downstream from Fuling, and yet occasionally the residents of these places have difficulty understanding each other. At a Fuling restaurant, if you want the dish known as *hundun* in Mandarin—translated in English as "wonton"—you have to ask for *chaoshou*, but if you go another thirty miles to Fengdu you'll have to call it *baomian*. Or, more accurately, *baomin*, because the folks in Fengdu slur the *ian* sound.

The result is a hell of a mess that I hadn't expected. I came to China hoping to learn Chinese, but quickly I realized there was no such thing. "Chinese" was whatever it took to communicate with the person you happened to be talking with, and this changed dramatically depending on background and education level. Educated people usually could speak Mandarin, especially if they were from the younger generation—the walls of our classrooms had enormous signs that commanded: "Use Mandarin!" But the vast majority of Fuling's population was uneducated and functioned only in the dialect. It made going to town a frustrating experience, because even the simplest conversations were difficult, and it also made my goal of learning Chinese seem impossible: I couldn't imagine learning both Mandarin and Sichuanese in two years. In fact, all I needed to do was improve my Mandarin, which would naturally enable me to handle the dialect, but in the early months I didn't know that. It seemed that I was in hopelessly over my head, and every trip into town was a reminder of that failure.

And Fuling was a frightening place because the people had seen so few outsiders. If I ate at a restaurant or bought something from a store, a crowd would quickly gather, often as many as thirty people spilling out into the street. Most of the attention was innocent

> ───────※───────
>
> Using a Chinese dictionary involves finding the *pinyin* (Romanized) spelling, whose section is subdivided into the four tones. First I had to decipher my teacher's handwriting, and second, remember the specifics as the other characters streamed before my eyes. Take the lesson on "Clothing." I would flip through the dictionary pages, searching for the word *xie*, and the appropriate tone section (fourth). First, I'd see "evil," then, "in harmony," and a little later, "to hold something under the arm." Finally, I might find "shoes,"—apropos to the lesson, but by now the class had moved on and I was lost again.
>
> —Nancy Pellegrini,
> "A Monolinguist Abroad"

curiosity, but it made the embarrassment of my bad Chinese all the worse—I'd try to communicate with the owner, and people would laugh and talk among themselves, and in my nervousness I would speak even worse Mandarin. When I walked down the street, people constantly turned and shouted at me. Often they screamed *waiguoren* or *laowai*, both of which simply meant "foreigner." Again, these phrases often weren't intentionally insulting, but intentions mattered less and less with every day that these words were screamed at me. Another favorite was "hello," a meaningless, mocking version of the word that was strung out into a long "hah-loooo!" This word was so closely associated with foreigners that sometimes the people used it instead of *waiguoren*—they'd say, "Look, here come two hellos!" And often in Fuling they shouted other less innocent terms—*yangguizi*, or "foreign devil"; *da bizi*, "big nose"—although it wasn't until later that I understood what these phrases meant.

The stresses piled up every time I went into town: the confusion and embarrassment of the language, the shouts and stares, the mocking calls. It was even worse for Adam, who was tall and blond; at least I had the advantage of being dark-haired and only slightly bigger than the locals. For a while we adopted the strategy of going into town together, thinking that between the two of us we could more easily handle the pressure. This was a mistake, though, because adding another *waiguoren* only increased the attention, and after a month of that we started making our trips solo. Finally, as the fall semester wore on, we did everything possible to avoid going to town. When I did go, I wore headphones. That was the only way I could handle it; I listened to the loudest and most offensive rap music I had—Dr. Dre, Snoop Doggy Dogg, the Beastie Boys—and it was just enough to drown out the shouts as I walked down the street. It made for surreal trips downtown, listening to Snoop rap obscenities while I dodged the crowds, but it kept me sane.

And so Soddy's question remained: How do you spend your spare time? When I finished teaching I would sit at my desk, which looked out across the Wu River to the city, and I would write:

学 学 学 学 学 学 学 学 学 学

While I wrote, I pronounced the word over and over, as carefully as I drew it:

"Xue xue xue xue xue xue xue xue xue xue xue xue xue xue xue xue xue xue xue xue."

I would write the same character about a hundred times total, and then I would think of ways in which it was used: *xuexi, xuesheng, xuexiao.* I would write it on a flash card and put it on a stack that grew steadily on my desk—between five and ten a day, usually. I listened to language tapes and reviewed the text that we had used during Peace Corps training. I flipped through the flash cards. By early October, when Dean Fu finally found two Chinese tutors, I had learned 150 characters. The signs on the way to Raise the Flag Mountain were still unintelligible, but the one in the center of campus had changed slightly:

Teaching 育 People, 管理育 People,

服务育 People, Environment 育 People

Our tutors were Kong Ming and Liao Mei, and we came to know them as Teacher Kong and Teacher Liao. They taught in the Chinese department, and neither of them spoke any English. They had never known a *waiguoren* before. Dean Fu had been unable to find tutors who spoke English, and at last we told him it wasn't important. We wanted to get started and we knew that Chinese department teachers had good Mandarin.

Teacher Kong was a short man who wore glasses and smelled of Magnificent Sound cigarettes. He was thirty-two years old, and he taught ancient Chinese literature. By Chinese standards he was slightly fat, which meant that by American standards he was slightly thin. He smiled easily. He was from the countryside of Fengdu, which was famous for its ghosts—legend said that spirits went to Fengdu after death.

Teacher Liao was a very thin woman with long black hair and a reserved manner. She was twenty-seven years old, and she taught modern Chinese. She smiled less than Teacher Kong. Our students, who also had some courses in the Chinese department, considered Teacher Liao to be one of their better instructors. She was from the central Sichuan city of Zigong, which was famous for its salt. Every city and small town in Sichuan claimed to be famous for something. Fuling was famous for the hot pickled mustard tuber that was cured along the banks of the rivers.

That was essentially everything we knew about Teachers Kong and Liao for months. We also knew about their Mandarin, which was very clear except for a slight Sichuanese tendency to confuse the *n* and *l* sounds. Other than that we knew nothing. To us they were like Chinese-teaching machines, or perhaps farm animals—a sort of inexpensive and bored draft horse that corrected bad tones. And to them we were very stupid *waiguoren* from a country whose crude tongue had no tones at all.

My first tutorial with Teacher Liao was scheduled for two hours, but I lasted less than sixty minutes. I went home with my head reeling—had a human being ever compressed more wrongness into a single hour? Everything was wrong—tones, grammar, vocabulary, initial sounds. She would ask me a question and I would try to process the language to respond, but before I could speak she was answering it herself. She spoke clearly, of course, and it was also true that during that hour not a word of English had been spoken. That was what I wanted, after all—a Chinese tutor. But I couldn't imagine doing that for seven hours a week and maintaining my sanity, and I looked at the pathetic stack of flash cards on my desk and thought: This is hopeless.

For a solid month it looked that way. I was too self-absorbed to even imagine what it was like from the other side, but later I realized that it was even worse for my teachers. They weren't under threat of execution for teaching the sacred tones to a *waiguoren*—that law, at least, had been changed since Qing Dynasty days. But theirs wasn't an enviable job. First of all, we underpaid them. This wasn't intentional: Adam and I had been given wrong information about the standard rate for tutors. Teachers Kong and Liao, of course, were far too polite to set us straight, which meant that for the entire first year they worked for two-thirds of what they deserved. Even worse, though, they were underpaid for seven weekly hours of boredom and frustration. The lessons in the book were simple—taking a train, going to a restaurant—and yet I botched everything, and they had no idea how to steer me in the right direction. How do you teach somebody to speak Chinese? How do you take your knowledge of ancient poetry and use it to help a *waiguoren* master something as basic as the third tone?

We were all lost, and that failure seemed to be the extent of our relationship. Other Peace Corps volunteers had tutors who spoke English, so at least they could chat together after class. They heard about their tutors' families; they ate dinner together; they became friends. My tutors didn't seem like real people—it was months before I learned that Teacher Liao was married and that Teacher Kong had a son. Here the language problem was compounded by the fact that at the beginning they were somewhat cagey and distant; they had never known a *waiguoren* before, and they weren't at all certain how to approach us.

Chinese teaching styles are also significantly different from Western methods, which made my tutorials even more frustrating. In China, a teacher is absolutely respected without question, and the teacher-student relationship tends to be formal. The teacher teaches and is right, and the student studies and is wrong. But this isn't our tradition in America, as my own students noticed. I encouraged informality in our classes, and if a student was wrong I pointed out what she had done right and praised her for making a good effort. To them, this praise was meaningless. What was the point of that? If a student was wrong, she needed to be corrected without any quibbling or softening—that was the Chinese way.

I couldn't teach like that, and it was even harder to play the role of student. Actually, this became worse after my Chinese classes started to feel productive, which happened more quickly than I expected. The characters in my book's lessons had always been elusive, odd-shaped scratches of black that drifted in and out of my head, calling up arbitrary allusions that were misleading. They were pictures rather than words: I would look at 木 and think of Kmart, and the twenty-seventh radical—厂 reminded me of the letter B, or perhaps an ax hanging on a wall. 大 looked like a man doing jumping jacks. 点 was a marching spider carrying a flag across the page. I stared so long at those odd figures that I dreamed about them—they swarmed in my head and I awoke vaguely disturbed and missing home.

But at a certain point it was as if some of the scratchings stood up straight and looked me in the eye, and the fanciful associations started slipping away. Suddenly they became words; they had meaning. Of course, it didn't happen all at once, and it was work that did it—I was studying madly in an effort to make the classes less miserable. But I was so busy that I hardly had time to realize that progress was being made.

One day after more than a month of classes, I read aloud a paragraph from my book, recognizing all of the characters smoothly except for one. I sat back and started to register the achievement: I was actually reading Chinese. The language was starting to make sense. But before this sense of satisfaction was half formed, Teacher Liao said, "*Budui!*"

I knew very little about China but, being a flaming liberal, I was sure that all hostility we felt toward the Chinese was a result of our biases and if we really got to know the Chinese, we would find them to be just like us. Error. It took me all of my first year in China to accept that I had been wrong in my assumptions and that we were vastly different people.

I'm not a China expert. I doubt if there is such a thing despite all those people you see on TV talk shows, hear on public radio, and read in newspapers and magazines. Just imagine a nation with about five times as many people as are in the United States, living in a space only slightly larger than our country, with most of the land unable to produce a crop. There are seventy-eight different races and hundreds of different languages and dialects. It is possible to live in one area all one's life and never travel more than twenty miles from one's home. Who could ever be an expert on such a people?

—Katherine Walker,
"Up Against the (Great) Wall"

It meant, literally, "Not correct." You could also translate it as no, wrong, nope, uh-uh. Flatly and clearly incorrect. There were many Chinese words that I didn't know, but I knew that one well.

A voice in my head whined: All of the rest of them were right; isn't that worth something? But for Teacher Liao it didn't work like that. If one character was wrong it was simply *budui*.

"What's this word?" I asked, pointing at the character I had missed.

"*Zhe*—the *zhe* in *zhejiang*."

"Third tone?"

"Fourth tone."

I breathed deeply and read the section again, and this time I did it perfectly. That was a victory—I turned to Teacher Liao and my eyes said (or at least I imagined them saying): How do you like me now? But Teacher Liao's eyes were glazed with boredom and she said, "Read the next one." They were, after all, simple paragraphs. Any school child could handle them.

It was the Chinese way. Success was expected and failure criticized and promptly corrected. You were right or you were *budui*; there was no middle ground. As I became bolder with the language I started experimenting with new words and new structures, and this was good but it was also a risk. I would finish a series of sentences using vocabulary that I knew Teacher Liao didn't expect me to know, and I would swear that I could see her flinch with unwilling admiration. And yet she would say, "*Budui!*" and correct the part that had been wrong.

I grew to hate *budui*: its sound mocked me. There was a harshness to it: the *bu* was a rising tone and the *dui* dropped abruptly, building like my confidence and then collapsing all at once. And it bothered me all the more because I knew that Teacher Liao was only telling the truth: virtually everything I did with the language was *budui*. I was an adult, and as an adult I should be able to accept criticism where it was needed. But that wasn't the American way; I was accustomed to having my ego soothed; I wanted to be praised for my effort. I didn't mind criticism as long as it was candy-coated. I was caught in the same trap that I had heard about from some of my Chinese-American friends, who as children went to school and became accustomed to the American system of gentle correction, only to return home and hear their Chinese-minded parents say, simply, *budui*. That single B on the report card matters much more than the string of A's that surrounds it. Keep working; you haven't achieved anything yet.

And so I studied. I was frustrated but I was also stubborn; I was determined to show Teacher Liao that I was *dui*. Virtually all of my spare time went to studying Chinese, and the stack of flash cards on my desk grew rapidly. By the first week in November I knew three hundred characters. I had no clear idea what I was shooting for—I had a vague goal of reading a newspaper, which would require between two and three thousand. But mostly I knew that I needed more knowledge than I had, and I needed it quickly.

In the mornings I ran to the summit of Raise the Flag Mountain, charging hard up the steps, my lungs burning high above the Yangtze. The effort was satisfying—it was challenging but uncomplicated, and at the finish I could look down on the city and see where I had gone. It was different from the work of learning Chinese, which had no clear endpoint and gave me more frustration than satisfaction.

There was a skill to running, and in some ways it was the only skill I had in Fuling. Everybody else seemed to have found something that he or she was good at: the owner of the dumpling restaurant made dumplings, the shoeshine women shined shoes, the stick-stick soldiers carried loads on their leathered shoulders. It was less clear what my purpose was—I was a teacher, and that job was satisfying and clearly defined, but it disappeared once I left campus. Most people in town only saw my failures, the inevitable misunderstandings and botched conversations.

And they always watched carefully. The attention was so intense that in public I often became clumsily self-conscious, which was exacerbated by my suddenly becoming bigger than average. In America I was considered small at five feet nine inches, but now for the first time in my life I stood out in crowds. I bumped my head on bus doorways; I squeezed awkwardly behind miniature restaurant tables. I was like Alice in Wonderland, eating the currant-seed cakes and finding her world turned upside down.

Mostly I longed to find something that I could do well. This was part of why the simple routines of the city fascinated me; I could watch a stick-stick soldier or a restaurant cook with incredible intensity, simply because these people were good at what they did. There was a touch of voyeurism in my attention, at least in the sense that I watched the people work with all of the voyeur's impotent envy. There were many days when I would have liked nothing more than to have had a simple skill that I could do over and over again, as long as I did it well.

Running was repetitive in this way, and it was also an escape. If I ran on the roads, cars honked at me, people laughed and shouted, and sometimes a young man would try to impress his friends by chasing after me. But crowds couldn't gather around, and none of the young men followed for long. I ran alone, and in a crowded country that sort of solitude was worth something. There was nobody in the city who could catch me.

Usually I ran in the hills behind campus, following the small roads and footpaths that wound around Raise the Flag Mountain. I ran past old Taoist shrines, and atop the narrow walls of the rice paddies, and I followed the stone steps that led to the mountain's

---

The surest test if a man be sane
Is if he accepts life whole,
    as it is,
Without needing by measure
    or touch to understand
The measureless untouchable
    source
Of its images,
The measureless untouchable
    source
Of its substances,
The source which, while it
    appears dark emptiness,
Brims with a quick force
Farthest away
And yet nearest at hand
From oldest time unto this
    day,
Charging its images with
    origin:
What more need I know of
    the origin
Than this?
        —Lao Tzu, *The Way of Life*

summit. I liked running past the ancient stone tombs that over-looked the rivers, and I liked seeing the peasants at work. On my runs I watched them harvest the rice crop, and thresh the yellowed stalks, and I saw them plant the winter wheat and tend their vegetables. I first learned the agricultural patterns by watching the workers as I ran, and I studied the shape of the mountain by feeling it beneath my legs.

The peasants found it strange that I ran in the hills, and they always stared when I charged past, but they never shouted or laughed. As a rule they were the most polite people you could ever hope to meet, and in any case they had more important things to do with their energy than scream at *waiguoren*. And perhaps they had an innate respect for physical effort, even when they didn't see the point.

The air in the countryside was often bad, because the Yangtze winds blew the city's pollution across the Wu River, and I knew that running did my health more harm than good. But it kept my mind steady, because the fields were quiet and peaceful and the activity felt the same as it always had. That old well-known feeling—the catch in my chest, the strain in my legs—connected all the places where I had lived, Missouri and Princeton and Oxford and Fuling. While I ran through the hills, my thoughts swung fluidly between these times and places; I remembered running along the old Missouri-Kansas-Texas railroad pathway, and I recalled the rapeseed blooming gold on Boar's Hill, and the old shaded bridge of Prettybrook. As the months slipped past I realized that even these Sichuan hills, with their strange tombs and terraces, were starting to feel like home.

But still the signs on the way to Raise the Flag Mountain were foreign and even as they slowly became familiar they reminded me how far I still had to go.

Peter Hessler went to China as a Peace Corp volunteer and taught English there from 1996 to 1998. His articles have appeared in The New York Times, The Philadelphia Inquirer, The Atlantic Monthly, *and* The Washington Post. *He is the author of* River Town: Two Years on the Yangtze, *from which this story was excerpted. He currently lives in Beijing.*

✳ ✳ ✳

The Walls Come Tumbling Down

Welcome to the new China!

"YOU HAVE TO UNDERSTAND. BEIJING WAS *WONDERFUL* during SARS," said Jeremy Wingfield, the manager of the CourtYard gallery. "Romantic, beautiful. The sky was clear, for once. Everything shut down. There was no smog or dust or traffic jams. No tourists. No cars." He looked at me closely, to make sure I was the sort of American who understood that, of course, he also knew that SARS was a terrible plague that killed people. But it was important nonetheless to acknowledge the marvel of the moment when Beijing stopped. "One day they announced SARS was over," he said, almost wistfully, "and it was as if nothing had ever happened."

Serendipity took me to the city twice in 2003, once in the spring when SARS was just emerging in public and then again in the fall. Most people described its impact in the same terms Jeremy did—as a surreal interlude. The authorities responded in the traditional way of Beijing: they built a wall. First to conceal the virus, then to stamp it out. All of Beijing became a forbidden city closed to travelers. People withdrew behind masks and the walls of houses and apartments. After the early days of panic, however, something unexpected happened: behind their walls, the healthy began to cultivate various internal gardens. "I read books," one said with wonder. "I listened to music." It was a parenthesis in time, strange and unlikely because building walls is no longer the business of Beijing. Tearing them down is.

Beijing is a city that wants to forget: the only important new wall being built is that between the past and the present. You cannot go to Beijing in search of some pristine encounter with history. You go to see a city in vital and vulgar flux, in the throes of what the Viennese economist Joseph Schumpeter famously called the "creative destruction" of capitalism, its people and tourists intoxicated by consumer goods, lucre, glitter, and glitz. Old China—the land of the emperors, including the emperor called Mao—seems an afterthought. The pressure of the contemporary is just too powerful. Beijing scrambles the like and unlike, the old and new. Broad avenues sit where city walls once were. Traditional *hutongs* [mazelike neighborhoods] are being razed, opening up grand new spaces, upon which modern buildings rise. The removal of walls gives the city a kind of jack-in-the-box explosiveness and the liberating, but also disorienting, sensation of there being no more boundaries.

Through the turbulent history of the twentieth century the stolid Chinese peasants had plowed ahead, kept their heads down, shrugged and hoped for the best through death and loss. Now their children are the young folk of potential and promise, their grandkids toddling around in the new century that could bring unimagined wealth and power to China. The old calligrapher just smiles when I ask him next day about the changes; it's good politics not to talk politics. Down in the street outside his shop, an open-air gallery is selling glossy framed lithographs of Marx and Lenin, Mao and Chou En-lai. A few younger Chinese men peer at the portraits like museum curiosities, then stroll away.

—Peter Delevett,
"Century Dust"

The reigning style is pastiche. Anything can mix and match. Foreign brand names are preferred to the indigenously Chinese, unless by indigenously Chinese you mean knockoffs. (There's more "Burberry" in China than wool in New Zealand.) Western tourists relish the city partly because, if things threaten to become too Chinese, there's always a Starbucks nearby. Although tourism fell to almost nothing during the actual epidemic—the Xinhua news agency reported that the number of overseas visitors dropped 50 percent for the full first half of the year—foreigners are back again, once more part of the city's collage. At night the new high-rises twinkle as if every day were Christmas.

There can be a madcap joy—sometimes innocent, sometimes clever—in playing with pastiche and artifice. I stayed at a hotel designed around a huge atrium that contained plastic palm trees, statues of naked nymphs in classical Greek style, and a white grand piano surrounded by pineapple lanterns. A Chinese woman sang Italian arias there. You could order a Manhattan.

Beijing has always been eccentric, unnatural and artificial. It did not develop in the way most human settlements did, with a lively market at its heart. The center of Beijing was instead a walled-off place where people could not go, the Forbidden City of the emperor. Mao added Tiananmen Square, the showplace of the revolution, where public behavior became as ritualized in its way as in the Forbidden City. In Beijing, there was a divine scale and a higgledy-piggledy scale—the vast space of the Leader and the gray honeycomb maze of walls, rooms, and streets where the people lived, called the *hutongs*.

Like most travelers, I went first to the Forbidden City and Tiananmen Square. I was unprepared not only for their scale, but also for their strange relationship. The revolutionary square is the existential reflection of the Forbidden City. How were the Communists, once they came to power in 1949, to match the elaborate scale of the Forbidden City? How were they to remove the crushing weight of Chinese history? By applying the great eraser that created Tiananmen Square.

Laid out in the early fifteenth century, the Forbidden City unfolds powerfully in courtyard after courtyard, as if the power of the emperor himself could never quite be reached. It is magnificent—but oppressive. The spaces press you down rather than lift you up. I wasn't really happy until I came to a garden of grottoes, pavilions, and shapely rocks and trees. Here, perhaps, the emperor could escape from himself. The garden contained some wonderful signs in English. One identified an artificial mountain with a temple on top as the "Hill of Piled Excellence." Not far away was a sign that in the United States would have said, "Do Not Touch." Here, it read, "A single act of carelessness leads to the eternal loss of beauty."

I wandered onto the empty endlessness that is Tiananmen Square. In my mind's eye, I imagined it seething with Red Guards as Mao reviewed the tanks, rockets, and troops. Or filling with the demonstrators who built "Democracy Wall"—how typical of Beijing that oxymoron is. But now it looked like a dead space, except for the aimless zigzagging of kites and tourists. Its

I looked for a back entrance and merely smiled at a cleaning lady emerging from a tiny side door way up along the twenty-foot-high western wall of the Forbidden City, chirped hello, indicated that I wanted to have a little peep and…I was in.

And the whole place was mine! No one else was about in the early morning silence except a swirl of swooping birds, a few cooing dove-couples, and the musty ghosts of emperors and princes and courtesans and courtiers moving almost tangibly through the shadows between the ornate palaces. This mildly illicit form of exploration added frisson and flavor to the rich reality of this amazing complex. Most tourist spots in China are inundated with visitors. Here, as soon as the main gates open off Tiananmen Square and the coaches roll up by the score, it becomes difficult to appreciate the power and mystery of such a unique place.

—David Yeadon, "In Beijing"

major buildings—Mao's mausoleum at one end and to either side
the Soviet-era Great Hall of the People and the National Museum
of Chinese History and the
National Museum of the
Chinese Revolution—are
pompous boilerplate.

The vitality of the city no
longer concentrates at its
center, but shoots out in glit-
tery sparks to the periphery.
From Tiananmen Square, I
took a taxi down Changan
Avenue to the boomtown
capital, the district of hotels,
condos, office blocks, embassies, and huge shopping
malls. "I went away for a
while," a Chinese woman
told me, "and when I came
back I didn't recognize
where I'd lived for years."
Cranes rise everywhere.
Many of the buildings brag
of affluence with silly pillars
and golden surfaces and pre-
tentious names like "Fifth
Avenue." Is Donald Trump
the city's architectural advi-
sor? The beautiful bicycle
swarms of Beijing are beginning to diminish, owing to
the exponential increase in
automobile traffic. Shopping
malls are everywhere, usually
organized around brand

<hr />

While building projects
proliferate like kudzu in
metropolitan areas, Beijing has
the added incentive of preparing
for the 2008 Olympics, and is
undergoing even more massive
reconstruction than usual. A fascinating perspective on this is
drawn by Jasper Becker, author
of *The Chinese*, who writes in
Travel & Leisure, "While parallels
could be drawn with Niemeyer's
Brasilia, Lutyens New Delhi, or
Haussmann's Paris, it is
Germania, Albert Speer's pro-
jected remake of Berlin as the
new capital of Hitler's Reich,
that comes closest to what is
being effected in China's capital.
The comparison is not inciden-
tal: the man behind a central
element of Beijing's new look is
none other than Albert Speer
Jr." Becker also notes that Speer's
design calls for a sixteen-mile-
long north-south axis that will
connect the Forbidden City to
the Olympic Village and major
transportation hubs.

—SO'R, JO'R, & LH

names. The Chinese craze for labels, even when ironic, is peculiarly passionate. Perhaps it comes from being confined for so long to one designer, Mao. Better architecture will come to Beijing—if only because the Chinese are beginning to regard architects, too, as brand names. If other cities have a Gehry and a Koolhaas, so must the capital of China. In the atrium of a Xi Dan mall last spring, I saw a cheap golden pillar or trunk that rose several stories. From it angled—goofily—dozens of plastic suitcases that held green apples or flowers. It was almost Edenic: a capitalist garden without a snake. Let a hundred designers bloom!

Occasionally, weary of the lights, I sought out unmoneyed Beijing. Before the fairy dust of capitalism, the dominant color of the city was a dour gray that sucked the light out of the air—an extraordinary gray that was not itself beautiful, but beautifully set off the lacquer reds of palaces and temples. That gray still suffuses the ground-hugging *hutongs* that provide such a contrast in scale to both imperial and consumer culture. Even the bicycles—there seem to be no new bicycles in Beijing—reflect this ancient hue.

You can take an official *hutong* tour, where someone will pedal you around while performing the role of colorful local Chinese man from the *hutong*. But it's more interesting, of course, to get lost. Houhai is an old district on a lake that's becoming a yuppie town. Bars, restaurants, and tea shops glitter at night around the water. Very nice. But you need walk only a few minutes down an alley into the *hutong*—and then turn a corner and turn a corner and turn a corner—and you will be lost in old Beijing. A woman washes her hair in a pail. Old men play games outside doors. A street vendor sells five or six pieces of fruit. Only by taking this kind of walk will you see that the new China is still only skin-deep. Once, deeply lost, I walked into a local restaurant—and every chopstick stopped. Even in Beijing.

One morning I went looking for Mao. His portrait still hangs in Tiananmen Square, but he is otherwise hard to find. His mausoleum is often closed. In crowded bookstores, I could not locate a new copy of the little red book. (The Chinese now buy other kinds of self-help books, including one by Dale Carnegie.) The Museum of the Chinese Revolution on Tiananmen Square has been temporarily closed for a long time, presumably because no one knows how to pretzel together today's capitalism with yesterday's communism.

Style can marginalize substance. Style can be a way to forget. It was Andy Warhol who first made Mao look stylish, in his celebrated portrait. The Chinese have taken the cue. The postmodern Mao is typically a figure to play with, which helps remove the sting from history. You can go to a restaurant that specializes in the food of the Cultural Revolution. The great Beijing flea market sells much Mao memorabilia, including old inspirational posters, caps and secondhand little red books. Much of the memorabilia is fake: the posters and little red book promising a new revolutionary man are now knockoffs distressed by workers, the better to hawk history to tourists.

In my search for something authentically Maoist, I made one inspired guess. What about the Military Museum of the Chinese People's Revolution? It's a run-down Stalinist palace with two large wings and a big star on top. In the museum parking lot, looking more beached than any whale, sits a passenger jet that used to transport Chinese VIPs. Inside the building, an enormous statue of the Great Helmsman welcomes visitors—at last!—to an exhibition filled with MIGs, machine guns, missiles, and assorted weaponry. On the second floor there's an exhibit about the Korean War. In contrast to most exhibitions in Beijing, no English wall labels describe the displays. (You would hardly know the United States was involved.) As I strolled around, I kept hearing a huge roaring sound. I walked up a grand staircase, pushed back a door and came upon a vast beehive filled with booths selling amusement park games—mostly toy guns that you shoot at cowboys or bears or, in one instance, MIGs.

On the plane, I'd read Lao She's *Camel Xiangzi*, a great novel written in the '30s about the crushing life of a Beijing rickshaw driver. It was only at Lao She's *hutong* courtyard house—now a dusty little museum devoted to the writer—that I could sense the painful tremors of Chinese history. It was an unshiny place, well thumbed like an old book. I stared at his worn furniture. He loved Dickens, Menchen, and American slang. As a man who wrote sympathetically about the working class, he tried hard to accommodate himself to the revolution; a photograph shows him laughing with Mao. In 1966, however, the Red Guards attacked and humiliated him, and he was either murdered or committed suicide.

Of course, I did the sights. And I had to see the wall of walls. "But don't go to Badaling," an expatriate told me. It was the worst place, he said, to see the Great Wall. Hawkers mobbed you. Tinny music rattled from loudspeakers. Tour buses belched. It was to Badaling, the expat confided—as if nothing more need be said—that Richard M. Nixon went in 1972 during his trip to China. It was at Badaling that the president, according to legend, observed, "This is a great wall."

The more he talked, the more I wanted to go to Badaling. Its ancient wall has been fully rebuilt and even improved. You could almost call it a zigzag work of modern art, by Christo perhaps. The moment I left the car, tourist shop owners were shouting "Hello! Hello!" and "Water! Water!" (One promised "Extra Special Water.") A troupe in costume loudly clanged Chinese instruments, promising a ride in a sedan chair. You can be the Emperor of the Car Park! On the actual wall, it was hard to move without interfering with someone's photograph. There were shops on the parapet, even a camel ride. In an effort to find some peace, I walked as far as I could, climbing a succession of remarkably steep steps until the way was blocked and the steps lay in ruins. I took a deep breath. I prepared my sensibility. Ahead of me, the dragon wall coiled ecstatically across the rugged hills, its artful engineering—but someone was tapping on my shoulder. A Chinese man pointed at the sky as a Boeing 747 passed overhead. "American science," he announced. "Good!" Then he gave me a thumbs up and answered his cell phone, which was playing "Oh Susannah."

For those who love to dream about the past, the great collection of Ming tombs outside Beijing is probably the best place to go, for even the chattering hordes of tourists cannot disturb the sublime quiet of these structures; they are so well sited under the mountains that they appear fixed for eternity. And those who love the eccentric should not miss the Dong Yue Mao or Eastern Peak Temple, a Taoist shrine in Beijing only recently opened to the public. It contains seventy-six rooms resembling little office-chapels, each occupied by sculptured figures who help the devout with any physical or existential problem. It is nothing less than God's bureaucracy. It includes a Department for Wandering Ghosts, a Department for Suppressing Schemes, and a Flying Birds Department. In each, the figures are designed for their assigned task. Some of the least interesting figures work, not surprisingly, in the Department for Promotion of 15 Kinds of Decent Life Style.

Although I always enjoy the monuments of the past, what inevitably moves me most during travel is the sight of an ancient place that still lives for people. In that respect, the great Lama Temple is the most stirring place in Beijing. Part of the Yellow Hat sect of Tibetan Buddhism, the temple is a beautifully composed series of courtyards thronged daily by practicing Buddhists. I went twice, startled by the devotion animating the architecture. One afternoon, I watched a woman in a slinky red dress, red boots, and a knockoff Prada bag prostrate herself before each of the many Buddhas. I wondered what she'd done the night before—and then I realized I knew what she'd done the night before. I'd seen her in a club at about 3 A.M.

On my last day, miraculously, Mao's tomb was open. For some of the people in the short line with me—many of them older peasants in ill-fitting suits—Mao obviously still remained a god. In the main hall, there was a large gift shop. I bought a Mao watch to go with my two other pop timepieces, a Betty Boop and a Bugs Bunny, and a Mao lighter that plays "The East is Red" when you lift the top. But I did not really want to end on kitsch. And so, with only a couple of hours to spare, I went to another garden.

In Jingshan Park behind the Forbidden City, I climbed a path to what a sign calls (but no guidebook does) the Pavilion of 10,000 Springtimes. Very nice. And a lovely view, too, over the glistening tile roofs of the Forbidden City. On the way down this timely hill, another sign warned: "Look out! The slope is steep and the road is slippery." How true. I crossed the street to Beihai Park and entered the "Round City," a little fortress enclosed by a circular wall. It contains a jade urn once owned by Kublai Khan and a ten-foot-high white jade Buddha. What I most wanted to see was its 800-year-old pine tree. According to the sign, an eighteenth-century emperor named this tree "the Marquis of Shade." I smiled to myself. A good place to while away half an hour, writing some notes under an 800-year-old tree. China seems so much older than America; but also so much younger. What time was it? I glanced at my new Mao watch.

Mark Stevens is the art critic for New York *magazine.*

PAULA MCDONALD

Waltz at the End of Earth

*Amazing things happen when you journey
to the edge of the map.*

TWO OF US WERE ON OUR WAY TO "END OF EARTH," THE
most remote beach on remote Hainan Island, the farthest south in
a string of Chinese islands in the South China Sea. A ridiculous
place to want to go; there's nothing there. But the ancient Chinese
believed the earth ended at the southern tip of this largest of
China's islands. Thus, to journey to "End of Earth" was to show
great "strength and courage," qualities of utmost importance to the
Chinese. To journey to "End of Earth" was to bring great good
fortune to yourself. In such a strange way, my journey did.

Getting to Hainan Island from Guangzhou isn't easy. Eighteen-
hour village-bus rides through the mountains with the inevitable
breakdowns in the middle of the night are followed by tedious ferries, incomprehensible transfers, and more tedious ferries.

But, we found our way to "End of Earth" eventually, a peaceful, serene place with an aura of great continuity. Beyond, with
quiet waves lapping at our feet, the sea seemed to stretch forever.
Like the ancient Chinese, who could know what was out there?
Or what would come next?

In a village nearby, we stopped for lunch at a roadside house,
a hovel actually, one of those one-room shacks that serve as

home, restaurant, and mini-zoo, a combination so common in rural China.

Joanne Turner, my fellow traveler, and I had eaten in many similar places in the few weeks since we'd met and completed a stint together as volunteers on a scientific project meant to catalog China's southern rainforests. We'd camped on remote mountaintops, sea kayaked the uninhabited Outer Islands, trekked through leech-filled jungles, and eaten, standing up, in every street market in Southern China it seemed.

Along the way, we'd become expert pantomimists, ready smilers, and absolute gourmands on the street-food scene. The shabbiness of the shack didn't bother us. The luxury of eating from an actual table instead of a rock seemed rather civilized, in fact.

This particular shack was poor even by Chinese standards though. It held only the bare wooden table, a rope bed, and several cages full of eight- and ten-foot snakes. The dirt floor was swept clean, and an old bicycle hung on the wall. Nothing more adorned the place. Cooking, as is customary in the countryside, was done out back on an empty oil drum with a wood fire below.

The eighty-year-old owner and her granddaughter immediately began to display their snakes. Out they came from their cages and were handed to us, one by one. Which did we want for lunch? We tried to pantomime that it was very hot, that we weren't very hungry after all, and that the snakes were very large. There would be so much waste.

Perhaps rabbit would be better, suggested our hosts. Or so we assumed as they took us to a shed in back where three

The southern Chinese, as any northerner will tell you with distaste, will eat almost anything. I have heard southerners themselves tell the story about the Indian and the Cantonese confronted by a creature from outer space: the Indian falls to his knees and begins to worship it, while the Chinese searches his memory for a suitable recipe.

—Paul Levy, *Out to Lunch*

rabbits were caged. Unable to look any bunny in the eye and then eat it, we politely tried to say that the rabbits were also too big. The only other choice seemed to be an old chicken pecking at the edge of the dirt lane, so we opted for him. Least of all possible sins, or so we thought.

Twenty minutes later, the food began arriving: the usual Chinese mystery soup, followed by several courses of vegetables, rice, and endless pots of steaming tea in the 100-degree heat. Finally the meat arrived.

It was unmistakably rabbit! Oh, lordy, where had we gone wrong? Perhaps we should have drawn pictures instead of doing charades. We ate it, of course. With grace and a good deal of hard swallowing. Not to would have caused a loss of face for the two gracious women whose humble hospitality we shared.

The heat was oppressive that day, as it is all over southern China in May, and even to sit still was to sit and drip. During lunch, the old woman kept smiling at me as if to say, "I forgive you for sweating in my house. There is no loss of face in this," and fanning me with a marvelously ingenious fan made completely of feathers. I had never seen anything like it.

Since there was literally nothing else in the one-room house, not even a change of clothes, and the fan seemed to be her only possession besides an old watch, I was careful not to admire it openly. Chinese custom demands the giving to guests of whatever they admire. But despite my intentional disregard of the fan, I was immensely grateful for the momentary illusion of coolness each *whoosh* brought.

Perhaps because I was trying so hard to ignore the feather fan, what happened next caught me completely by surprise.

Suddenly, for no apparent reason, the old woman broke into a great grin, hugged me hard, handed me the fan, and then hugged me again. I was stunned. It was obviously a gift, but her generosity, under the circumstances, was astonishing. What had prompted the act? What could I, a lanky, perspiring stranger with a sunburned nose, in her life for so short a time, have possibly done to deserve the gift of one of her few possessions? Nothing that I could conceive of, but something had changed dramatically in the little room. The old woman now sat smiling beatifically as though I had pleased her more than I could ever imagine. But I couldn't, for the life of me figure out how.

Despite the baking heat inside the house, we lingered awhile after lunch and drank more tea just to stay and not seem to rush away. And then, to our amazement, when her granddaughter finally left to take care of other chores, the old woman began to speak in halting English, obviously a language she had not used for decades. Bit by bit, straining to understand the stumbling words, we learned her story.

Her husband had been imprisoned under Mao for being a follower of Chiang Kai-shek and had died a prisoner. She had watched as he was led away. She never saw him again.

Before the Cultural Revolution the woman had been a teacher, the daughter of educated diplomats, one of the new regime's despised intellectuals. After the Communist victory in China, she had been exiled from Shanghai to the remote island village for the double sins of being educated and being the wife of a political enemy. She had lived in the isolated village for decades surviving as best she could by cooking and selling the snakes and rabbits she and her granddaughter were able to trap.

Her story, told with no rancor, captured our hearts, and despite the need to get on, we stayed. The long-forgotten English words seemed to get easier for her as we asked questions about her life and encouraged her to reminisce. She told us of her childhood, of traveling and learning English at embassies as a youngster. Memories of another, so very different life. Yet, for all her losses, she truly seemed to have no bitterness. With one strange exception. When I asked her directly if she had regrets, she could think of only one: that she had never learned to waltz.

One of her most vivid childhood memories was of being taken, as a young girl, to a grand ball in Hong Kong where there were many English guests in attendance. The music was international that night, the first time she had heard anything besides the harsh, sharp cacophony of China's music, and suddenly the ballroom was filled with swirling skirts and the sweetest sounds she had ever heard. Couples were waltzing, and, to the young Chinese girl, it was the most beautiful sight in the world. Someday she would grow up to become one of those graceful waltzing women.

She grew up, but China changed. There were no more waltzes. And now there were no more illusions in her life.

In the silence that followed the story, I took her hand across the table. Then I quietly asked if she would still like to learn to waltz. Here. Now.

The slow smile that spread across her face was my answer. We stood and moved together toward our ballroom floor, an open space of five feet of hard-packed dirt between the table and the bed. "Please, God," I prayed, "let me remember a waltz. Any waltz. And let me remember how to lead."

We started shakily, me humming Strauss, stepping on her toes. But soon we got smoother, bolder, louder. "The Blue Danube" swelled and filled the room. Her baggy Mao pajama pants became a swirling skirt, she became young and beautiful again, and I became a handsome foreigner, tall, sure, strong…perhaps a prince who carried her away. Away from her destiny at "End of Earth."

The feather fan hangs on my office wall today, next to her picture. Next to our picture. The two of us, hands clasped, smiling strangers from such different worlds, waltzing around a steaming hut in a forsaken spot I visited by chance that day. That day I met strength and courage at "End of Earth."

Paula McDonald lives on the beach in Rosarito, Mexico. On the clearest of days, if she squints, she likes to think she can see China's "End of Earth." When the waves are quiet, she can certainly hear Strauss.

ARTHUR ZICH

Before the Flood

The Yangtze River defines China—
but the definition is changing.

Jiang Zaiying bounced her thirty-ton dump truck over the lip of a mammoth crater beside the Yangtze River. Around us stretched a moonscape of granite palisades reduced to gravel. The truck rumbled down the rain-gouged slope and splashed to a stop where a front-end loader filled the bed of the vehicle with rocks and muck. Then Jiang rammed the rig into gear and roared back up the crater to deposit one more earthen load toward construction of the Three Gorges Dam. When it is completed—in 2009—Three Gorges will be the most powerful dam ever built, the biggest project China has undertaken since the first ramparts of the Great Wall went up 2,000 years ago.

"The whole world is watching this project," Jiang said. "It's an honor to be part of it—an experience I'll cherish the rest of my life."

Some Chinese do not share Jiang's enthusiasm for the Three Gorges Dam. According to journalist Dai Qing, whose book decrying the project, *Yangtze! Yangtze!*, earned her ten months in prison, the dam is a monstrous disaster waiting to happen. "There is only one Yangtze River," she has written, "and we have already subjected it to many stupid deeds."

But no such sentiment clouds the patriotism and devotion one hears among Jiang's fellow workers in the village of Sandouping, where the great dam is slowly rising, a thousand miles up the Yangtze from the sea. Nearly 3,000 miles more separate the dam-site from the Yangtze's headwaters, making this river the world's third longest, after the Nile and the Amazon. Yangtze waters irrigate China's "land of fish and rice," the great central valley where close to half the nation's food is grown. On it has been written much of China's history and myth. Yet at the same time the river has brought China misery. Devastating floods have repeatedly inundated thousands of square miles and claimed more than 300,000 lives in this century alone.

To most Chinese the river is know as Chang Jiang—Long River. On maps it traces the sinuous line of a dragon. Its serpentine tail curls out of the ice of the Tibetan Plateau and tumbles to China's largest city, Chongqing. Its torso twines through the fabled Three Gorges, celebrated by centuries of poetry and art; its neck winds across the flatlands to the river's mouth near Shanghai.

This piece was first published in 1997, and the dam is much closer to completion, but the author gives a sense of the awesome scale of the project and the changes it is bringing.
—SO'R, JO'R, & LH

Beijing's plan to harness this dragon—to control its furious flooding and transform its raw power into electrical energy—is daunting. The dam will stand 607 feet high and more than a mile wide. It will create a reservoir 370 miles long, with a system of locks designed to bring prosperity through maritime commerce to China's interior. There are taller dams and there are wider dams, but none has this might: At peak load, twenty-six turbines of perhaps 400 tons each, the largest ever built, will generate 18,200 megawatts of electricity, equivalent to the output of eighteen nuclear power plants.

The government claims all this will cost 17 billion dollars. But opponents of the dam—foreign and domestic—challenge virtually every aspect of the government's plans. Critics contend that the region would be better served by a series of smaller dams on Chang Jiang tributaries; that sedimentation will make Chongqing's deep-draft harbor unusable and impede generation of electricity; that an annual flow of a quarter-trillion gallons of raw sewage, together with effluents flushed from abandoned factories left to drown, will kill aquatic species and turn the reservoir into an open sewer the length of Lake Superior; that incalculable relics in unexplored archaeological sites will be forever lost; that before the project's scheduled completion date in 2009 no fewer than 1.9 million people will be forced from ancestral homes and farms and relocated elsewhere. All told, opponents charge, project costs could run as high as 75 billion dollars; already much has been lost to official corruption. Many international lending institutions have refused to help finance the project, largely out of concern for potential environmental problems as well as for the dam's risky financial viability.

To assay the dam and its impact on the region, I embarked on a six-week, 400-mile odyssey down the middle Yangtze, covering the stretch where the new reservoir will be. I hitched rides on a variety of vessels—sampans and hydrofoils, excursion boats and ferries—and put in at a dozen cities along the way, talking with government officials, scientists, technicians, and the farmers and city dwellers who will be most directly affected when the waters rise. I heard many expressions of enthusiasm and pride, like Jiang Zaiying's. But I also heard voices of anger and foreboding. All along the way I saw new construction on a scale that boggled the imagination—new cities, bridges, and highways being thrown up on the river's mountain flanks. It is all predicated on the success of the dam, and it told me as graphically as the awesome construction of the dam itself that the Chinese government intends to finish this project, whatever the cost.

Chongqing, my first stop, was on a building binge. Heavily bombed during the war Japan launched against China in 1937, the city looks like something of a war zone again as new buildings rise from towering heaps of rubble and trash. Construction cranes dangle over Chongqing's jagged hills like sci-fi movie insects. Apartment blocks with gaily colored terrace awnings sprout where once pagoda-roofed pavilions stood. Shops hawk home furnishings—bathtubs, water heaters, fancy beds. On street corners, handymen in from the countryside to claim a share of the boom times cluster with signs touting their skills. Smog billowing through Chongqing's canyons is so foul that it's said one can flavor food with it: The city's rain is the most acidic in China.

On the riverfront, at the confluence of the Chang Jiang and the Jialing Jiang, the deep-water port will be expanded to handle vessels ten times larger than those now navigating the river and increase commercial traffic in coal, tung oil, silk, and an array of agricultural products that southwest China would like to ship to markets on the coast and the world beyond.

But the Chang Jiang is one of the most sediment-filled rivers in the world. Plunging 21,700 feet from its mountain source, it flattens out at Chongqing and, despite the flushing power of its current, leaves immense bunkers of vole-gray sand along the city's riverbanks when monsoon floodwaters recede each year. Opponents of the dam contend that a still-water reservoir will cause even more sediment to be deposited, obstructing the passage of deep-draft vessels.

> Those who would take over the earth
> And shape it to their will
> Never, I notice, succeed.
> The earth is like a vessel
>   so sacred
> That at the mere approach of
>   the profane
> It is marred
> And when they reach out
>   their fingers it is gone.
> —Lao Tzu, *The Way of Life*

I stood on a promontory overlooking the port-to-be. The muddy banks were jammed with blue-and-white excursions boats. The worn stone steps leading to them was alive with ticket hawkers, pancake peddlers, cargo loaders, swarms of passengers clambering to get aboard. I found a gang of diggers pitching a two-story mountain of sand into battered blue dump trucks. One of them, a spry, muscular fellow named Hu Hongrong, put down his spade and told me that the sand had been left by last year's floods, that it was going to construction sites in the city, and that he did this work six months a year, then waited for the monsoon and the rushing river to replenish their sand dune.

Hu earned the equivalent of twenty-five cents a truckload, about two dollars a day, he said. He lived with his co-workers in a hillside shed without water or toilet facilities. Home was a village sixty miles downriver. He had last seen his wife and five-year-old daughter on the Chinese New Year three months before. "The dam will make life better for our children," Hu said. "They'll have electric lights, TV, be able to study their lessons. With luck they'll go to university and bring honor upon our family."

I left Chongqing bound for Fuling aboard a double-decker river ferry jam-packed with people and every conceivable cargo that could be slung from the shoulder poles of ubiquitous porters known as *bangbang-jun*, "the stick army." Our skipper threaded the vessel through a gaggle of motorized sampans in a fine falling mist. Behind us a giant stone Buddha, right hand raised in the wisdom position, gazed down from the river's south bank—just one of the relics that will be lost to the reservoir that the Three Gorges Dam will create.

As the city fell away, terraced fields of wheat and potatoes appeared on the slopes above the river. Here and there the lone figure of a man or woman, slightly stooped, tilled the land with a hoe.

Fuling, like most of the Chang Jiang's cities, is flung across slopes so precipitous that its narrow streets can run only parallel to the river. They are linked up and down by slippery stone stairways. And like most of the river's cities, Fuling is grimy with coal dust, wet from the mist, and destined to be largely inundated as the reservoir rises. It is a city of unceasing noise—tooting riverboats, quacking taxis, blaring dump-truck air horns, an incessant rattle of stereo speakers and television sets.

A billboard on the mountain above the city proclaims, "Fuling pickles bring everlasting love." Fuling is the pickle capital of China.

So I went ashore to meet a pickle king. Nimble and sharp-eyed, Zhang Yonglin presides over acres of mustard tuber. He employs a dozen families that produce more than a thousand tons of tart pickles a year. As a measure of his success he carries an expensive pager inside his old blue Mao jacket and uses it to keep in touch with his daughter, the factory manager. But since Zhang's property lies precisely on the reservoir's 700-foot elevation mark, his days on the ancestral farm will be measured by rising waters.

Zhang is not alone. Half the people destined to be moved are farmers. At rough estimate the reservoir will take as many as 240,000 acres of cropland out of production, including many of the orange groves that grace the river's lateral valley. "It's a pity that so much fertile land must be lost," Zhang said as we toured his fields and fermentation pits. He pulled a dripping tuber from a pit, cracked it open, sniffed it the way a connoisseur would savor cognac, and pronounced it fragrant.

Back at his house Zhang's daughter served us tea. "My family has been here since the Ming dynasty," Zhang said. The Ming dynasty, I reflected, ended more than 350 years ago. I asked him what the government would be offering in return for his land. "I don't know," he replied. "I don't know when we'll have to move. Or even where we'll be moved. You have to take what the state gives you. There is no bargaining."

Zhang's daughter added softly, "Mama died here. We hope that we can move her grave."

Below Fuling the river cleaves yet another stretch of green terraced slopes, where tiny farm villages perch atop stony ledges, isolated, save for the river, from the rest of the world. Along this middle reach of the Chang Jiang, the landscape conveys a simple message: that China is a nation of peasant farmers, always has been, and perhaps, given the imperative of human numbers, always will be. Yet the great dam rising at Sandouping seemingly sends a different message—that China is a nation in transition to another kind of society altogether.

"Farmers find it hard to survive in an industrialized society," Pang Xiaolong was saying. I met this imperious young business-man aboard a crowded hydrofoil plowing toward the city of Wanxian, 125 miles downriver from Fuling. Pang was a branch manager of a company hoping to win government contracts for resettlement housing. His tailored green plaid suit stood in marked contrast to the drab peasant garb of the other passengers.

"Farmers want to work in the factories, but the transition is dif-ficult and few of them adjust," Pang went on. "They have no skills. They lack education. They lack the attitude one needs to learn. They have no sense of time, of living by the clock."

The vessel cut its engines and coasted toward the barge that served as Wanxian's landing. "There's competition for positions these days," Pang shouted over the crush of passengers moving to-ward the exit. "A new generation is taking over. If you want to keep your job, you have to produce!"

I asked how he had managed to reach such an exalted position at such a tender age. "My father is manager of the company," he said.

Wanxian, at the midpoint between Chongqing and the dam, stands so high above the river that porters with red-curtained sedan chairs queue up at the landing to haul tourists up its 183 steps. But its elevation will not save the ciy. Beside Wanxian's old clock tower and a leafy park in the center of the city stands a red-and-white sign indicating the level to which the waters will rise. All below it—two-thirds of the city proper, embracing 8.5 square miles and 900 factories—will be drowned. A quarter million peo-ple will be uprooted and moved to an unknown location. Wanxian will be the reservoir's costliest victim.

The good news is that a new Wanxian will rise above the reser-voir. A railway, the city's first, will tie Wanxian into the major east-west trunk line, ninety miles to the north. A riverside highway linking Shanghai with Chengdu, the capital of Sichuan, will cut through the city. An airport capable of handling jumbo jets will be built atop a mountain on the south side of the river. Tying the airport to the city, one of the world's longest single-arch bridges will span the Chang Jiang.

At the bridge site I met Zhang Mingtai, general manager of SOTE Ltd., the region's largest industrial complex. Zhang is one of the new breed of Chinese entrepreneurs, a salesman for "market socialism." We stood at the edge of the precipice above the river, and Zhang swept a hand across the vista—the doomed city, the Chang Jiang running red with iron-rich soil, the immense valley reaching back into distant mountains. "This is central China," Zhang said over the wind. "The resources here are unknown to outsiders. We're enormously rich in coal, salt, and natural gas. Right here we'll have a population of 570,000 hard-working people. When the dam is built, the opportunities here will be limitless!"

"Without the dam?" I asked.

"Without the dam," he said brusquely, "we'll have nothing."

If Zhang embodies Wanxian's future, young, exuberant Li Liang bears responsibility for its past. Li's grandiose title is Director, Sichuan Work Station, Cultural Relics Preservation Team, National Cultural Relics Bureau. His resources do not match his desk plaque. Li has but five men, no certain budget, and precious few years to find and excavate the region's relics along a 300-mile stretch of the river valley.

Li's team has discovered 1,208 historical sites that face certain inundation—more than 300 of them in Wanxian alone. Among these are temples and other structures dating back to the Han dynasty, around the time of Christ; more than thirty Stone Age sites 30,000 to 50,000 years old; and what appears to be the seat of the little-understood people known as the Ba, who settled in the region some 4,000 years ago.

Li took me to one of the sites: a small pagoda beside a stone slab surrounded by a shallow moat right in the midst of Wanxian's busy downtown. There, a thousand years ago, Tang dynasty poets gathered beneath the moon and sipped wine from floating cups. I thought of time and the river flowing—time that was, for sites such as these, swiftly running out. The Beijing government, reluctant to spend money to salvage these relics of China's glorious history, is doing little more than minimizing the losses. "So many places cannot be saved," Li said. He gazed off in the direction of the river. "In less than a decade, they'll be gone."

It is impossible to summarize all that the Chang Jiang has meant to the millions of Chinese who have lived and died beside it and its tributaries over the years. Its watershed encompasses 700,000 square miles, a fifth of China's total land area. It irrigates more than a third of China's agricultural output and carries three-quarters of China's internal waterborne commerce. It divides the country north and south in matters as fundamental as culinary taste and religious perspective.

Only recently have scholars recognized that the Three Gorges region represents one of the true seats of Chinese civilization. In the demi-world where history intersects with myth, it's said that the gorges were created by the ingenious folk hero Yu, who—with the help of a troop of dragons—reconfigured China's hills and valleys to drain the land and make it habitable for humans.

"But for Yu," goes an old Chinese saying, "we should all have been fishes."

The gorges made Sichuan a nearly impenetrable redoubt for the kingdom of Shu during China's Three Kingdoms era 1,800 years ago—and did so again for Chiang Kai-shek's Nationalist government when Japan invaded in 1937. With pinnacles soaring up to 4,000 feet, the gorges have inspired China's greatest landscape artist, moved poets to reflect on the insignificance of humans in the face of nature, and offered the modern traveler some of the most spectacular scenery on the planet.

A few miles below Wanxian the Chang Jiang narrows, runs ragged between giant slabs of black rock. Scattered farmhouses rise from lush green promontories shrouded in mist. A sign proclaims: "The new site of Yunyang County welcomes you!"

But for me, old Yunyang city was all there was just then. And Yunyang was a page out of time gone by. Cooks sold deep-fried *doufu* from charcoal-fired woks at the river's edge. Narrow alleys

Paintings of Chinese land-scapes are delicate portrayals of magical kingdoms. Behind tree limbs one can see, far below, the waters of a winding stream emerging from distant misty hills. A fisherman holding a pole stands on his bamboo raft. The magic always comes from the mist which surrounds tall sharp mountains, one perhaps capped by a small temple. These seem like allegorical paintings—there could be no such mountains, no such wraiths of mist. Yet, this is Guilin, south of the Yangtze. Approaching by plane, the ground rises to meet you in monstrous rows of teeth. These hills are karst limestone, taller than they are wide, standing on an alluvial plane through which shallow rivers flow. Each tooth has gaping cavities where the limestone has been etched away by rain or rivers, so that they appear to be man-made. Some even have steep winding lines of steps carved into their sides, which add to the illusion of being the handicraft of an ancient artisan.

—John Graham,
"The Classic Landscape"

twining off the steps were crowded with stalls displaying straw sandals, cheap metal kitchen utensils, plaster Mao busts. Old men smoking foot-long pipes lolled in old-fashioned slat chairs outside old-fashioned teahouses. The first sound I heard came from a loudspeaker in a tree—China People's Broadcasting Station, the same dawn-to-dusk instrument of propaganda harangue I'd heard in China twenty years ago.

I also heard the first voices of discontent among people scheduled for resettlement—a sense of outrage that would grow sharper as I neared the dam. I hailed a cab to Bao Ta (Precious Tower), a village on the city's outskirts scheduled for resettlement. When that would happen was uncertain, the driver told me. "Some officials invested the resettlement money in other projects," he said. I asked him who the officials were. "I don't know their names," the driver said, "I'm only *laobaixing*"—the Chinese term for common people. "Officials don't care about the *laobaixing*."

*

In Bao Ta village, beside a vegetable patch redolent of orange blossoms, the local people crowded around, eager to voice their anger. "We're supposed to get 5,000 yuan [US $600] a head for resettlement," a farm woman shouted. "The central government gives the money to our provincial officials. They give it to the county, and the county gives it to the city bosses. But as it goes down the line, each official takes his cut. Who knows what will be left by the time it gets to us?"

Another woman spoke up: "They're supposed to give us jobs, but if you don't have connections, you can't get one." *How do you acquire connections?* I asked. "You want connections, you give them cigarettes and wine," she replied.

Then an old man spoke with the courage of years. "There is corruption here," he said with a resigned, ironic chuckle. "And the more money there is, the more corruption there'll be."

Not all the villagers along the river were as disenchanted as Bao Ta's residents. Some expressed simple resignation, in the centuries-old tradition of the Chinese common man who has learned to accept whatever card fate—or the state—might deal. In Zigui, farther downriver, I met an orange grower named Qu Zharun, who claimed to be a direct descendant of Qu Yuan, the third-century B.C. poet revered to this day. But not even Qu's august lineage was going to save his farm and the mud house he'd built for his wife and sons thirty-four years ago. His plight exemplified that of so many elderly in the Chang Jiang Valley. "Where will I go?" Qu asked, passing a bowl of fresh-picked cherries. "I'm old. I can't read. I have no skills. I'll have to decide which son to live with." He smiled wryly. "Or maybe I'll become a doorman at one of our fancy new hotels."

Options are likewise limited for Long Zhiyi, a barrel-chested innkeeper in the village of Dachang, some fifty miles up the Chang Jiang's Daning River tributary. He views the dam in the context of China's economic reforms and newfound prosperity. "My name means 'one-knowing dragon,'" Long boomed. "The one thing I know is how to make money! Before the reforms it was illegal to own your own business. We were poor. I worked in the field. Now? I'm rich! I have six guest rooms. Tourists and big shots come!"

And the dam?

"For me? No good!" he roared. "I was born here. I built this house with my own hands. I'll lose my inn! My goldfish pond! My street! For me, it's terrible!" Then he put his arm around his eighteen-year-old daughter and gave her a fatherly hug. "But for her, it's wonderful! After the dam we'll have a fish farm beside the reservoir! Maybe a bigger inn and a restaurant!"

The prospect of rising waters has already improved the lives of some displaced families. Consider the case of Li Chenling, a former farmer now resettled in a new high-rise apartment. Before the move, her family had lived in a mud-walled, dirt-floored house in an impoverished river village of some hundred households. They had no glass in the windows, no heat in the winter, an outdoor privy. Until she became pregnant, Li worked in the field alongside her husband, growing their own food. But when the Southwest Synthetic Pharmaceutical Factory relocated from the Chongqing riverfront to the higher ground of her village, the couple were given the apartment to compensate for the loss of their land, and Li's husband qualified for a factory job as a chemical machine operator.

The couple moved in the day their daughter was born. "We've become city people now," Li told me. "We pay fifteen yuan [$1.80] a month rent, including water, gas, and electricity." What of their newfound lifestyle most delights her? "Tap water," she replied happily. "And indoor toilet!"

Qutang, the first and shortest of the three gorges, was almost hidden in rain, but I sat snug and dry in the pilothouse of a creaking old river ferry. Through mists tumbling over the north bank, I could see Baidicheng—the White Emperor City—with its stately mountaintop temple dating back almost 2,000 years.

For a moment it seemed that the river had reached a dead end, that the boat would smash head-on against a charcoal-streaked, copper-colored cliff at the entrance to Qutang Gorge. The pilot put the wheel hard over. We sluiced sidewise into the racing current of a watercourse barely 350 feet wide—the narrowest point in the gorges. There was no room for error. The pilot wheeled hard right. Our old bucket shuddered and slid into the gorge. Precipitous sandstone cliffs soared above us, leaving high a splinter of sky.

High on one wall hung a cedar coffin, a burial of the ancient Ba people whose unstudied ways will be obliterated by the reservoir. On the other wall the remains of a recessed towpath ran like a scar. On it as many as 300 brute trackers, naked and roped together like animals, once hauled cargo junks of a hundred tons and more upstream against the surging current. That time ended in the 1950s when Chinese engineers blasted out the riverbed boulders that had made their arduous toil up the gorges necessary.

Now, in the pearl gray dawn, one could almost hear echoes of their soulful cadence, "Ayah...ayah!" And looking up at gnarled pines clinging to the cliffs, I could imagine the once abundant monkeys crying "ceaselessly on both banks," as the poet Li Bai described them 1,200 years ago.

Then, as quickly as we had entered Qutang Gorge, a scant five miles downriver we were out of it. The river broadened, the current slowed to a muddy pace, and life on shore resumed its eternal pattern. A sampan with a lattice cage of ducks lay up on the riverbank. A woman knelt on the rocks beating her laundry with a stick. The land beyond the shore opened out in verdant farms. Ahead of us, still more cliffs crowded the gray sky, and behind them the jagged peaks of Wu Xia, Witches Gorge.

Twenty-five miles long, this gorge is perhaps the most forboding of the three. A dozen 3,000-foot limestone peaks with names like Climbing Dragon and Flying Phoenix soar from the river to shut out the sun. During our passage, eddies whirled across the water and gusts of wind hooted through the narrows. I felt a touch of relief when we emerged into a stretch of open river valley.

Ahead lay Xiling Gorge, the last and, at forty-seven miles, longest of the three gorges. Once Xiling's threatening shoals all but closed the river. Junks running downstream at twenty miles an hour often splintered apart on submerged boulders. Dredging and blasting have eased much of that danger. But landslides continue to break off huge chunks of unstable shale; only a few months earlier half the face of a mountain fell on a south shore village. Fortunately a seismic warning evacuated the residents from harm's way. But the rubble we saw from the river was unsettling. Where whitewashed farm buildings once stood, rocks the size of houses huddled in the deep shadows, massed one upon the other.

Chinese seismologists who support the dam say that it is safe from rock slides and earthquakes. But in this village we were only forty miles from what will be one of the world's most powerful rivers ever dammed. And China's dam-building record on far lesser waterways has included a number of tragic failures.

The new and the old strike an ever more disquieting contrast the closer one comes to Three Gorges Dam. A twisted pine gripping a riverine cliff, a lone fisherman casting his net from a rock-strewn shore, an old man sitting in silent meditation atop a misty crag—such vignettes evoke poetic visions of China's past. But then you see the freshly minted cities rising to replace the towns doomed by the reservoir.

What impact might these changes have collectively on the river? Opponents of the dam, such as Probe International, a Canadian environmental group, have described the chemical poisoning of the river that will come from industrial toxics—arsenic, cyanide, methylmercury, among others—leaching out of drowned factories. For their part, government officials in China point to strict environmental laws governing industrial pollution, including stiff fines for repeated violations. But an environmental control officer at a pharmaceutical factory dismissed these safeguards with a shrug. "It's cheaper to pay the fine than to build a treatment plant," he told me. Moreover, right now, fully 80 percent of China's cities have no sewage treatment—and nowhere in the plans for these brave new cities did I find mention of building any.

Such matters are of little concern in Sandouping, the once tiny village where the great dam will rise. The single goal of the 60,000 workers assembled there is to build the thing. I stood in a driving rain on the dam site's highest point, looking out across the river. Directly below, men and machines were digging a trench for the five-stage lock system. Giant drills had sliced almost 300 feet straight down into solid granite. Beyond, dump trucks and bull-dozers, tiny as toys in the distance, scurried up and down a maze of gravel roads. And this was only the cofferdam—a kind of giant river-spanning bowl inside of which work will then proceed on the permanent dam and its hydroelectric hardware. I tried to imag-ine what the dam would look like when completed: a gleaming concrete barrier, almost a mile and a half long, holding back an unimaginable weight of water; the river's thundering spill; power lines singing overhead; great ships gliding through the locks; and untold millions of homes and farms downstream, presumably se-cure at last against the ravages of flood. What price, I wondered, could anyone put on such an achievement? And what cost in human terms?

I found at least part of the answer to that a few days later, below the damsite at a riverside village called Zhicheng in the flat central China rice lands. There, Zhu Guobing and wife, Gao Yuren, had just resettled after being forced from their home in the gorges— one family among the hundreds of thousands of households the dam will eventually displace.

Generations of Zhus had lived in the mountains above Xiling Gorge. On moving day the couple had loaded their meager pos-sessions—two pigs, five chickens, several bags of grain—aboard a crowded government boat and gathered with friends and relatives for a farewell dinner. "We told them to tear down our house and take anything worth taking," Zhu told me. "I couldn't bear it. I was crying in my heart."

So I came to the end of my journey—left to ponder this dam that spawns such patriotic fervor and furious opposition. Time will tell which side is right. But for all the controversy that attends construction of the Three Gorges Dam, one fact seems indisputable. Unless changes in national leadership bring anti-dam forces to power, the dam will be built. For better or worse, colossal, timeless China is rising at last to join the modern world.

Arthur Zich is a graduate of Dartmouth College and Yale's Institute of Far Eastern Languages, and was a Mandarin Chinese linguist in the U.S. Air Force Security Service. He has also served as a foreign correspondent for Time-Life, a writer and editor for Newsweek, *and a freelance writer for* National Geographic *and other publications. He is a recipient of the Professional Journalism Fellowship from Stanford University, and he lives in Northern California.*

STEPHANIE ELIZONDO GRIEST

The Tao of Bicycling

Like so many things, it's made in China.

EVERYBODY IN BEIJING HAD A BICYCLE BUT ME. AND I wanted one. Bad. Preferably a proletarian model forged from industrial steel that weighed fifty pounds and had a basket for cabbage storage and a tinny silver bell. That way, I would be just like everyone else.

Liu—my colleague at *China Daily*, where I worked as an editor—was my first recruit in the purchase. Whereas the other reporters fawned over my tones, she put me in my place my second day on the job with: "I know you are just learning Chinese, but you keep mispronouncing my first name. I am not an 'Evil Fish.'" So I trusted her to tell me if I was getting a good deal or not.

Envisioning Chinese bicycle salesmen to be as wily as American car salesmen, I decided a male should tag along, too. Xiao Yang happily agreed. His name means "Little Sheep," but I liked to call him—in English—"Lambchops," to which he cheerfully replied: "I am a sheep, not a lamb."

The three of us went to the canteen to discuss the purchase. Lambchops asked a few questions between bites of chicken and cashews and—after determining that I really did not want a model "more appropriate for foreigners"—said he knew just where to go.

51

After washing our plates and storing them in the lockers, we headed out to the street to hail a taxi. Legions of cabbies inhabit Beijing's streets, but the cheapest were the yellow vans known as Miandi, or "Breadboxes." Lambchops flagged one down and hopped in the front seat to keep the driver company. Liu and I shared the back seat: a tire with a towel draped over it. Off we roared, dodging daredevil Xiali cabs to the left and jam-packed buses to the right, and eventually pulled up to a department store that advertised its wares on colorful banners that spilled down its facade. Dozens of bicycles were parked in its front rack, guarded by an eighty-year-old attendant with a wispy white beard who nodded as we walked past.

The first floor largely consisted of women's apparel that would strike many a blow to my self-esteem in upcoming months, as I could never pull any of the Asian-sized pants past my knee caps. We rode the escalator to the basement and there—between the washers and the dryers—stood a rack of Chinese bicycles, solid as tanks and twice as heavy. Black Forevers anchored one side; purple Flying Pigeons the other. Lambchops disentangled a Forever for me and, with considerable effort, turned it upside down. I rotated the pedals and squeezed its brakes. "Let's take it out for a spin," I suggested.

Giggling nervously, Lambchops translated my request to the two salesmen who had just joined us. The one with Coke-bottle glasses grunted before shouting, first at Lambchops, then at me.

"Ah, Stephanie. It is not permissible to ride this bike until you buy it," Lambchops translated.

"But how am I supposed to know if it is a good fit?"

The men folded their arms across their chests and glared. Apparently, I wasn't.

When I lived in Moscow as an exchange student, I generally did as I was told, largely because people there intimidated me. Being half a head taller than most everyone in China, however, felt oddly empowering. Deeming that orderly department store in need of some civil disobedience, I turned to the sales clerks and, in staccato Mandarin, declared: "I ride before I buy."

With that, I uprighted the bike, straddled its seat, rode past the dryers, and headed toward the refrigerators in the neighboring aisle. The clerks were stunned. Lambchops was mortified. Evil Fish was amused. And I was the proud owner of a Chinese bicycle. All I needed now was the basket. And the bell.

In the month that followed, not one cyclist passed me on the road. This had less to do with my athletic prowess than the fact that Chinese rode at the same pace they did *tai chi*. And yet, everyone I passed always caught up with me at the traffic lights, which were interminable. I would bolt ahead as soon as the light turned green, but they rejoined me at the next red light a block away. Even though I rode twice as fast, we all arrived at the same place at the same time.

Moreover, my Chinese Forever couldn't be ridden like my mountain Mongoose back home. There was no hunching and pumping on

> I waited about five hours before setting out on my own. My first order of business was, of course, to secure a bicycle. I didn't waste time shopping around, as the only model available was the Fei Ge. Huo Baoji based his classic model on the 1932 English Raleigh roadster. He had Flying Dove in mind when naming his creation, but due to a glitch in the translation, the bike became known as the Flying Pigeon. Weighing in at nearly fifty pounds, the Flying Pigeon was a beast of a bike. It was also a work of art in its simplicity. Pedals, chain, wheels, frame, seat, and handlebars— that's all you got. Handbrakes were included, but rarely worked. And like Henry Ford's Model-T, the Flying Pigeon came in any color you wanted, as long as you wanted black.
> —Stephen Ausherman, "Flying Pigeon, My True Friend"

this set of pedals: when I tried to stand, the bike threatened to keel over. For the longest time, this exasperated me: how else was I supposed to burn off those yummy pork buns I devoured for breakfast? But biking is a meditative endeavor in China, even when used for utilitarian purposes. Life is hard enough—why exert more energy than absolutely necessary?

Eventually, I learned to sit in a fully upright position like everyone else and ride slowly, with the flow, taking in the peoplescape as it glided past. Barbers tended to their customers beneath shade trees, their combs and clippers peeking out of their pockets. Bicycle repairmen squatted in the middle of the sidewalk with their tools and pumps, waiting for someone's tires to blow. Black marketeers spread out their pirated CDs, DVDs, and computer software atop tarps. Blind men read palms and told fortunes. Provincial-looking men dug ditches in tattered suits and ties; construction workers pulverized dilapidated buildings wearing only hard hats for protection.

The most enterprising roadside capitalists were the food vendors. Peasants roasted chestnuts over open fires and baked sweet potatoes atop oil drums. Old men in Mao jackets shish-kebobbed hawberries and dipped them into syrup that dried into a candied crunch. *Baozi* ladies sold dumplings straight off the bamboo steamer. Noodle ladies doused your choice of rice, egg, or glass noodles with vinegar and soy sauce and served it in a styrofoam box. There were duck egg ladies, phallus-shaped fried bread ladies. My favorite was the pancake lady, who parked her cart just outside my compound. With a ladle, she spread her batter over a pizza-sized griddle and cooked it like a crepe. Once it solidified, she expertly flipped it over with a spatula, added green onions, sauces, and spices, cracked an egg on top, and let it cook a couple seconds more. Then she folded the whole thing into quarters, scooped it into a piece of brown paper, and handed it over, hot and delicious.

Alongside these *xiao chi*—"small eats"—vendors stood the produce peddlers. Each morning, peasants pedaled cartfuls of fresh fruits and vegetables into the city, and you could tell the season by their selection. When I first arrived in August, there were bright orange persimmons, scarlet pomegranates, and clumps of sweet lychees. Farmers hauled in cabbages by the truckload in November, which everyone left in the sun to dry a week or two before storing them for the long winter ahead. During the cold season, carts yielded carrots, potatoes, radishes, and lotus roots shaped like baby arms. Cherry blossoms and wild vegetables announced the arrival of spring; strawberries, pineapples, mangoes, and melons meant summer was near. Bananas were perennial and foreigners apparently had a reputation for liking them, because every time I rode past a guy selling some, he'd grab one and jiggle it at me. (Female banana vendors, incidentally, never did this.)

Rounding up the food sellers were the meat mongers, whose offerings were equally fresh. Schools of eel quivered in half-filled wading pools; too many fish crammed into murky tanks. Crabs, lobsters, and crawfish attempted escape by forming decapodan pyramids and boosting each other out of their bins. Hens, ducks, geese, and pigeons scrunched into chicken-wire cages; carving blocks were strewn with bloody chunks of pork and beef.

Equally vivid was the scene inside of the bicycle packs. Like eating, working, showering, and shitting, cycling was a communal activity in China. Couples held hands as they rode side by side. Girlfriends chatted about their day. Street chefs toted their kitchens; guys, their dates; husbands, their wives; mothers, their children. Businessman talked on cell phones, toddlers rode in bamboo seats. Bicycles were an indispensable mode of transportation for millions of residents, and their numbers didn't waiver with the weather. When it started raining, cyclists simply pulled over and broke out the brilliantly-colored ponchos designed especially for them, with extra long fronts that stretched over their handlebars and covered the contents of their baskets. Then they continued with their journeys, a kaleidoscope of yellow, orange, red, green, and purple polka dot. These were the times I felt most part of this world: cruising down the street with a basket full of eggplants, dodging a downpour in a peacock blue poncho, on my way to where I needed to be, with no better way of getting there.

I have yet to discover the road to understanding the birthplace of Maoism and Taoism. But I'm fairly certain that it can only be traversed by bicycle.

Stephanie Elizondo Griest has belly danced with Cuban rumba queens, mingled with the Russian Mafia, and edited the propaganda of the Chinese Communist Party. "The Tao of Bicycling" was excerpted from her first book, Around the Bloc: My Life in Moscow, Beijing, and Havana. *She has also written for* The New York Times, The Washington Post, Latina Magazine, *and* Travelers' Tales Cuba, Travelers' Tales Turkey, Her Fork in the Road, *and* Hyenas Laughed at Me and Now I Know Why. *She once drove 45,000 miles across the nation in a beat-up Honda, documenting alternative U.S. history for a children's web site. You can visit her own web site at www.aroundthebloc.com.*

KATHLEEN LEE

✳ ✳ ✳

Into the Heart of the Middle Kingdom

She roams the vastness of Chinese culture.

LIAO INHALED ON HIS CIGARETTE LIKE HE WAS BLOWTORCHING his lungs, tapped a hard fingernail against one of my tiles, and said in Chinese, "You should have played that one." I was playing mahjongg—badly. The other players—two men who played fiercely and rapidly and a woman wearing the latest Chinese fashion, a tight chiffon dress slit to her hips and a pair of heels with ankle-length nylon socks—smoked while I contemplated my tiles. The woman played coolly, as if she didn't care who won. They were all patient, which is typical of the Chinese, who seem to have levels of sheer tolerance that would elevate most people to nirvana.

I couldn't concentrate: too much was happening on this weekday afternoon at the Jin River Park. Liao's constant conversation, for instance. "In the summer, tea is my savior," he said, twisting off the lid of his tea jar and drinking. He had lustrous thick hair and bad teeth. We spoke a mix of Chinese and English, Liao interjecting "Do you understand?" with manic regularity. I had talked to him every day since I'd arrived in Chengdu, the capital of Sichuan Province, but he had an endearing amnesia. Today he said, "You live in Brazil, right?" No. His conversation required no prompting. "Chinese people are more concerned with social rules. Westerners are more honest." Was he talking about the way I played mah-jongg?

A few feet from our concrete table under a shady elm, a troop of soldiers marched into the park, dropped to their bellies, and began desultory target practice with unloaded weapons. They appeared to be aiming at pedestrians strolling along the opposite bank. Mysterious. How could they lie with their noses so close to the stinking waters of the Jin River, peppered with garbage and bubbling with methane? From a nearby primary school came the sweet innocence of children singing "Twinkle, Twinkle, Little Star" in Chinese. Itinerant barbers snipped people's hair. Beneath the sounds of bicycle bells and honking horns from the street were the clicks of mah-jongg tiles, the sharp clap of wooden chess pieces. Nobody appeared distracted, except me. Perhaps the ability to focus in the midst of bustle is what living in China, among an intimate mass of a billion people, teaches you.

When I first came to the country—and to Sichuan Province—in 1987, I was really just in transit. China hardly figured in my imagination: I was going to India. But you can't just pass through this land; it takes you by the throat.

At first I thought everyone was angry, an exoticized anger in a language that sounded like music sans melody. Then I realized that the Chinese were like my Italian relatives: loud. I began to like the country and its people; the chaos and noise of human exchange was oddly familiar, while nearly everything else, from the language (which I didn't yet speak) to the bedding (towels for pillowcases), was delightfully strange. From that first trip, Sichuan Province stood out as extraordinary. Chengdu was livelier, Sichuanese people warmer, the markets more colorful, the countryside more vivid than other places in China. Sichuan satisfied every expectation I unconsciously held about the country: peasants in emerald rice fields, mountains laced with mist, temples with tiled, upcurved roofs. In Sichuan, you can experience the China of the twenty-first century and the old China of willow-patterned plates and the wild

China that we rarely imagine. This was the China that I knew I had to return to.

Sichuan, meaning "Four Rivers," is roughly the size of France, and landlocked near the center of the country. In the eastern part, where most of the province's 110 million residents live, lies the fertile Red Basin, with a subtropical climate and rich soil. Three harvests a year are produced here in a rigorous cycle from muddy fields to luscious greenery. Sichuan is China's Iowa, California, and Kansas: a combination heartland, breadbasket, and gateway to the west—minus John Deere. Instead of tractors and combines, you see men with wooden plows slung over their shoulders leading water buffalo into muddy fields, and women bent between rows of plump cabbages. China relies on Sichuanese agriculture, profits from which power the economic success of the province.

There's a saying: "When the rest of the country is at peace, Sichuan is the last brought to heel." In China, Sichuan is famous for its spicy food and its residents' independent-mindedness, a stubborn quality connected to the province's main physical feature: mountains. Sichuan is ringed and sliced by forbidding alpine ranges. The west, in particular, with more herd animals than humans, is pleated with wild, high peaks. These have served to both isolate and insulate Sichuan from mainstream China. Little surprise then, that it was Sichuan native Deng Xiaoping—tenacious, peppery, inventive—who orchestrated China's economic metamorphosis from communism to the present idiosyncratic blend of capitalism and socialism.

As you move from the farmland of eastern Sichuan into the mountains and high plains of the west, civilizing influences thin, cowed by the untamed sweeps of exhilaratingly empty land beneath plattered skies. This is China's Wild West. The pressures of materialism dwindle as the pressures of survival intensify. Produce grows in patches hewn from the raw, luminous terrain, and unfenced grasslands surge, oceanlike, to the horizon. The fiercely autonomous people who inhabit these immense distances are Tibetan, Hui Muslim, and Qiang, three of China's ethnic minority groups. From western Sichuan, the central government feels remote, and residents do what they like. In response to the atmosphere of lawlessness that prevails in the region, Chengdu is thick with soldiers poised for trouble, either in Sichuan or to its west in Tibet.

Visiting a Chinese city is like deboning a fish: if you do it right, it's terrific; if not, you eat bones. Within fifteen minutes of my arrival in Chengdu, I began to think that all of China was under construction. Buildings were rising and falling—it was often hard to tell which. Chengdu's old half-timbered structures—resembling sixteenth-century English cottages—were disintegrating or were being sledgehammered away without nostalgia. Blocky new white-tiled buildings fingered the skyline, and I was convinced that their blue windows were meant to give the illusion of blue skies, because in Chengdu, they say dogs bark when the sun—an intruding stranger—emerges. Chengdu's skies weren't blue, but the sun lit the gray unto an opalescent brilliance gone powdery with pollution.

The way to experience a Chinese city is to wander its streets, and the way to wander its streets is on a bicycle. So, on my first morning, I rented a Flying Pigeon and wobbled into the mass of bicyclists maneuvering among food carts, pedestrians, cars, buses, pedicabs, motorbikes, fruit sellers with baskets of peaches swinging from either side of shoulder poles all coming from different directions. Fortunately, people in Chengdu ride at a conversational pace; unfortunately, they appear to daydream. Traffic lights are loosely adhered to, and lane dividers are merely decorative; it was a hip-to-bumper, face-to-windshield scrum.

After running into only two cyclists, when I swerved to avoid someone spitting (the signature habit in China), I arrived at the massive concrete statue of Mao planted at the top of Renmin Nan Lu (People's Road South). The chairman's statue resembles the smaller plastic one of Colonel Sanders outside a KFC several hundred yards away: two big-chested men, one with an arm outstretched in welcome, both apparently benevolent. They meet across a huge square where nobody is allowed on the grass. Of the two, Mao is the controversial figure.

"Mao was a great man who made mistakes," said a woman with a sparse puff of white hair. "He improved life for the peasants. Everyone was equal—no rich or poor. Yes, there were terrible things." She shrugged and chased after her grandson, who was heading for the forbidden grass. Clearly, the present was more absorbing than the past.

A few moments later, I met Liao for the first time. He refused to absolve Mao. "He was selfish, an egomaniac. I can never forgive him," he said. "During the Cultural Revolution I learned nothing, the schools were closed, and other, worse things happened." For a minute he looked as if he might cry or punch somebody. Abruptly he switched from Mao to mah-jongg and asked if I could play; he too had little desire to review the past.

Back on my bike, I headed south down Renmin Nan Lu, stopping to watch department store employees performing exercises to a routine blasting from the PA system. Lined up in their uniforms outside the store, sullen young women twisted and flapped beneath the stern gaze of a manageress. They were not happy Socialist workers forging a healthy Socialist future. These group calisthenics used to be carried out with a willed desire to believe in socialism. Now what was there to believe in? China has changed quickly and deeply, and with the changes came cynicism, born of the gap between Socialist rhetoric and capitalist reality. These women understood the vacuousness of a Socialist activity attached to a capitalist enterprise.

Next came the street markets between Renmin and Hongxing streets, selling lychees, freshly folded dumplings, blue-skinned chickens, pet crickets woven into basket cages, frothy pink hair ribbons. A woman talked on her cellular phone while the duck she had purchased was dipped in a vat of boiling water and then plucked. New technology was in everyone's pockets, but the Chinese people were not about to buy their meat wrapped in plastic on a foam tray in a fifteen-aisle supermarket.

I bought a triangle-shaped bread from a woman selling them warm from a basket on the back of her bike. She had a broad, placid face and wore her hair tucked into a white cotton cap. Soft and flat, the bread had scallions and a sprinkling of crushed cardamom and anise; two pie-shaped slices cost less than ten cents. When I opened my wallet, the vendor spotted a picture I carried of myself at the age of five. "That's you," she shouted. A delighted crowd gathered to examine and comment on my younger self; they love children, they loved my former innocence.

At Wangjianglou Park I stopped for a rest: instant relief. The noise of traffic was held at bay, replaced by the susurrus of breezes through bamboo. I dutifully viewed the sluggish Jin River from the pagoda-style Ming Dynasty River Viewing Pavilion, which had thick pads of moss growing on its roof tiles. (Dates and dynasties: I attach people to time periods. Tang is Charlemagne, Ming is Shakespeare, Qing is Napoleon.) Then I strolled curved paths beside lotus-flowered lakes and watched a ballroom dance class. Nobody appeared self-conscious; the Chinese can dance badly in front of anyone. Beside the dancers, a shirtless man practiced tai chi, arms sweeping the air, legs lifting and landing as if he might fall through the earth if he weren't careful.

> A German-American teacher at the University, who was married to a Chinese woman, liked to tell the story of the time he got lost in the country. Riding his bicycle up to a house, he asked for directions (in fluent Mandarin) from the couple who answered the door. But instead of helping him, the old farmer and his wife just shook their heads at him in silence. Perplexed by their unusually rude behavior, the teacher turned to walk away when he heard the man say distinctly to his wife, "If I didn't know any better, I would swear that young devil was trying to speak to us in Chinese."
>
> —Katherine Lee Clark, "A Teacher's Journey to China"

At a teahouse pavilion of dark, polished wood overlooking a quiet lake, I settled into a reclining bamboo chair and, for fifty cents, drank an endless cup of fragrant tea refilled by a roving band of pourers. It was served in a handleless porcelain cup fitted into a tight saucer. You sweep the curved lid over the surface of the water, brushing back floating tea leaves. Sip, sweep, sip. I was surrounded by the warm din of conversation, the scraping of chairs being arranged, the cracking of sunflower seeds, and the rustling of newspapers. A middle-aged woman offered me a loquat, somebody else wanted to know who I thought would win the World Cup. While I eavesdropped on conversations about prices, illness, and love, several people hovered nearby to see the novelty of English being written, and two ear pickers persistently offered to pick my ears.

Beneath China's convulsing urban landscape lay the unperturbed, ancient heart of Chengdu. Back on my bike, I turned down a narrow alley and found people playing games and gossiping. It's easy to imagine these scenes a hundred years ago and a hundred years from now. Something remains untouchable in Chinese culture; it is the oldest continuous civilization, and it has the distinction of converting conquerors—the Mongols (thirteenth century) and the Manchus (seventeenth)—to its own beliefs, rather than the other way around.

At one table, Zhao, a chemist with orange, tobacco-stained fingernails, played Chinese bridge and talked, cigarette trembling between his lips. His troubles began in the 1950s, when Mao encouraged intellectuals to speak freely during the Hundred Flowers Campaign. "I said some things and was sent to Gansu Province for two years of reeducation."

I wanted to know what he'd said, but he concentrated on the elegantly narrow cards in his hand. "It was a hard life, but simple—only survival mattered." Things worsened: First, his wife died, and then, in 1958, a three-year famine began in the countryside, killing 30 million people—a famine brought about by corrupt and irresponsible government policies. "I was lucky," Zhao said. "I lived near a lake and we ate fish but nothing else."

Eventually Zhao's name was cleared and he was invited back to the science institute where he worked. But an intellectual life was too complicated, so he returned to Chengdu and became a furniture maker. He lived a calm life until 1967, when the Cultural Revolution propelled the country into chaos. "But I didn't worry," Zhao said, squinting through his own cigarette smoke. "If I was a tiger, I was already a dead tiger." He inhaled and held the smoke carefully, luxuriously. "We got our food with coupons and did nothing. Many people suffered, especially in Sichuan. For me, I was already dead." He threw a card with a sharp crack. "After Mao died, I got a job as a chemistry teacher in a middle school."

I looked at the other players in that shadowed alley, each with his own story of suffering. How was it that Zhao, and others, weren't bitter and angry? "Chinese people don't complain, they accept things as they are," Zhao explained. "That's why we aren't angry."

I rode into the sunless streets where the action never ceased: a Chinese-medicine doctor applying glass cups to a man's back, blind fortune tellers awaiting customers, a masseuse performing a head massage. People sat on bits of newspaper; families strolled and talked. Some women wore slippers and pajamas, as if they were in their own backyard. This was nothing like life in America, with its locked doors and fenced yards.

Swift bats swooped over the darkening river water. At the park beside the Jin River, Liao was still playing mah-jongg. "We meet again," he shouted. "It's destiny." His eyes blinked rapidly behind his tilted glasses, and he smiled crookedly with the air of a slightly crazed comedian.

Long-distance bus travel in China is like a Zen meditation: an exercise in uncomfortable concentration. At the end of a ten-hour ride to Songpan in the Min Mountains north of Chengdu, I was actually reluctant to leave my fellow passengers. We were dirty and tired of being close, yet a strange bond had developed between us. I said goodbye to the mother with whom I'd shared snacks, and whose baby had wet my lap, and my seat partner who'd slept with his head bumping my shoulder. I thanked the bus driver, a heroically calm man. While competing for his piece of the busy road, he had argued with passengers over fares, scrambled for change from a metal box, and fought back mounds of luggage that threatened to collapse onto him.

I came here to do a horse trek into Sichuan's legendary mountains. Songpan, a scrappy town that was once a Qing dynasty garrison, is demarcated by meat. One half of the main street is Muslim, where mutton and yak are sold; the other is Chinese, where pork is sold. Besides the majority, who are Han Chinese, Tibetan, Hui Muslim, and Qiang people live in the area, and they do so harmoniously, though this hasn't always been true.

I wandered along the main street, past a Hui man wearing a white Muslim skullcap and enthusiastically hawking yak and mutton kabobs. He threw his head back and flashed a mouth full of gold teeth; the mutton was surprisingly tender, but I chewed on the yak until my jaw ached. Two Tibetan men with horses in tow sauntered by, wearing long black coats, one shoulder free of a coat sleeve, as if for easy access to the knives tucked into their red sashes. I took their disheveled hair as evidence of a wild ride into town. In an open-fronted shop, I tried on a heavy Tibetan necklace of turquoise and coral chunks strung between carved silver beads, and made the solemn-faced shopkeeper laugh when I bent under its weight. Back on the street, a yak carcass—dinosaur-sized bones and gaping, airy nave of a rib cage—marked a corner. Was it that I had never seen such enormous bones or was it that I rarely saw an entire carcass?

Cowboys and China do not mix easily in the imagination. I had no notion what to expect the next morning when I met my Songpan cowboys: Li, the head wrangler, had dreamy eyes and an Elvis lock of hair on his forehead; Ermao blushed easily and tried to disguise his boyish charm behind cigarettes. They slouched sloppily in saddles that were really just big pads, their feet, in thin tennis shoes, dangling free of the carved metal stirrups. They did not wear hats. I was dismayed to notice that the horses were already tired and caked with mud, and I didn't like the jitteriness of

my assigned mount—a belligerent black gelding. I swung into the
saddle, and the horse rolled his eyes and promptly dumped me in
the middle of the street. Li and Ermao dismounted, mortified at
the sight of me lying on my back; I lay for a minute, watching the
tails of two yaks as they insolently swished past.

After Ermao and I switched horses—he didn't want to ride the
black horse either—we climbed steeply away from Songpan, past
Tibetan villages with prayer flags beating rhythmically in the sharp
wind. The sun was dim in a flat, pale sky. I tried conversing with
Tibetan women wearing their braids wrapped around their heads
with scarves and coral beads, but they didn't speak Mandarin and
I don't speak Tibetan. A group of high-spirited Tibetans trotted
past in a burst of laughter behind a train of lumber-loaded yaks,
heavy heads swinging with a gloomy, romantic air.

At the top of a pass, Li pointed out the ruin of a stone corral.
"We used to work in a commune," he said. "All the horses were
kept here. Nobody owned animals." He looked disapproving, and
I had to admit that communal cowboys didn't sound like a happy
combination. He continued, "Now that we have an economy, I
want to buy a car." The difficulties of the past only moved Li to
pursue his goals with greater energy.

We dropped into a valley where the Tibetan town of Munigou
rested between folds of forested hills and a wrinkled river.
Munigou was as pristine and tidy as anything made in Switzerland:
neat fields fenced with delicately woven slender branches. Wood
piles, whose size attested to the wealth of the owner, looked as if
they had been stacked by mathematicians. The white disks of satellite dishes, sprinkled among the houses, advertised the village's
prosperity, the source of which was farming and animal husbandry.
Still, there was no farm machinery, just the bent backs of women
in the fields. The traditional two-story houses had a first floor for
animals, made of stone, and a second floor for people, made of
wood, with carved verandas and wood shutters; all boards planed
by hand, all joints wood.

We rode out of Munigou, passing a red-robed monk on a bicycle wearing a white mesh fedora with the letters CORLDW DUP

on the band. Secret code for "World Cup"? Ermao, too young to care about life before private ownership, talked blithely about the two cows, three horses, and forty goats his family owned and the girlfriend he had just broken up with: "If you sleep with a girl, you have to marry her." Meanwhile, I wondered where we were going to sleep. My saddle was a canvas bag packed with a Tibetan tent (no floor) and a quilt. No sleeping bags, no pads, no cook-stove. I didn't know where we were or what would happen next, yet I relished the anticipation of the unexpected. I like travel that resembles a chaotic Christmas, with mysterious gifts awaiting un-veiling. Impending surprise turned my surroundings exotic: the blazing clarity of pines against an aqua sky, the slanting lemon afternoon light.

We didn't camp out, we slept on plank beds in a plywood hut at the top of a valley north of Munigou, where three of Li's friends had a small shop and a restaurant. Ermao led the horses into a high pasture, while Li and his friends waded into the stream to catch lizards, like boys. I wondered if they were groping around slick stones in search of dinner: stir-fried lizard? The thin-lipped man in charge threaded a line through the chin of each of the five cap-tured creatures, then strung them between two saplings to dry, where they wriggled and flipped their tails. As it turned out, they were not slated for our dinner but were to be sold in town for use as medicine.

Mr. Thinlips deftly chopped vegetables on a log, then kneaded dough. He built a fire in a wood-burning stove and began prepar-ing Tibetan noodle soup while Li spread a quilt over a board in a corner of the hut, then threw a Tibetan coat, lined with a mangy sheepskin, on top of it: my bed and bedding. I lay down for a rest and sighed. It was just as it looked—hard and cold.

After dinner, we sat beside a sparking campfire; the rustling of water, the snapping of pitch, a few stars between clouds softening the edges of the night, the sound of horse's teeth crashing through fava beans. It was beautiful; it was China. A generator started up in the building across the stream, and karaoke drowned the night sounds, disco lights colored the trees overhead. The Chinese are

masters of one-stop entertainment. If a place has one feature—
beautiful scenery, say—it can only be enhanced by the addition of
other attractions: karaoke, children's rides, balloons that can be shot
for prizes. This means that temples, parks, or scenic areas might
have the atmosphere of an amusement park. China's recent history,
notably devoid of entertainment, seems a reasonable enough excuse for the excess.

In the lobby of my hotel back in Chengdu, an old-time China
traveler told me, "Get on a bus in Xiaojin. Go over the snowy
mountain, and get off in Siguniangshan. There's a guesthouse and
three valleys. Spectacular."

"Over the snowy mountain" sounded like directions to a fairy-
land. Then, when I discovered that Siguniangshan, in the Qionglai
Mountains, wasn't on my map, and that there was no road drawn
to Xiaojin, I had to go. Maps are my downfall: I'm enticed by small
print or an isolated name far from roads. I can't resist going
"nowhere." Still, the bus to Xiaojin was crowded—so crowded that
I had to sit on the board over the engine, beside the driver, which
gave me an arresting view of our approaching fate.

Five hours outside of Chengdu, the pavement ended and we
started to climb a half-built road. For three hours, including stops
to cool the boiling engine, we pitched up a rock-and-mud strip
about as wide as dental floss cut into the mountainside, scraping
past trucks going in the other direction and swerving to avoid
frightened yaks. Except there was no room to swerve. I couldn't
see the bottom of the valley, just thousands of feet of sharp air. The
driver snacked nervously, fiddling with drinks and bags of salted
plums; I watched the road and strategized a disaster plan. If we had
rolled, I would curl up and cover my head with my hands. I held
my pack in my lap, hoping to avoid being impaled on the gearshift.
Work crews stood beside their tents, perched on the road's sheer
lip. I was awed by these unheralded men and women, hacking
China's infrastructure out of this severe landscape.

We drove into the blindness of clouds, and I put my head in my hands; I was in an old bus that sounded like a beast in pain on an abysmal road with zero visibility. When we emerged abruptly into clarity, only the driver and I were awake to witness frothing clouds ascending the mountains in fat, languorous swells. The surrounding peaks cut into the sky in splintered piles with needle-sharp silhouettes. At the crest, I imagined the prayer flags were flapping for us as we began to hurtle down the other side at a speed that shook the entire bus almost to pieces. I got off in the dusty one-street town of Siguniangshan, stunned to have arrived. That ten-hour bus ride was all-consuming: I had forgotten that I had a destination.

Siguniangshan (Four Girls Mountain) is the name of both the town and the pyramid-shaped peak above it. Legend has it that four sisters turned themselves into a mountain in order to protect the local villagers. As I trudged up the street, tucking my chin to keep swirling dust out of my eyes, Tibetan women peered from shops selling tools, yarn, rope, cigarettes; men lifted their heads from inside truck

---

We're speeding down a steep stretch towards a no-look left turn. We draw near the hairpin and Lamdo, the driver, waits. We reach the turn, Lamdo waits. At the edge he whips his forearm across the steering wheel, but it slips. His arm slips all the way off the steering wheel instead of turning it. Straight for the edge. Death, a bold stare. My mind flashes a childhood memory of a sunny soccer game and I thank God for the interesting life I've had. Lamdo brings his arm back around. Places an open palm on the wheel, and turns with all his might. Death disappears off to my right and is replaced by another stretch of muddy road. My heart beats again.

But no one speaks for several minutes.

—Tony Brasunas, "A Slippery Shelf Above the World"

engines; all squinted at me with surprise and suspicion. "One person?" they asked. Obviously, few came here alone. I now understood the romance and power of Sichuan's mountains—this had not been an easy place to get to.

In the morning, I teamed with a sister, brother, and wife trio from Shanghai in a jeep going to Changping Valley. They put a live chicken they'd bought for lunch into a box and then into the jeep, where it sat meekly at my feet. Our Tibetan guide wiped his forehead with his sleeve; he looked hung-over.

We entered Double Bridge Valley through a rock-walled slit that widened into pink-carpeted meadows cut by a clear, hard-running stream. Herders—the women spinning and knitting as they walked—followed sheep and pigs up the mangled dirt road. A boy in overly large pants sang a mournful song syncopated by sheep bells. Higher up, the waterfalls began: fat, white spouts; thin slides of sweat on the mountain's brow.

We stopped for the driver to tighten bolts in the engine, shaken loose by the rough road. Yu, the sister, told me, "My teacher used to say, 'If you travel, it must be to seek difference.'" She brushed mud off her white tennis shoes and straightened her crisp blue slacks. We discussed culinary differences and changes within China. Born in 1968, she vividly remembered a time when all she ate was cabbage and rice. But, like everyone I met in Sichuan, she focused on the present. "Now there is so much meat and so many choices, though I'm afraid I've only eaten Chinese food."

At lunchtime we entered a stone hut. Three pots hung over a central fire, the walls were furry with soot, a lump of yak cheese sat in a damp corner. The guide wrung and slit the chicken's neck, the Tibetan owner of the hut went to pick mushrooms, I hiked up past horses and yaks poking their heads through bushes to gaze at me.

The sheer, high grandeur could have been Yosemite, except that no tourist in Yosemite would bring a live chicken for lunch. At the top of the valley there were vertical rock faces, a cream and cappuccino glacier, and spiky peaks piercing a cobalt sky. I stopped in a spear of silvery light, delighted to have found this empty, magical place where the sounds of wind and water fluttered at the edges of a delicious solitude.

Kathleen Lee has traveled extensively in Asia, South America, and the Middle East. She sometimes writes for Condé Nast Traveler *magazine and her work appears in* Best American Travel Writing 2001 *and* 2002. *She's the author of* Travel Among Men, *a collection of stories.*

SEAN PRESANT

Six Lessons in
Communist Travel

A second-class ride turns into a first-class experience.

COMMUNISM IS A STRANGE BIRD. OUR HISTORY SEEMS TO
be a long war against it, so one would expect that when you get
near it, it should make itself known with grenades and hellfire.
Maybe a parade. Some tanks.

Turns out, communism is a much more subtle animal, as I was to
discover on the first leg of my travels through mainland China. It's
a neverending war, yes, but a quiet one—one that you never see but
always feel—a kind of push and pull between want and allowance.

My first encounter with the big "C" was on a northbound
overnight train traveling from industrial Guangzhou to the pastoral
city of Guilin. Always one to take interest over comfort, and to save
a few bucks, I was traveling second class. The Chinese call it "hard
sleep" in reference to the row upon row of hard, vinyl-covered
boards mounted five high that double as beds. As it happens, my
board was in the exact center of a car packed to capacity with
mainland Chinese travelers—all of whom were staring at me. My
presence, you see, was an accident. The Chinese government goes
to exhausting pains to keep foreigners and nationals in separate
spaces, but since I had a travel agent book my ticket and he
neglected to mention that I was American, I was in the national

car. And while I usually prefer to be with the locals, there's something unnerving about sixty people staring at you like you're on fire.

So, two hours into the trip, tired of smiling like an idiot at no one in particular, I wandered a few cars down to where I thought I'd glimpsed a lock of blonde hair upon boarding.

Lesson #1: When adherence to order is militant, expect the military.

The great thing about train travel in China is that once you remove yourself from the beehive of activity in the stations, you land in a place that, while often crowded, has a dependable sense of order to it. You know without fail when you're getting on a long Chinese train that there will be a metal thermos of hot water in every berth, and you know that it will be refilled whenever it gets low. This is to service the dry noodles everyone carries. You pour the boiling water on the noodles and you have not only hot food, but a bit of order in the chaos.

That sense of order has a dark side, though, for beyond the thermos you'll find something else on every train— People's Liberation Army guards and railroad officers.

On the rails in China, there is no privacy. You must interact. The atmosphere in a Chinese train, as Paul Theroux observed in his book, *Riding the Iron Rooster*, is that of a traveling living room. For the Chinese, a long train ride is an event, and they make themselves at home in order to enjoy it: people roam the aisles in their pajamas, drink themselves into oblivion, play cards, eat lavish banquets, and generally annex vast sections of the train as their own. It's perhaps the best way to enter a Chinese home without actually being invited into one.

—Jeff Vize,
Pigs in the Toilet (and Other Discoveries on the Road from Tokyo to Paris)

Sometimes they wander through your car, sometimes they stand very still in opposite corners, watching you—the guards to make sure you don't violate rules of government, the railroad officers to make sure you don't violate rules of the railroad.

It's one of the few pieces of visible evidence you get that China's history of governmental oppression isn't entirely history. And while you can search the guards for signs of humanity, you won't find much. The penalty for cracking is severe.

I found the blonde, a young architecture student named Frieda, and her female companion, a Hong Kong native named Wei-In, halfway down the train. They had an entire car to themselves, having bought their ticket at the window designated for foreigners.

Of course when I say "by themselves," I mean "by themselves with a PLA guard and a railroad officer."

"We were wondering when you would show up," Frieda shouted as I entered. Apparently they'd seen me get on the train and knew it was only a matter of time before I went looking for conversation.

I took a seat on the bench next to Frieda, who was smiling flirtatiously at the PLA guard in the corner. He was a young guy, probably no more than twenty, and this made him blush.

"Turtle Jell-O?" Wei-In offered.

I looked down at a plastic pudding cup filled with what looked like dark green Jell-O.

"Turtle?" I asked, thinking maybe it was called that because it was green.

"Yes, made from turtle."

Never one to refuse a new food product, I gave it a try. It tasted like nothing. Not like nothing I'd ever tasted before, but literally like nothing.

I looked out the window. The sun was starting to fade, and the terrain was still industrial, brown, and uninteresting. I started to worry that Guilin was going to be more like a theme park than the old scroll paintings that extolled its beauty.

Lesson #2: Nothing is simple.

"You should move your things in here," Frieda said.

Since I was fairly sure the rest of the trip in the crowded car would be nothing but me sitting by myself, and since I had been told when the lights go off everyone downs the cots and sleeps, in one big motion like a drill team, I thought there was no harm in moving.

Wei-In said she'd explain to the train representative standing in the corner what we were going to do. She approached, a few words were spoken, and she returned.

"She said she can change your ticket, but not while we are in the tunnel."

I looked out the window. We were nowhere near a...

Tunnel.

Suddenly the world went dark.

I'm not exactly sure what this tunnel went through, but we were in darkness for half an hour. I thought about the saying "dig so deep you hit China" and wondered if there was an equivalent saying in Chinese, something like "dig so deep you hit Reno."

Regardless, when we emerged back into the dwindling light, the woman changed my ticket, or rather, the plastic chip that had been given to me in exchange for my ticket, which I would receive back at the end of the trip when I gave the plastic chip back, so that I could show my original ticket and be let off the train. (See my previous note on adherence to order.) I moved my bag, bought some Pabst from a rolling cart, and was ready to go.

This is where things got interesting.

Lesson #3: There really are people under there.

As the night crept on, Frieda continued smiling at the PLA guard. She told us she thought he was cute and was going to try to lure him over.

Wei-In warned her that if he flirts with her, the hawkish railroad woman could turn him in for fraternizing sexy-like with a Westerner and he would be kicked out of the military. His family would be shamed.

"Shaming?! People still do that?"

Apparently.

But you can't stop German passion. It's like a tank. Frieda batted her eyelashes. She added a little wave. The guard smiled.

We continued with the Pabst and the turtle Jell-O. The sun had since set, so there was nothing visible out the windows. No city lights. No highways with cars. Nothing. It was just the three of us, sitting center-car, the two officials on either side.

It was like Brecht.

About half an hour into the darkness, Frieda gave up her pursuit and we talked about architecture. When I looked up, however, I noticed that the guard had wandered from his post in the corner. Just a few feet closer, and still hugging the wall, but definitely closer.

Frieda took this as a small victory and continued her conquest. She held up her large beer as if to offer some. He shook his head no.

"Houston. We have contact."

I looked back at the railroad woman. She hadn't moved and she wasn't smiling. But she was watching.

Frieda told Wei-In to tell the guard she wanted to talk to him.

Wei-In turned and said something to the guard. He said something back.

"What did he say?"

"He said you have pretty hair."

Frieda stroked her pretty hair.

"He wanted to know where you're from. So I told him."

Frieda turned up der Klunker. Using Wei-In to translate, she found out that the guard was only nineteen, but already had a wife and a child.

With each question the guard moved a little closer, and the scowl on the railroad officer grew more surly.

I decided it was my duty to save this poor fool from shaming, so I set about trying to lure in the railroad officer. She was pretty in a kind of "Good morning, I am a stop sign" sort of way.

I don't have long blonde hair to flip, so I thought I could grunt in a masculine way that would say "I am utilitarian." Or I could just smile and lift my glass. Which is what I did.

She looked straight through me. No smile. No reaction.

This dude is in for one bad shaming, I thought.

And then the lights went out.

I don't remember it if was nine or ten, but it was either exactly nine or exactly ten which, according to the government, was the time when people go to sleep.

Wei-In flipped on a small reading light, which lit up our bunk area and spilled weakly into the aisle.

The guard used this as an excuse to move in closer.

The thought crossed my mind that if Frieda and this boy made love, he would need to wear padding to prevent injury. Perhaps a helmet.

As the night crept on, though, I realized that this kid's drive wasn't lust. He didn't want to leave his wife and he didn't want to go to bed with Frieda. He just wanted to talk to someone from a land other than the one he spent his every day traversing.

His drive was quite simple. He was nineteen and bored.

Lesson #4: There are two things which cross all cultural barriers—love…and boredom.

As the train continued plodding its way through the darkness, the guard started spilling information about his family life.

Turns out his wife wore the pants in the family. And based on how he described her, I had no doubt we were talking about actual pants.

At this point I wanted to learn some Chinese, so the guard and Wei-In set about teaching me how to say the guard's favorite phrase, "I can only do what my wife lets me." I, in turn, taught him the English equivalent, "I am whipped."

"I am weeped!" he said proudly.

I laughed so hard I shot Pabst through my nose.

And that made him laugh. Which made Wei-In laugh. Which made Frieda laugh. We were like the U.N., if it worked.

Only one person wasn't laughing.

The ice queen in the corner.

The kid looked at her, and she stared him down. His humor ran off like a squirrel fleeing a car tire. He grew quiet and, without a word of departure, went back to his post in the corner.

He had gone too far.

The ice queen dropped her shoulders and lifted her head, as if to acknowledge she had done her work. No reverie would be had on her watch.

Lesson #5: There is sadness.

The thought that this poor kid might lose his job and his family pretty much ended the party. We put the empty bottles of beer under the window, beside the thermos of hot water. I pulled down a cot and laid down on the hard, sticky vinyl surface.

Wei-In flipped off the small reading light, and there the three of us lay, silently knowing that even in the darkness the ice queen and the kid were standing at their posts. What he was thinking, I don't know. But I was worried for him.

I awoke in a puddle of drool. I think everyone in hard sleep awakes in a puddle of drool. How can you not? You're on vinyl. There's no pillow. It happens.

And this would be unpleasant, save for what was out the window.

Somehow the night had brushed away the rusted oblivion of Guangzhou and left us in an indescribable green paradise. Like the hills of Ireland, or perhaps turtle Jell-O if you put a 100-watt bulb behind it, the land seemed to breathe. Far in the distance sharp peaks rose up like spikes on a dragon's back, a heavy white mist clinging to them like something remarkably unpolluted.

I looked down and saw Frieda staring out the window, equally awed. Wei-In had a broad smile on her face as well, as if she'd just come home.

I felt great. Excited. Awake. Far away from everything I knew. I had gotten myself halfway around the world and that made me feel somehow proud.

But then I remembered the guards.

I looked out and saw that, as expected, they were still standing in their corners. This was going on ten hours now that they'd been standing. Maybe when we fell asleep they sat down, but based on the way they leaned against the walls, I doubted it.

The landscape eventually gave way to cityscape as we pulled into the city of Guilin.

My mind was immediately abuzz with the day's plans. The first order of business was to get a hotel, then find a boat to take us up the river the next day—which is the main attraction of the area. Frieda said that they were going to meet up with two other German students, but if I wanted to share a hotel room and a boat with them I would be a welcome addition. I agreed because, well, that's what's fun about traveling alone. New friends at every turn. New possibilities. A chance to start over every few days, hop a train and speed into some great unknown.

It was not something I ever thought of as a great privilege. But now, looking at the kid standing in the corner, I was suddenly aware of how much of a privilege it really was. Not everyone can just escape life for a couple weeks a year—money or not. That's something we take for granted.

We headed sadly off the train. As we passed the guard, I nodded, as if to say "sorry we got you in trouble."

It was a guilty moment, one I was going to have to blur over when I told people of amazing mainland China.

But as I passed, the guard slapped me on the back and said brazenly…

"I am weeped!"

And he laughed.

And that was amazing. But not as amazing as what followed…

Lesson #6: When you live in a place where the government is always present, like a domineering parent, victories are often so small you can miss them.

The ice queen laughed too.

Sean Presant has crossed the globe writing for the Let's Go series, making the world safe for adventurous travelers seeking relics of the ancient world and all-you-can-get pizza. When not questioning the air supply in crowded Egyptian pyramids, tripping over confused iguanas in the Galapagos, or biking with chickens through Asia, Sean is a Los Angeles-based director and screenwriter.

FERGUS M. BORDEWICH

Master Kong

*More than a decade ago, a return to Confucian values
indicated big changes ahead for China.*

THROUGH THE WINDOW OF FANG LIZHI'S APARTMENT, I could see row upon row of indistinguishable brick tenement blocks receding into the smog of modern Beijing. "Confucianism is somewhat like Newtonian physics," Fang was saying. Fang, an astrophysicist and one of China's most outspoken dissidents, made headlines several months later when he was stranded in the U.S. embassy in Beijing and finally released by the Chinese government. "There are people who say that Newton is finished and we ought to throw him out. But some of his thinking is quite valuable. So is much of Confucius's. Confucius unfortunately emphasized order over democracy. But if you take away that emphasis, what remains is quite compatible with human rights and individual freedom. What we have to do is reevaluate a few of his first principles."

What Fang was saying about Confucius seemed less remarkable to me than the fact that he was talking about him at all. In 1949, the Communist Revolution chucked the sage into the dustbin of history and replaced his teachings with the gospel according to Mao. Today, however, the vestiges of an older China are starting to become visible through the disintegrating superstructure of communist faith. Most disillusioned Chinese, including Fang, look first to the West for new inspiration, but many are also beginning to take a new look at the man whose teachings virtually defined Chinese civilization for almost twenty-five centuries. The communist regime itself has quietly rehabilitated Confucius as if he were a disgraced commissar, and would like to draft him for service in China's post-Maoist modernization.

Meanwhile, Chinese tourists in astonishing numbers are flocking to the small city of Qufu, where Confucius lived and taught, and where his progeny dwelled without interruption until his seventy-sixth direct descendant saw the red handwriting on the wall and fled to Taiwan in 1947.

Qufu (pronounced *CHU-FOO*) is the nearest thing to a slice of Old China that still survives in the People's Republic. Thanks mainly to the superstitiousness of the seventy-fifth Yancheng duke, as the direct descendants were known, Qufu was spared the ham-fisted industrialization that has turned much of urban China into a vast Dickensian Coke-town. When the duke learned in 1904 that a railway was to enter the city, he protested to the emperor that the rigid iron tracks would interfere with the sacred and benevolent energies that were believed to flow around Confucius's tomb. The main Beijing-to-Shanghai line, and with it the twentieth century, was obligingly rerouted several miles to the west, bequeathing Qufu a sort of languid solemnity that curiously recalls the time-polished quietude of Assisi.

An instinctive dignity that has virtually disappeared elsewhere in China still suffuses even the most trivial bargaining of the peasants who hawk slabs of fleshy bean curd, racks of noodles, pears, apples, and the weird obscurata of Chinese medicine in the town's gray-brick lanes. Qufu's citizens know there is something different about them; when I asked a vendor of skewered hawthorn fruit what Confucius had given to the people of Qufu, he readily replied, "He made us more civilized."

There is no more hallowed ground in all China than the great Temple of Confucius and the 460-room Kong family mansion that still form Qufu's core. Showered with titles and land, sheltered for

twenty centuries by imperial fiat from the cruel vicissitudes of
Chinese history, the sage's clan ramified beyond belief. Today, more
than a hundred thousand of
the half-million inhabitants
of Qufu's county bear the
surname Kong (the sage's
name, Kong Fuzi—"Master
Kong"—was Latinized to
"Confucius" by sixteenth-
century Jesuits). Kongs are
everywhere; they drive
Qufu's taxis, change money in its back alleys, till the flat, dusty
fields outside town, and serve as loyal apparatchiks in the local
communist administration.

> When the land was ruled
> with wisdom, the leaders
> were selfless as melting ice.
> —Lao Tzu, *The Way of Life*

Kong Fanyin had one remarkable stroke of good luck in his life.
He also had one remarkable stroke of bad luck. Unfortunately, they
occurred almost simultaneously. In 1947, the escaping duke ap-
pointed him overseer of the labyrinth of secluded courtyards, ornate halls, and serpentine passageways that was the ancestral home
of what must surely be the oldest family on the face of the earth.
That was the good news. The bad news was that less than two
years later, the Communist Revolution overthrew everything the
family had represented through more than two thousand years of
feudal Chinese history.

Kong Fanyin was first brought to the mansion in 1936 as a play-
mate for the duke, in the days when the palace teemed with indo-
lent Kongs and hundreds of servants, guards, and secretaries who
managed the clan's immense holdings. After the new regime
declared the mansion a museum in the 1950s, Kong Fanyin was
allowed to remain as its vice-director. When I visited, he was a
stout man of sixty-four, with silvery hairs sprinkling his lip and
chin, and he bore himself with the stately weariness of a man who
only barely survived the trauma of revolutionary politics. Despite
the autumn heat, he trundled gamely along in a Khrushchevian

overcoat squeezed over the high-buttoned suit that was *de rigueur* among provincial Chinese officials.

When I asked him if he had become a communist, he evaded the question. Chinese are embarrassed by communism now; it has become a code word for backwardness and failure. All over China, I kept meeting people who looked toward Western culture or Christianity or the Chinese past for an identity beyond the reach of the commissars. The discontent would climax a few months later, when millions of Chinese filled Beijing's Tiananmen Square, demanding democracy.

On the night of June 3, 1989, the People's Liberation Army crushed the popular democracy movement, killing between five hundred and a thousand people on the streets of the capital. Tens of thousands were arrested all over China in the days that followed, and the Chinese instinctively fell back on the advice of Confucius, which for nearly 2,600 years has given them guidance in difficult times: "See much, but ignore what is dangerous to have seen, and be cautious in acting upon the rest." Repression since then has restored China to the same kind of predictable, if somewhat artificial, stability that travelers knew in the late 1970s and early 1980s, an atmosphere that is unlikely to change until more flexible leaders may arise.

All this was still in the future as Kong Fanyin and I stepped across the mansion's ancient threshold. He led me behind the high white wall that had enclosed the forbidden realm of the Kongs, past the Gate of Reenlightenment with its sculpted cargo of dragons and billowing clouds, and into the lofty hall from which the dukes had ruled as imperial magistrates over the surrounding countryside. All around us on the ends of wooden staves stood the gilded emblems of power: stylized dragons, carved melons, stirrups, symbolic halberds, pikes, and clubs.

What a sight it must have been when the dukes traveled out into the world of lesser mortals! Trembling townsmen melted into the alleys or froze with their faces to the ground as runners hurtled by with vermilion boards on which gilded calligraphy proclaimed the awesome privileges of a bygone age: "Wearer of the two-eyed peacock feather," "Possessor of the yellow ribbon of the first grade," "Duke of the continuing line." The duke swung magisterially along in their wake, suspended from the shoulders of his porters in a silver sedan chair, surrounded by silk-clad retainers whose sole purpose was to awe.

We probed through doglegged passageways into courtyards plumbed with lilacs and punctuated with ornamental rocks that boiled and foamed like frozen surf. The largest—a monster ten feet or more in height—seemed less to be stone at all than a raw slab of the Tao itself set on a pedestal, as evanescent as mist or steam. Kong Fanyin told me it had earth's benevolent energies, to prevent them from seeping out and trickling away; it was the linchpin of the entire mansion, a sort of mystical fulcrum on which the Kongs believed the safety of all their elegant halls and their own lives turned.

In hall after hall, the vestiges of a vanished world hung in musty suspension like fruit in aspic. Confucian austerity blended with patrician opulence to produce compositions of extraordinary power and grace. Slim rosewood chairs confronted each other beneath scrolls that exploded with monochromatic bursts of calligraphy. Marble tables teemed with cloisonné elephants, grave ivory sages, porcelain vases, rococo clocks, ornamental trees carved of medicinal fungus, and life-size chrysanthemums made of coral, jade, and lapis lazuli. On the walls hung paintings of butterflies, wrens, peach blossoms, strange rocks, and plums. I disliked one painting of a vased peony, and I remarked on its surprising coarseness. "It was a personal gift from the empress dowager to the seventy-fifth duke," Kong Fanyin said. "For an empress it's perhaps not so bad."

Chinese tourists, spitting a hail of melon seeds and gobbling slabs of poppy-seed candy, clambered on each other's backs to press against the windows of a suite that had been left untouched since the duke's 1935 wedding. Dusty red silk swathed every table and chair, and the walls still spoke with faded felicitations from forgotten or executed Kuomintang dignitaries. Here were their gifts, now mesmerizing a proletarian generation for whom hand-wrought beauty was just a historical memory: scepters of sandal-wood and jade, bundles of never-opened silk, cut glass, goblets, silverware, and, incongruously, pink porcelain hurricane lamps. The wedding had been the Kongs' final extravagance before the twentieth century's politics at last brought an end to their power.

I asked Kong Fanyin how it felt to be a member of the "first family under heaven," as the Kongs used to be called.

"One was honored to belong to the line of the most important Chinese who ever lived," he replied. "But one was expected to be-have perfectly in accordance with the sage's teachings. Anything less was considered a sin."

I wanted something more, to know what kind of inner con-nection he felt with Confucius himself.

"It's difficult to say," he said, employing the familiar formula that Chinese use to deflect unwelcome questions.

We sparred for a while longer. I knew my curiosity intruded on that hidden courtyard of the self where every Chinese lives his real life. But more than anything else, it was a craving to touch the dis-tant past that had brought me here in the first place.

"Confucius lived a long time ago," Kong at last said, expres-sionlessly, leaving me to make of it what I would. "But I can see him very close to me, intimately. He has not gone away."

Though almost 2,500 years separated us, Confucius did indeed seem startlingly real. His home has been memorialized for so long that the monuments had become virtually indistinguishable from the things they honored. A few hundred feet from where I stood with Kong Fanyin, a gray-brick cottage of antique design marked the site of Confucius's house and opened on a patch of the cob-bled lane he had walked. Nearby, a red-columned hall stood where the sage had taught his son rites and poetry, and beyond it lay the family well, along with a five-hundred-year-old commemorative wall where his teachings were hidden during China's first book-burning Cultural Revolution, in the third century B.C. As late as the beginning of this century, the Kongs possessed a carriage that they believed Confucius himself had driven through the streets of Lu, as Qufu was then known.

Confucius was born in 551 B.C., a generation before the Buddha, to a family of impoverished aristocrats; he died in 479, a decade before the birth of Socrates. He wandered for years without success among the feudal states of eastern China, in search of a prince who would allow him to put his theories of government into practice. But he always returned to his house in Qufu, where he became the first professional teacher in Chinese history, holding forth beneath a backyard apricot tree to aspiring young politicians in what I like to imagine as a sort of École National d'Administration of its day.

Confucius's ideal world was one of perfectly ritualized order, as exquisitely motionless as the stone I saw framed in a round moongate at the end of the courtyard where we stood. "Speak nothing contrary to the rites; do nothing contrary to the rites," he told his disciples. There were, he no doubt discouragingly added, no fewer than three hundred rules of major ritual and three thousand minor observances that had to be mastered before a

---

If it were not improper to be critical toward so venerable an old gentleman, one might voice the suspicion that Confucius did not suffer severely from lack of self-confidence, for he repeatedly stated that he would produce a faultless administration and do away with all crime within three years in the domain of any prince who would hire him. Alas, if only he were back, be it only in the principality of Lu! No present member of the human race, unless perhaps a "practical politician," will have the cynicism to suppose that the offer of this wandering Luluite was not eagerly competed for from the eight points of the Chinese compass. Yet the truth is far worse than that: he found no takers whatever!

—Harry A. Franck, *Wandering in Northern China* (1923)

man could even hope to govern. But there was more to Confucius than the seeming reactionary who declared, "The prince is like the wind and the people like grass; when the wind blows, the grass bends." There was the proto-democrat who believed that any properly educated man could become a sage, no matter how low his birth. He also espoused the novel idea that the purpose of government was to make people happy, and that those who ruled should do so by moral example rather than force.

Confucius's teachings became the official state cult during the Han dynasty (210 B.C. to A.D. 206) and remained so until the last emperor was overthrown by the Republican Revolution in 1912. They provided a system of public ethics, private morality, and family values so comprehensive and so tenacious that it has survived, if only half-acknowledged, even in Communist China. "We still live under a system that emphasizes order at any price," Fang Lizhi had said to me. "What China suffers from most today is the psychology of Confucian feudalism blended with socialism." At the same time, the so-called Confucian nations of Taiwan, South Korea, and Singapore attribute their modern economic success in large part to the self-discipline and cooperative ethos of Confucian education.

The symbolic heart of the whole Confucian system was the great temple at Qufu. You enter it today as every temple has been entered since the dawn of Chinese time—from the south—stepping through a tunneled gate in a rose madder wall onto a marble causeway that progresses symphonically through solemn courtyard after courtyard like the eerie and majestic music of ancient China. You pass through a forest of eight-hundred-year-old cypresses, across a camelback bridge whose balustrades fly on sculpted clouds, and into a courtyard filled with age-splintered junipers, to a wall still scarred with the slogans of the Cultural Revolution.

You pass through a theatrical gate into a forest of stelae (one of them says, CONFUCIUS IS LIKE FOOD AND CLOTHES; WITHOUT HIM CHINA NEVER CAN PROSPER) mounted upon snarling tortoises, to step at last, in grand crescendo, into the very navel of Confucian China, where the great frigate of the sage's sanctum cruises upon an elevated sea of marble, its upswept eaves billowing like wind-filled sails against the cerulean sky of east China.

Few people were permitted to enter its precincts in imperial times, and those who were came breathless and atremble. Even Confucian rationalism succumbed to the impulses of an epoch when panoply was power. Twice a year the gates were flung open and the sage's spirit was invited in, as if it hovered, palpable as the smoke of the city's cook fires, in the air outside. Great drums boomed into the night. Torches threw flickering shadows across the opulent robes of the officiants; in the half-light, the gilded dragons seemed to writhe and leap from the temple's colonnade, while boys brandishing pheasants' feathers danced with infinite gravity to the stony echo of jade chimes. A chorus chanted: "Oh, great Kongzi! Prior in perception! Prior in knowledge! Coequal with heaven and earth! The sun and moon are sustained by thee. Heaven and earth are kept pure by thee. Thou art what never else was since men were generated!"

The sanctum now shelters a rather garishly painted plaster image of Confucius; a museum of Han stone carving occupies the galleries that formerly contained the gilt name tablets of the seventy-two Confucian sages. Today's celebrants are Chinese tourists, who surge with an ear-cracking roar through the lofty halls. I asked a buck-toothed miner who was there with a busload of his mates why they had come. "Because we don't have to condemn Master Kong any-more," he shyly replied. "Because he is permitted."

I rode out one day to Qufu Normal University to meet Li Jinshan, who is the director of the Confucius Foundation of China. He was in his fifties, and flat-bodied and compact, like a well-shaped tool. It was immediately clear that he was a cadre, a party official, whose main job was probably to ride herd on the genuine academics, who sat in silence through the entire inter-view. It was people like Li who kept Chinese communism well-oiled and humming, and would see that it cruised along nicely again after the Tiananmen massacre. I wondered how the official attitude toward Confucius had changed since 1949.

"There has never been an official line," Li declared.

He was lying, of course. As he spoke, his right knee began to jog up and down. It was a tic that recurred every time I touched a sensitive political nerve.

After the 1949 revolution, Confucius was regarded simply as a more or less contemptible mouthpiece for feudalism. During the Cultural Revolution, which began in 1966, his works were banned completely, and the mere accusation that a person had been influenced by Confucianism was sufficient to ruin a career.

"What happened in Qufu during the Cultural Revolution?" I asked.

"Things were abnormal," Li replied. His knee was now pumping violently. "There were complications."

What exactly did that mean? I wondered.

I waited for an answer. The silence lengthened painfully. Li's whole leg was bouncing wildly, almost out of control. Everyone in the room was staring at it.

The truth is, the Red Guards invaded the Temple of Confucius. They scoured the tablets of Confucius, of the sage's parents, of the four great disciples, of the seventy-two sages, from their crimson altars and, like so much kindling, burned them to cinders. They hitched a truck to the bronze images of Confucius and his disciples, pulled them out like tree stumps and dragged them in a procession through the streets of Qufu, shouting, "Down with the Confucian curiosity shop!" Then they smashed the statues to pieces with sledgehammers. Kong Fanyin and some of the clan's old retainers were publicly tortured on the Drum Tower at the center of town. Later, the Red Guards marched to the clan cemetery, where every Kong for the last twenty-five centuries has been buried. There they looted the tombs and threw the shriveled corpses of the sage's descendants on the ground amid their yellowed and crumbling silks, jades, and ivories.

"As time goes on, we find that more and more people are interested in Confucius," Li said disingenuously. "Nowadays, we must study Confucius in order to further the country's modernization. We must carry on our traditions so that we can realize both our material and spiritual civilization."

Li's knee stopped jogging. He was back on the safe ground of official policy. Nevertheless, it struck me as an extraordinary admission.

"We take a pragmatic view now," he said. "We should take what we can from Confucius. We mustn't throw the baby out with the bathwater."

You can hire a horse-drawn taxi to take you to the Kong family burial ground; however, I preferred to walk the two or three miles down the road that was the city's main street in Confucius's day. It now stretches arrow-straight between flat and stubbly autumn fields. It was the day upon which offerings were traditionally made to the dead. Men and women, most of them dressed in peasants' blues, were streaming lumpily toward the vast walled enclosure to pay their respects to their more illustrious ancestors. In the past they would have made offerings of rice liquor and food, and burned quantities of printed "spirit money" so the dead might buy all they wanted in the netherworld. But that had all been banned by the Communists as superstition. Police with bullhorns were stopping everyone at the gate and searching them for wads of concealed toilet paper that was intended to serve as make-do "spirit money"; whatever they found, they confiscated and threw into an oven at the side of the road.

The gate debouched into a forest of cypresses and pistachio trees. It was a very strange place, intensely grave and beautiful, dense with the spirits of the wisest and noblest dead that had ever walked the Chinese earth, and populated with heraldic ranks of mandarins and soldiers, lions, hounds, and camels carved in stone and poised in weathered pairs before hundreds of stone altars. Confucius's tomb was a simple mound marked by a slender stela, a place utterly free of pomposity and emphasizing instead the modesty and humility that the sage insisted were the deepest virtues of truly good men. Overgrown holes still gaped where the Red Guards had done their work.

Somehow, some of the Kongs had smuggled their wadded paper through the cordon. Telltale gusts of smoke rose from little fires in front of the graves, while ghostly figures in blue boilersuits wandered amid a rain of yellow leaves, searching for relatives' tombs. Police in sidecars were patrolling the forest roads, on the prowl for worshipers, and even as I watched, a pair of them appeared and snatched away a heap of smoldering paper from a shamefaced man as he knelt before some ancestor's tomb.

As I wandered through the forest, I wondered what the new Confucianism might turn out to be. I doubted that even amid a ruined communism Confucius could ever be venerated with the superhuman awe that he enjoyed through more than two thousand years of Chinese history. It seemed safe to say, however, that he would be an important part of the Chinese future. Before my eyes, Kongs were climbing over the cemetery wall, passing their bicycles over from hand to hand along with great bales of paper, surging in twos and threes and groups of half a dozen through the perfumed trees toward the ancestors' graves, smiling and unstoppable.

Fergus M. Bordewich is the author of the critically acclaimed books Killing the White Man's Indian *and* Cathay: A Journey in Search of Old China. *He was also the general editor of* Children of the Dragon, *an anthology of eyewitness accounts of the Tiananmen Square massacre. His articles have appeared in many national publications, including* American Heritage, Smithsonian Magazine, The Atlantic Monthly, The New York Times Magazine, Reader's Digest, *and others. He lives with his family in New York's Hudson Valley.*

JEFF BOOTH

The Fourteenth Tower

An ancient monument lives in the modern age.

CHINA IS FULL OF TOUTS—AGGRESSIVE SALESMEN WHO HOUND you, the *lao wei* (foreign tourist), to buy souvenir junk at every step. And nowhere do they cling with more tenacity than at the Great Wall. My goal was to find the essence of the Great Wall, but I had to escape them to get away from the merchandising. I planned to camp overnight to experience the Wall without post-cards and t-shirts. I found more than I expected.

A few years earlier, a friend and I had gone to the Great Wall at Simatai, about three hours northwest of Beijing. It was a desolate, beautiful site, with the stone parapets snaking along a dragon's-back mountain ridge. The original Great Wall was cobbled to-gether from various mud barriers by Emperor Qin ShiHuang about 210 B.C. The discontinuous, overlapping sections of the Wall were finally linked most completely by Ming emperors during the fourteenth century. The Great Wall at Simatai was "unspoiled," however well that elitist backpacker term can be applied to a struc-ture that the entire world knows about.

During my second visit, another friend from Beijing and I planned to hike from Simatai to Jinshanling, another section a long day's hike to the west. Returning to the site, I found Simatai overrun with Chinese and foreign tourists. It was becoming another Badaling, the spot nearest Beijing where one can pose with a costumed Ghengis Khan and check the Wall off your "to do" list.

On the dirt pathway leading to the entrance, saleswomen swarmed toward us, raising souvenirs high overhead instead of Chairman Mao's little red book. Beyond a new gate and its entrance fee, the Yan Mountains soared above it all, with the Wall lining its highest ridge.

Simatai makes you earn your "I Climbed the Great Wall" t-shirt. The actual climbing part is challenging. Crumbling, foot-wide, scrambling sections of the Wall with a fifty-foot drop on either side leave you panting and shaking from exertion and excitement. Despite recent changes, it's clear this is still not Richard Nixon's Badaling.

Unfortunately, it is hard to enjoy the hard-earned thrill of the climb when lines of visitors inch slowly up the steep steps, or worse, take the recently installed, multi-colored chairlift to be whisked nearly to the summit in a matter of minutes.

I wanted none of that. My friend and I turned left as we reached the Wall. Everyone else turned right, up the immediate path to the first peak. We tramped down

We hurried up a rugged stairway, hoping but failing, to escape the swarm of vendors. My blond hair, which always seemed to promise the most foreignness, thus the greatest likelihood of a sale, did not go unnoticed. No less than an hour later I finally bought a Great Wall picture book from the woman who had followed me all that time. With her saleswoman's zeal and sheer perseverance, she deserved to be rewarded. Besides, her face was lined and worn, and I had the discomforting awareness that I have so much more in my life than some books to sell. But apparently I overpaid, and the rumor flew, and every other vendor came to point at me, exemplar, to convince others of the rightness of an excessive price.

—Anne Calcagno, "Emboldened by Women in High Heels"

toward the reservoir, towards the setting sun and Jinshanling. We left everyone behind except for two tourist hawkers, a peasant and his wife. We'd already told them, politely, in Chinese and English, that we weren't going to buy anything. The woman continued to skip ahead of me to show me her wares. I repeated, "No thanks, we want to go off on our own. We don't need souvenirs, we want experience." I'd never said more naive words.

One of the most frustrating aspects of these vendors is when they shift gears from in-your-face sales tactics to simply following you, quietly, for a long time. The entire point of my friend and me trekking out here was to sleep under the moon, to feel the time-lessness and emptiness that ruins and nature hold hand in hand. And here were two wiry, sun-worn *nongmin*, Chinese peasants, with heavy sacks full of souvenir books, trudging behind us, the haunt of sales threatening to ruin all of my narrowly defined "experience."

Luckily, I had no idea where I was going, and we were completely unprepared for what might lie ahead.

We walked for several hours, never forgetting that they followed us. The mountains were fantastic—crumpled waves of green that crashed away into the blue haze on all sides. The sun was low, and the light was warm on the ancient stone; the sky deep blue and edged with dark storm clouds that threatened, but never delivered.

At one point, I asked the peasant his name. He was Zheng, his wife was Xiao Hua. Whenever I stopped to take photographs, the two of them also stopped. My friend rested, she was a city girl, and Beijing's pollution doesn't help anyone's lungs. Zheng stood to the side, and if it looked like I'd be a while (fumbling with tripod, film, filters) he pulled out his long, thin golden pipe, a *yan gan*, packed some tobacco in, and had a smoke while watching me. He and his wife didn't offer to sell anything anymore. The low sun, great for photos, also meant approaching night. I wasn't exactly sure how far Jinshanling was. There were no watchtowers in sight, and we'd hoped to find one to sleep in since we were only had a few ba-nanas, a bottle of water each, and two sheets for blankets.

We had planned to camp, of course, so psychologically it wasn't a problem that we were in the middle of nowhere. But at several thousand feet altitude, even in August, when night falls so does the temperature. And it fell much more than I had anticipated (to about 50 degrees), and more than I cared to face without a roof over my head (even if it was a wind-funneling, open-faced, cold Ming Dynasty brick roof).

So I asked Zheng, in Chinese, where we were.

He seemed surprised, maybe at the innocence of my question, maybe that I had finally spoken to him again, and wasn't telling him that we weren't going to buy anything.

"Chang Chen," he replied. The Long Wall, literally.

I changed tactics and asked how far to Jinshanling, where we hoped to get off the Wall and catch a bus back to Beijing. About sixteen more towers, he said. Not too far. How many towers have we passed since Simatai, I asked. About twelve, Zheng said. Not too far. We'd already been hiking since mid-morning, so "not too far" didn't sound encouraging as the afternoon grew long.

Maybe Zheng, puffing gently on his pipe, noticed the look of slight concern pass across my face. He asked if that was too far for us to walk. "I walk back and forth along the Wall every day," he said. "From my village to Simatai, forty towers a day. It keeps me strong. It is the way I go to work."

> Chinese people will always say "yes" when you ask them something. In their culture it is disrespectful to say "no" to an older person. So you have some funny things happen. You will say, "Would you meet me on Tuesday at 2:30 P.M. at…." They will say "yes." You then go to the stipulated place and alas, they are not there to meet you because they have said yes, had no intention of meeting you, but didn't want to say "no."
>
> —Esther Stafford,
> "Diary of a Foreign Devil"

They were on the way to Zheng Cai Jun, their village, near the fourteenth tower, where they planned to cut into the valley below, another eight kilometers until home. They weren't following us to sell anything, we were simply traveling together on the only road around. I felt a little embarrassed at my earlier pace, hoping to put distance between them and ourselves. My friend explained to her countrymen our idea of camping in one of the watchtowers. The fourteenth tower wasn't far, his wife said, though she looked at me with a gaze I'd become accustomed to; it meant "Crazy foreigner, why would you want to do that?"

The rest of the hike became increasingly difficult. At several points, the Wall climbed so sharply up a cliff face that we had to pull ourselves up with our hands, pseudo-bouldering on distinctly unstable stones. Finally, Xiao Hua pointed to the tower capping the next ridge, practically silhouetted by the sinking sun.

The fourteenth tower (and I still am unsure if this is simply Zheng's reference scale or a more acknowledged numbering scheme) had a dozen arched windows on its four sides, a bare stone floor, and nothing else. Before leaving, Zheng asked if we had enough food, did we know how to build a fire? Sure, I said. He didn't believe me. Xiao Hua offered to bring us back some food. I hesitated.

It's a difficult balance, and sometimes an outright contradiction, between being open and trusting and being wary while on the road. I was unsure if she was offering to bring us food, as friends, from the rapport we'd developed over the past few miles, or if she was looking to make another sale. I'm intensely conscious of saving every yuan possible, and particularly sensitive to the oft-practiced technique of taking foreign travelers for five times the normal Chinese price. So suddenly, at the entrance to the fourteenth tower, the sun sinking below the clouds and hanging, just for a moment, along the rim of the far mountains, I didn't know if I was facing friendship, or just another sales pitch.

I realized it didn't really matter, not while standing on the Great Wall at sunset. We agreed, and thanked them. Zheng and his wife disappeared over the side of the Wall somehow, and headed off towards their home.

After the sun set, the large stones and red bricks quickly lost the heat of the day they'd stored up. I couldn't get a fire going. It was gorgeous still, and the silence and austerity were exactly what I had wanted, or thought I wanted. But an hour later, when we heard Zheng's voice from the darkness, I couldn't have been happier. Soon we were sitting around a roaring fire Zheng stoked in one of the alcoves of the tower, his wife spreading bamboo baskets of stir-fried eggplant, boiled potatoes and cabbage, and egg-fried rice on the flagstones. We all ate together, Mrs. Zheng repeatedly encouraging me to eat more. My friend explained to me in English that this was probably a week's worth of food for their household. Zheng told me he was frustrated with the way local officials ran his eldest son's school, and that one of the reasons he and his wife sell tourist books and t-shirts is to make more money to send him to a better school. His wife then talked about how she hasn't been to Beijing in a long, long time.

"Why should I go to Beijing?" Zheng retorted. "Everyone from Beijing comes here, foreigners and Chinese alike." He tapped the ashes from his pipe into the fire, and leaned back against the stone, humming a folk tune.

Zheng and his wife packed their baskets and gathered their chopsticks eventually. Before there could be an awkward pause, I offered them some money. They protested, and I insisted, and they protested, but eventually accepted it. It all seemed quite regulated and proper. And though they hoped for, and maybe expected payment, that didn't lessen our enjoyment of dinner at all, or the sincerity of our thanks. It didn't negate the warmth of the fire in this sole lighted watchtower for hundreds of miles along the ancient Wall.

We wrapped ourselves in our individual sheets, lay near the fire as it died out, and slept. There is nothing like sleeping on centuries-old stone, both for what it does for your back, and what it does for your sense of history.

At dawn, the sun rose over the battered stones of the Wall just as it has for centuries. White fog lay like secrets in green valleys, and we walked on towards Jinshanling. Almost immediately we could see Jinshanling's winged towers in the distance. This stretch of the Wall is particularly famous for the unique gabled rooftops to its watchtowers, tightly clustered along a particularly devious serious of switchbacks. We met a group of Chinese hikers heading towards Simatai, the reverse of the hike we'd just done. Parts of the Wall are partially restored here because it's another tourist site. Walking became easier. But I wasn't just hiking along an architectural wonder anymore. I understood the difference between ruins, and history that's still alive.

Jeff Booth is the editor of Student Traveler *magazine, and has contributed to* New Traveler, In-Singapore Magazine, *and* Transitions Abroad. *He prefers chopsticks to forks, gondolas to cars, and the journey rather than the destination.*

MARK SALZMAN

The Master

Like the song says, everybody was kung fu fighting—
a young foreigner in China learns the martial arts.

I WAS TO MEET PAN AT THE TRAINING HALL FOUR NIGHTS A
week, to receive private instruction after the athletes finished their
evening workout. Waving and wishing me good night, they politely filed out and closed the wooden doors, leaving Pan and me
alone in the room. First he explained that I must start from scratch.
He meant it, too, for beginning that night, and for many nights
thereafter, I learned how to stand at attention. He stood inches
away from me and screamed, "Stand straight!" then bored into me
with his terrifying gaze. He insisted that I maintain eye contact for
as long as he stood in front of me, and that I meet his gaze with
one of equal intensity. After as long as a minute of this silent torture, he would shout "At ease!" and I could relax a bit, but not
smile or take my eyes away from his. We repeated this exercise
countless times, and I was expected to practice it four to six hours
a day. At the time, I wondered what those staring contests had to
do with *wushu,* but I came to realize that everything he was to
teach me later was really contained in those first few weeks when
we stared at each other. His art drew strength from his eyes; this
was his way of passing it on.

After several weeks I came to enjoy staring at him. I would break into a sweat and feel a kind of heat rushing up through the floor into my legs and up into my brain. He told me that when standing like that, I must at all times be prepared to duel, that at any moment he might attack, and I should be ready to defend myself. It exhilarated me to face off with him, to feel his power and taste the fear and anticipation of the blow. Days and weeks passed, but the blow did not come.

One night he broke the lesson off early, telling me that tonight was special. I followed him out of the training hall, and we bicycled a short distance to his apartment. He lived with his wife and two sons on the fifth floor of a large, anonymous cement building. Like all the urban housing going up in China today, the building was indistinguishable from its neighbors, mercilessly practical and depressing in appearance. Pan's apartment had three rooms and a small kitchen. A private bathroom and painted, as opposed to raw, cement walls in all the rooms identified it as the home of an important family. The only decoration in the apartment consisted of some silk banners, awards and photographs from the set of *Shaolin Temple*. Pan's wife, a doctor, greeted me with all sorts of homemade snacks and sat me down at a table set for two. Pan sat across from me and poured two glasses of *baijiu*. He called to his sons, both in their teens, and they appeared from the bedroom instantly. They stood in complete silence until Pan asked them to greet me, which they did, very politely, but so softly I could barely hear them. They were handsome boys, and the elder, at about fourteen, was taller than me and had a moustache. I tried asking them questions to put them at ease, but they answered only by nodding. They apparently had no idea how to behave toward something like me and did not want to make any mistakes in front of their father. Pan told them to say good night, and they, along with his wife, disappeared into the bedroom. Pan raised his glass and proposed that the evening begin.

He told me stories that made my hair stand on end, with such gusto that I thought the building would shake apart. When he came to the parts where he vanquished his enemies, he brought his terrible hand down on the table or against the wall with a crash, sending our snacks jumping out of their serving bowls. His imitations of cowards and bullies were so funny I could hardly breathe for laughing. He had me spellbound for three solid hours; then his wife came in to see if we needed any more food or *baijiu*. I took the opportunity to ask her if she had ever been afraid for her husband's safety when, for example, he went off alone to bust up a gang of hoodlums in Shenyang. She laughed and touched his right hand. "Sometimes I figured he'd be

> How can a man's life keep its course
> If he will not let it flow?
> Those who flow as life
>   flows know
> They need no other force:
> They feel no wear, they feel
>   no tear,
> They need no mending,
>   no repair.
> —Lao Tzu, *The Way of Life*

late for dinner." A look of tremendous satisfaction came over Pan's face, and he got up to use the bathroom. She sat down in his chair and looked at me. "Every day he receives tons of letters from all over China, all from people asking to become his student. Since he made the movie, it's been almost impossible for him to go out during the day." She refilled our cups, then looked at me again. "He has trained professionals for more than twenty-five years now, but in all that time he has accepted only one private student." After a long pause, she gestured at me with her chin. "You." Just then Pan came back into the room, returned to his seat and started a new story. This one was about a spear:

While still a young man training for the national *wushu* competition, Pan overheard a debate among some of his fellow athletes about the credibility of an old story. The story described a famous warrior as being able to execute 1,000 spear-thrusts without stopping to rest. Some of the athletes felt this to be impossible: after 50, one's shoulders ache, and by 100 the skin on the left hand, which guides the spear as the right hand thrusts, twists and returns it, begins to blister. Pan had argued that surely this particular warrior would not have been intimidated by aching shoulders and blisters, and soon a challenge was raised. The next day Pan went out into a field with a spear, and as the other athletes watched, executed 1,007 thrusts without stopping to rest. Certain details of the story as Pan told it—that the bones of his left hand were exposed, and so forth—might be called into question, but the number of thrusts I am sure is accurate, and the scar tissue on his left palm indicates that it was not easy for him.

One evening later in the year, when I felt discouraged with my progress in a form of Northern Shaolin boxing called *"Changquan,"* or "Long Fist," I asked Pan if he thought I should discontinue the training. He frowned, the only time he ever seemed genuinely angry with me, and said quietly, "When I say I will do something, I do it, exactly as I said I would. In my whole life, I have never started something without finishing it. I said that in the time we have I would make your *wushu* better than you could imagine, and I will. Your only responsibility to me is to practice and to learn. My responsibility to you is much greater! Every time you think your task is great, think how much greater mine is. Just keep this in mind: if you fail"—here he paused to make sure I understood—"I will lose face."

Though my responsibility to him was merely to practice and to learn, he had one request that he vigorously encouraged me to fulfill—to teach him English. I felt relieved to have something to offer him, so I quickly prepared some beginning materials and rode over to his house for the first lesson. When I got there, he had a tape recorder set up on a small table, along with a pile of oversized paper and a few felt-tip pens from a coloring set. He showed no interest at all in my books, but sat me down next to the recorder and pointed at the pile of paper. On each sheet he had written out in Chinese dozens of phrases, such as "We'll need a spotlight over there," "These mats aren't springy enough," and "Don't worry—it's just a shoulder dislocation." He asked me to write down the English translation next to each phrase, which took a little over two and a half hours. When I was finished, I asked him if he could read my handwriting, and he smiled, saying that he was sure my handwriting was fine. After a series of delicate questions, I determined that he was as yet unfamiliar with the alphabet, so I encouraged him to have a look at my beginning materials. "That's too slow for me," he said. He asked me to repeat each of the phrases I'd written down five times into the recorder, leaving enough time after each repetition for him to say it aloud after me. "The first time should be very slow—one word at a time, with a pause after each word so I can repeat it. The second time should be the same. The third time you should pause after every other word. The fourth time read it through slowly. The fifth time you can read it fast." I looked at the pile of phrase sheets, calculated how much time this would take, and asked if we could do half today and half tomorrow, as dinner was only three hours away. "Don't worry!" he said, beaming. "I've prepared some food for you here. Just tell me when you get hungry." He sat next to me, turned on the machine, then turned it off again. "How do you say, 'And now, Mark will teach me English?'" I told him how and he repeated it, at first slowly, then more quickly, twenty or twenty-one times. He turned the machine on. "And now, Mark will teach me English." I read the first phrase, five times as he had requested, and he pushed a little note across the table. "Better read it six times," it read, "and a little slower."

After several weeks during which we nearly exhausted the phrasal possibilities of our two languages, Pan announced that the time had come to do something new. "Now I want to learn routines." I didn't understand. "Routines?" "Yes. Everything, including language, is like *wushu*. First you learn the basic moves, or words, then you string them together into routines." He produced from his bedroom a huge sheet of paper made up of smaller pieces taped together. He wanted me to write a story on it. The story he had in mind was a famous Chinese folk tale, "How Yu Gong Moved the Mountain." The story tells of an old man who realized that if he only had fields where a mountain stood instead, he would have enough arable land to support his family comfortably. So he went out to the mountain with a shovel and a bucket and started to take the mountain down. All his neighbors made fun of him, calling it an impossible task, but Yu Gong disagreed: it would just take a long time, and after several tens of generations had passed, the mountain would at last become a field and his family would live comfortably. Pan had me write this story in big letters, so that he could paste it up on his bedroom wall, listen to the tape I was to make and read along as he lay in bed.

Not only did I repeat this story into the tape recorder several dozen times—at first one word at a time, and so on—but Pan invited Bill, Bob, and Marcy over for dinner one night and had them read it a few times for variety. After they had finished, Pan said that he would like to recite a few phrases for them to evaluate and correct. He chose some of his favorite sentences and repeated each seven or eight times without a pause. He belted them out with such fierce concentration we were all afraid to move lest it disturb him. At last he finished and looked at me, asking quietly if it was all right. I nodded and he seemed overcome with relief. He smiled, pointed at me and said to my friends, "I was very nervous just then. I didn't want him to lose face."

While Pan struggled to recite English routines from memory, he began teaching me how to use traditional weapons. He would teach me a single move, then have me practice it in front of him until I could do it ten times in a row without a mistake. He always stood about five feet away from me, with his arms folded, grinding his teeth, and the only time he took his eyes off me was to blink. One night in the late spring, I was having a particularly hard time learning a move with the staff. I was sweating heavily and my right hand was bleeding, so the staff had become slippery and hard to control. Several of the athletes stayed on after their workout to watch and to enjoy the breeze that sometimes passed through the training hall. Pan stopped me and indicated that I wasn't working hard enough. "Imagine," he said, "that you are participating in the national competition, and those athletes are your competitors. Look as if you know what you are doing! Frighten them with your strength and confidence." I mustered all the confidence I could, under the circumstances, and flung myself into the move. I lost control of the staff, and it whirled straight into my forehead. As if in a dream, the floor raised up several feet to support my behind, and I sat staring up at Pan while blood ran down across my nose and a fleshy knob grew between my eyebrows. The athletes sprang forward to help me up. They seemed nervous, never having had a foreigner knock himself out in their training hall before, but Pan, after asking if I felt all right, seemed positively inspired. "Sweating and bleeding. Good."

Every once in a while, Pan felt it necessary to give his students something to think about, to spur them on to greater efforts. During one morning workout two women practiced a combat routine, one armed with a spear, the other with a *dadao*, or halberd. The *dadao* stands about six feet high and consists of a broadsword attached to a thick wooden pole, with an angry-looking spike at the far end. It is heavy and difficult to wield even for a strong man, so it surprised me to see this young woman, who could not weigh more than one hundred pounds, using it so effectively. At one point in their battle the woman with the *dadao* swept it toward the other woman's feet, as if to cut them off, but the other woman jumped up in time to avoid the blow. The first woman, without letting the blade of the *dadao* stop, brought it around in another sweep, as if to cut the other woman in half at the waist. The other woman, without an instant to spare, bent straight from the hips so that the *dadao* slashed over her back and head, barely an inch away. This combination was to be repeated three times in rapid succession before moving on to the next exchange. The women practiced this move several times, none of which satisfied Pan. "Too slow, and the weapon is too far away from her. It should graze her back as it goes by." They tried again, but still Pan growled angrily. Suddenly he got up and took the *dadao* from the first woman. The entire training hall went silent and still. Without warming up at all, Pan ordered the woman with the spear to get ready, and to move fast when the time came. His body looked as though electricity had suddenly passed through it, and the huge blade flashed toward her. Once, twice the *dadao* flew beneath her feet, then swung around in a terrible arc and rode her back with flawless precision. The third time he added a little twist at the end, so that the blade grazed up her neck and sent a little decoration stuck in her pigtails flying across the room.

I had to sit down for a moment to ponder the difficulty of sending an object roughly the shape of an oversized shovel, only heavier, across a girl's back and through her pigtails, without guide ropes or even a safety helmet. Not long before, I had spoken with a former troupe member who, when practicing with this instrument, had suddenly found himself on his knees. The blade, unsharpened, had twirled a bit too close to him and passed through his Achilles' tendon without a sound. Pan handed the *dadao* back to the woman and walked over to me. "What if you had made a mistake?" I asked. "I never make mistakes," he said, without looking at me.

Mark Salzman is the author of Lost in Place, True Notebooks, *and* Iron and Silk, *an account of the time he spent in China studying martial arts and teaching English. He has also written three novels,* Lying Awake, The Laughing Sutra *and* The Soloist, *which was a finalist for the* Los Angeles Times *Book Prize for fiction. An amateur cellist, he lives in Los Angeles with his wife.*

PART TWO

SOME THINGS TO DO

KARIN FAULKNER

Pleasure Tips

Who could have known it would feel so good?

BECAUSE I LIVE ALONE WITH A CAT, MY GREATEST MOMENTS of sensual pleasure since living and teaching in China have come from having someone diddling around in my ears with a Q-tip. I think the whole experience at the "hair shop" is the most surprising experience, and the best bargain in China. It is an opportunity to close my eyes for most of an hour, yield myself up to others' hands and to feel like a queen. A spoiled and indulged queen. A queen who moans.

Recently the textbook for my English classes had a unit on health called "Grandma Knows Best." It was on traditional remedies around the world, the kind of remedies that "Grandma" knows. So I began the class asking everyone to tell the group what they would do for themselves if they had a headache. Many of the students said they would go to the hair shop for hair washing. Me too. It works.

The first time I had this treatment, in Ningbo, I thought I was just going to the barber's for a haircut. Of course it would be washed, too. A Chinese friend took me there and asked if I would like a massage of my head and shoulders as well. I asked what it would cost. All of it, wash, cut, massage would be about $2.50. Less than a gin and tonic. I thought I would be out of there in less than half an hour.

The young girl sat me in a chair (the only one in the place) put a big splat of cheap shampoo in her hand, smeared it around on the crown of my head, added a squirt of water and started rubbing it around, lathering it up. And then she rubbed it around and around here and there on my head using a variety of finger maneuvers. She seemed to be thoroughly rubbing every follicle and centimeter of my scalp. I stole a look at my watch. Ten minutes. When was she going to rinse me? She scraped all the suds off so I thought rinsing was imminent, but no, she added another splash of water and whipped up a fresh array of snowy mountain peaks on my head using her repertoire of strokes, flicks, scratches, tugs, and rubs. She also rubbed my neck, temples, forehead, and shoulders. That was when I decided to stop checking my watch for some time warp of a mistake until the end. It lasted a full hour before the haircut. And there was no misunderstanding about money as I had feared. It was that cheap.

Since then I have had many, many hair washes in China, with no haircut. In Xiamen, they cost less than $1.50, less than a cup of coffee. They last about an hour. Someone rubs your scalp, neck, shoulders, back, and arms in an infinite array of strokes that have all been taught by some official organization because there is a basic set (like they all make little tiny squeezes all along the outer edges of the ears several times) with some variations, just a little individuality.

And some room for genius. The people who do this are the lowest of the lowly employees in the beauty salons and hair shops (men and women go to both), where they are not allowed to cut or comb or style hair, only massage and shampoo. I have found two of these young people who have miracle hands, doing the kind of massage we pay $40 to $60 an hour for in America. Healer's hands. And for each of them, after the first "hair washing" I dug into my little pocket dictionary and found the characters for "medicine" and "hands." They each understood and grinned and blushed and bowed. But I bowed lower. They were healers.

It was one of these medicine-hand people, a woman about thirty, who first stuck a Q-tip in my ear. All the hair washers before had handed me a few Q-tips and I dried in there all by myself. But she snuck up on me with the Q-tip. I was surprised, felt a little invaded, slightly alarmed, but managed to relax. It felt wonderful. When she began on the second ear I had a picture in my head of my old dog from my childhood, a dog whose impeccable dignity could only be ruffled by one thing—rubbing his ears. He would moan. He would drool, seeming to lose control of his lips. I kept as much control as you must being a stranger in a strange country. I think I did moan just a little.

Today I was in the barber's in my little neighborhood. I was hoping that the boy who couldn't be past nineteen, who has washed my hair and rubbed me all those other places many times while I sat in his chair, would be there. But it was Sunday and he was not. Lots of men were in there sitting around smoking and talking loudly over the blaring TV which no one was watching. No one was

One blustery Beijing morn, I got in a taxi driven by a guy with a ponytail's worth of glossy black hair. He seemed the strong, silent type, but when we slowed, he rolled up a sleeve, rubbed a smooth arm, and grinned. "*Wo mei you maoer!*" Look—no hair! I rolled up my sleeve and twisted a patch of my Latina-black arm hairs. "*Wo you!*" I have some! He leaned over and caressed it. Then he lifted up his pant leg to expose a second hairless limb. "*Hai mei you!*" he said. None here either! Since I hadn't shaved (it was winter, after all), I had quite a collection in store for him. "*Wo you!*" I cried as I pulled up my jean cuff. "*Aiya!*" he cringed in horror. We rode on in silence. I assumed my gorilla girl legs had been a turn-off, but he slipped me a piece of paper when I got out of his cab. A phone number was scrawled across it. I looked up in time to see him blow me a kiss before he sped away.

—Stephanie Elizondo Griest, "The Stranger"

having anything done to their hair. I thought maybe it was a closed-for-business day. But a young woman in a very short, pale-pink dress and extremely high, hot-pink platform shoes appeared through the cigarette haze. She looked like an angel who had gotten past the fashion police and then she made that beautiful Oriental gesture of open reception with her hand, the gesture that led me to a chair.

At first I thought that the whole experience was going to be shot down by all the noise. Everything the Chinese do is LOUD. I am used to that, but the TV today was alive with gunshots and other sounds of violence and the group of men were all talking louder than that and the pink angel who had her hands in my hair was also unabashedly watching the tube. I just closed my eyes like I always do. I am at that age where there is little pleasure in sitting in front of a mirror in a well-lit room for an hour.

I was grumbly at first, meditating on the "fatal flaw" in nearly all Chinese experiences. The sublime touching that goes on in the barber's is always held in check from complete bliss meltdown by the noise in those places. But the girl in the pink outfit just wrangled all the grumpiness right out of my head in just a few moments. She knew where it hurt. She knew where the grumble-loops were. Her fingers knew where to go to make the dragons scram out of their stinky little caves under my shoulder blades. She rubbed my temples in firm circles until they were as smooth, calm and full of serenity as lily ponds. She did little things with her fingernails all along my eyebrows that no one has ever done before. I was putty, Silly Putty. I could not stop smiling with my eyes closed, something like the Buddha trying not to crack up.

And then she rinsed me. This rinsing is always one of the very best parts of the whole event. Lying back supine with my head cradled in the black basin as unconscious and thought-free as if I had been beheaded while still smiling. They choose the right temperature for the day and my mood, they lift my head, turn it slightly for proper run off, slide their snaky little fingers all through it. And then they slide a finger into the ear canal to block it while rinsing the outer ears. There is a slight quality of bodily invasion each time, but, oh, oh, it feels so good. So intimate. I think maybe the pink girl today knew I felt a lot of pleasure about that. She did it three times. I think I lost consciousness for a few seconds there. *Petit mort.*

She spent at least three times longer than anyone ever has rinsing my hair. She wiped my neck and forehead several times with a hot washcloth. I wanted to lick her hand a few times. I was limp when she raised me up toward my feet again. That old posture where I must carry my head around on top of my body. It really wasn't my first choice right then. But I did walk back to the chair and submit to hair rubbing with some gratuitous shoulder squeezing tossed in again. Then she snuck up on me with the Q-tip. I felt it start to slide in my ear canal like a very familiar animal, something like a domesticated and affectionate pussy willow bloom. I just closed my eyes. I did not feel invaded this time. I had more than an inkling of what this girl could do to me.

She did that. And more. Finally I was glad for all the noise in the shop. I did moan. I consciously tried not to do my version of the "I want what she ordered," scene in the restaurant from "Harry Meets Sally," because that belongs to Meg Ryan for all time. But, if people could have heard me over the din, they would have all wanted it with a Q-tip then and there, too.

She combed me. I waved away the blow dryer. She flicked my hair into the right places with her fingers. She patted my little head to show she was pleased with how it looked. I nodded like the mute I had become, still agog from how it all felt beneath my hair and up my ear canals. I paid the little bit of money, and I knew better than to try to tip. I squeezed her hands, but did not kiss them. I might have lost control of my lips and drooled.

Karin Faulkner is an expat who settled first in Indonesia and now has been writing and teaching E.S.L. in China since 1999. Before leaving the USA, she taught with California Poets in the Schools for eighteen years and also ran her own small press. Her essays and newspaper columns appeared regularly on the Mendocino Coast. She is hard at work on a book about China, and there is more of Asia that she wants to know.

A Leg Up on Fate

Can the gods reveal the future?
Inquiring minds want to know.

NOISY, TEEMING, INCENSE-FILLED WONG TAI SIN IS HONG Kong's largest and most popular temple, a one-stop supermarket of Taoism, Buddhism, Confucianism, folk-myth, magic, and supernatural practices. While most temples have a resident soothsayer, Wong Tai Sin has a fortunetellers' alley, a warren of 161 stalls, each with its own metal door that clangs down at closing time just like any other shopkeeper's.

Such commercialization of a place of worship is not at all bizarre to the pragmatic Chinese. The fortunetellers pay rent and attract droves of people who drop donations into the slotted box by the temple entrance and buy the paraphernalia of prayer from the temple keepers. Thus, shrines can be built and charitable works maintained.

Perhaps no Westerner can ever fully understand the religion of the ordinary Chinese—the pursuit of worldly success, the appeasement of the dead, and the seeking of hidden knowledge about the future. Ghosts and spirits must be kept happy lest they become restless and return to plague the living; the living must forge links with the dead and those yet unborn; numerous deities must be courted in order to avoid their displeasure. If misfortune occurs despite one's best efforts, answers and remedies are sought before the altar—and in the fortunetelling stalls of Wong Tai Sin.

Few outsiders rummage about in this mystical, supernatural underside of Hong Kong. If one attempts to do so, it is essential to have a Chinese-speaking guide who is willing to talk openly. Mine was Perry Wong.

As the incense and cacophony of worship swirled about us, I was acutely aware, even with Perry by my side, that I was an interloper, a Caucasian voyeur in the midst of those intent on the ancient yet ongoing business of attracting good luck and averting disaster.

Adding to the babble at Wong Tai Sin was the incessant rattling of fortune sticks, one of the most popular methods of divination. Kneeling before the altar, a worshiper holds a round container filled with as many as one hundred bamboo sticks and shakes it until just one works its way free and falls to the floor. A Chinese numeral is inked on each stick to correspond to a numbered fortune, called chim. Several soothsayers in the alley specialize in chim interpretations—and relay additional information from the temple's deities and spirits.

"Would you like to try?" asked Perry. To do so, I had to have several questions in mind—not just one, because the word "one" in Cantonese sounds much like that for "poison," and that would not do.

Since no real concern had brought me, I searched my mind for a pair of questions that would not appear frivolous to the temple's deities, spirits, or whatever might be listening. Finally I settled on inquiries about my future health and happiness.

But first the incense. I had to buy joss sticks, light three, and bow one time each to heaven, earth, and humanity.

That done, I collected a canister from the supply on the altar and found a few unpopulated inches in which to kneel. On my right, a man was fervently thrusting a fistful of incense toward the heavens; on my left a woman, tears rolling down her cheeks, touched her forehead to the ground before tossing *bui*, two pieces of wood, worn smooth by uncountable hands, that could be read "yes" or "no" according to their fall; two out of three would settle her fate.

Now I was shaking the canister, concentrating on my first question and fearful that more than a single stick or, heaven forbid, the entire supply would tumble to the floor, a sure sign that I was not serious. At last one stick emerged from the pack, teetered at the edge of the canister, and fell—followed, as I zoomed in on my second question, by another.

Lam Ching Yee, the most popular reader of chim at Wong Tai Sin, was easy to find; hers was the stall flanked by a queue of occupied stools. An assistant recorded my chim number, asked my birth date, collected my money, and estimated that it would be an hour before we could be seen. We took a number from a dispenser, as if waiting our turn to buy bread at the bakery, and left to look for the stall of Chui Shu Kong, highly regarded among Wong Tai Sin's palm readers.

We found him—his queue of stools unoccupied at the moment—at stall 92. He looked to be in his mid-thirties, with a neatly clipped mustache, crisp white shirt,

---

Another strategy for predicting the future is called *sing pei* or confirmation by Buddha's lips. Two carved pieces of wood, joined by a string or cord, are thrown in the air. When they land, if both "lips" land in the same position, with Buddha's mouth "closed," it means Buddha is saying "no." If one lands up and one down, his mouth is open and it means "yes." There seemed a 50-50 chance to this option, so I asked the lips all my questions. As the smooth pieces of wood moved against each other, it was like Buddha was whispering. Half the time I got yes, half the time, no. Once we knew what they were, we began to see *sing pei* everywhere: in temples, antique and gift shops, and booths on the street.

—Judith Babcock Wylie, "The Whisper of Buddha's Lips"

---

burgundy tie tucked into navy vest. His gray suit jacket hung on a hook on the wall. His fee: HK$100, or about US$13 at the time.

I laid my hands palms up on his table and felt them begin to tremble as Perry translated Chui's reading of my character. The soothsayer accurately saw in my hands that I was a near-workaholic and that I tended to pinch pennies. He added that I negated the pinching with extravagant splurges. He noted my impatience with those less mentally or physically quick than myself. Yet he reported that I was a sociable creature who had many friends, that I loved to read (yet would rather be outdoors than in), that I played respectable games of golf and tennis. He told me about my siblings, my children, my parents, and, with Perry squirming to find euphemistic ways to phrase the information, precise details about my female organs.

"I have told you about yourself and your past so that you will believe me when I tell you about your future," he said. I would soon become seriously ill, and, unless I took precautionary steps, my life would not be long. Despite my protestations that I was always well and fit, a telltale vein at the base of my thumb told Chui a different story.

We left stall 92, me in stunned silence and Perry, who had learned more details about me than he'd bargained for in his role as guide and translator, acting inscrutably Chinese.

But this was Hong Kong, where positive fatalism is practiced. Here, no fate is written in stone. If one's fortune is good, there is nothing to fear. If it is bad, steps can be taken to change it. All I had to do now was find out what spirit I'd alienated and how I'd come to be out of tune with myself and my surrounding world.

Perhaps my house was sited poorly, with bad *feng shui,* and I should have a geomancer come in to correct the placement of windows and doors.

Perhaps my chi, body energy, was in need of bolstering and I should embark on a program of acupuncture, t'ai chi exercises, or meditation.

Perhaps I should consult a *fu kay* practitioner, who would receive a medical prescription from the spirit world for me to have filled by an herbalist.

But right now I had the opportunity to tackle the problem in

Western style—a second opinion—derived from the pair of questions I'd asked of the fortune sticks.

A glass door slid discreetly behind us, shutting out the hub-bub of Wong Tai Sin as we took our seats across the table from Lam Ching Yee. A middle-aged woman wearing a brown print dress with a lace collar, she was already at work on my two chim, selected by her assistant from an array of bright pink paper rectangles printed in red that hung on the wall. Each chim, written in archaic characters and style, told a story, almost a riddle, with obscure references to old Chinese legends.

Inexplicably relayed through a microphone, since we were seated but inches away, Lam Ching Yee dealt first with my future happiness. The fable she told—"Kwan Kung, the respectable and good, helped to send his two sisters-in-law to meet his brother safely"—appeared meaningless to me, but was unhesitatingly interpreted to mean that my future happiness depended on a consultation with two people before I took action.

Which two people? Before taking action on what? I would know, I was told.

On to my second question, which between the shaking of the canister and the reading of the chim had metamorphosed from cliché to concern. This time the text told of a farmer who discovered that his field was full of diamonds. Perry smiled as he relayed the interpretation: my years would be many, and each would sparkle with good health.

For a nonbeliever, I felt an inordinate rush of relief. Yet I also trusted the palm reader who had related so much that was accurate. A third opinion might tilt the scales one way or the other.

At stall 84, I sat across a small table from Richard L. H. Tsui, Life Member of the Society for the Study of Physiognomy, Hong Kong and London—so read his business card. For HK$200, I heard that my face revealed a person of intelligence, warmth, and beauty. I'd weathered rough spots in my life, but now I was like a fine horse running strong and free. I was surrounded by friends and family who loved and respected me; my financial future was secure; my career upward bound.

And, yes—why would I even question it?—of course I would have a long and healthful life.

Tsui's manner was that of a benign and wise grandfather. His face glowed in the reflection of my good fortune. I liked him immensely.

"What did you think?" I asked Perry once we were out of earshot of 84.

"I think," said Perry, "that he tells people what they want to hear."

That evening after dinner, Perry and I were wandering the Temple Street night market, Hong Kong's vast, clamorous, bazaar of improvised stalls dedicated to cut-price seconds, fake designer watches, and over-runs. Midway, the market split into two sections with the walls of jackets and jewelry continuing on up Temple Street, while to the right, following the edge of a small park, something quite different was taking place.

Amidst the incense and the chanting faithful at the Wong Tai Sin Temple, I took the divination sticks and shook them as I saw others shaking them. A stick with the number four written on it popped out. Four is the symbol for death. A sudden wave of emotion washed over me. I felt connected with some universal force that pressed a message upon me: "You face death." Later, I realized that I must face death without fear, that it was something that I had been ignoring in my life. The realization had nothing to do with religion, but was more an issue of yin and yang—and suddenly I was in balance.

—Sean O'Reilly, "City of a Million Dreams"

In the street fronting the park, teams of child acrobats were bouncing and twisting in the glow of kerosene lamps.

Next door, amateur Chinese opera was under way, voices wailing to the chop and clash of wooden blocks and cymbals.

Farther along, a freelance dentist practiced his trade. His stoic patient was sitting on a tiny stool as the dentist prodded about in his mouth.

Next to him a bare-chested man flexed his muscles to demonstrate the effectiveness of the tonic he was selling, and down the block a letter writer was composing an epistle for a client.

Across the street, encircled by onlookers and seated at a fold-up table, was a man wearing round-rimmed glasses, his bald head shining in a pool of hissing gaslight. On the table was a small coop constructed of bamboo dowels and partitioned to house four matched white birds with bright red feet and beaks. Fanned in front of the birds were what appeared to be thick, brown playing cards. "Fortuneteller," Perry whispered as we joined those gathered around. "I think this is one you should try."

I moved up on the queue of stools until I, too, was bathed in gaslight. The soothsayer's eyes widened quizzically as he looked up and into my Western face. Paying a reasonable HK$5 and abandoning my health concerns, I asked what my prospects for financial advancement might be in the coming year.

My question became an incantation to the birds. Then one was chosen for release, and the soothsayer pulled up several dowels at the front of the cage. With endearing efficiency, the bird hopped down the fan of cards until it stopped to tug one free of the pack with its beak. Task completed, it accepted a bite of birdseed from a matchbox and hopped directly back to its cage.

The soothsayer pulled what looked to be a Chinese version of a tarot card from its brown cover, took one look, and threw his head back in laughter, his stainless-steel teeth shining in the lamplight. According to the fortune translated by Perry, my prospects for wealth were nil because, speaking allegorically, I had abandoned my fruitful apple orchard in favor of chasing after jackrabbits. I laughed, too, albeit hollowly.

"Would you like a second opinion?" Perry asked, because right over there at another table bathed in gaslight was a diviner whose method involved the tucking of three old Chinese coins into a tortoise shell. I shook my head. The day had been long, and I'd poked about enough in a world where I did not belong.

Perhaps I'd do well to simply invest in a bag of fortune cookies.

And keep a watchful eye on that telltale vein at the base of my thumb.

Yvonne Michie Horn is a travel writer whose work has appeared in newspapers and magazines in the U.S. and abroad. She lives in Santa Rosa, California.

JOHN KRICH

* * *

The Revenge of
the Snake People

Is that thing kosher?

QING PING MARKET IS NOT FOR ANYONE WHO HAS EVER
felt the slightest urge to join a chapter of the S.P.C.A. The bulk
of this covered gallery, running crosswise through old Canton at its
most crowded, is taken up with the world's greatest variety of exotic flora and fauna offered up as edible. The covered streets are
claimed by sacks of medicinal herbs, a hundred types of dried
fungi, aquarium fish, and tropical birds. It takes a bit of effort to
spot anything offensive to foreign sensibilities, but of course, that's
just what foreigners come here to do. On a good day, there are
caged monkeys, raccoons, civets and, worst of all, fluffy kittens rubbing their noses against the wooden bars. They are not here to be
sold to the zoo. Yes, Virginia, they really do eat anteaters by the
truckload, wise old hoot owls, freshly stunned baby deer with open
starlet eyes still seeking a gentler fate.

Everywhere, the leitmotif of Canton [now called Guangzhou]
is the unidentified, decapitated carcass, all glazed and shiny; the
hanging rodent flank, tail included; the steam-pressed pig head
complete with steamrolled eyeballs. Though a number of overseas
Chinese will insist that eating dog is entirely illegal, the barbeque
shops of Canton are hung with stripped torsos too small to be

pork and too big to be rabbit. "Woof! Woof!" is the explanation which I both expect and dread. Apparently, poodles and schnauzers are out. According to ancient texts, young "yellow dogs"—but not golden retrievers—are considered the tastiest brand of so-called "fragrant meat." One time in Korea, I'd been tricked into trying the stuff myself. As my hosts suppressed their giggles, I had nibbled on oddly stringy strips of flesh carefully disguised in a fiery sauce. The flavor had hardly been memorable, but that could be said about a lot of meals.

If "nature is one huge restaurant," as Woody Allen once put it, then no place in Canton makes the point so vividly as the Snake Restaurant. On our last night of furtive, vaguely creepy scavenging through China, Mei has to inquire three or four times to find the place. Of course, it's down a fittingly dark and serpentine street in the old city. But no identification is more obvious than this restaurant's ground-floor entry. To get upstairs to a table in the cushy mezzanine, even one's own banquet room where the snake comes with electrified sing-along, you have to pass through a frequently blood-bathed and hosed-down area. This tiled butcher shop is lined with snake cages. But in the center are strikingly clinical dissection tables manned by more enthusiastic young snake handlers than could ever be found in an Indian bazaar. Each are certified trainers, we're assured, and deft slaughterers, choppers and strippers. Only in China would this show be meant to stimulate, rather than put off, one's appetite.

But Chinese appetites come from village life, as these snakes come from a farm near the Hong Kong border. As in ancient times, when Southerners were scorned for their love of frogs, a younger generation is enthusiastically carrying on the snake tradition.

"After you try it, you'll like it!" we are urged by an assistant manageress with a four-foot-high black beehive hairdo, a flashy, denture-regular set of choppers and cheeks as rosy and polished as a Washington State apple. So we follow her recommendations for a soup of snake, chicken, and cat, pieces of barbequed snake, a stir-fried snake with greens, and whole ginger in snake broth. A bonus comes in the form of snake spleen, excised with a knife from a caged garden snake brought to the table, then squeezed into a shot glass of *mao tai*. Talk about swallowing bile! But this bitter medicine is considered another boost for virility, one gamble which few men over thirty can refuse.

"The spleen contains vital element NA-3, C1," says the manager cheerily. But isn't that salt? Fortunately, she isn't pushing Stewed Three Different Snakes with Chicken Feet in medicinal herbs, the ever-popular Stewed Fur Seals, or the Stir-fried Ophicephalus Fish Ball and Stewed Frog.

"The entire snake is treasure," purrs the politburo Nefertiti on her return. "It increases blood circulation, cures cough, builds the blood and organ, tones the skin and hair. Make everyone feel energy, woman get beauty!" Apparently, we've come at the right time of year, too, since she hastens to rhapsodize, "When the autumn winds start, the snakes all grow meaty. That's the best time to eat!"

Now I know the origins of the term "snake oil." Not only is snake meat very *yang* or hot, in the Chinese system, but this woman claims it helped save the lives of some Cantonese injected with experimental serums by the occupying Japanese. And she herself seems unusually pumped up. For a state-run place especially, morale in the Snake Restaurant sure is high. The whole staff is its best advertisement—

> ━━━━━ ✸ ━━━━━
>
> In Canton, and more strongly in Nanchang, I didn't sense the slightest trace of Marxism in the atmosphere: I felt that apart from a government that proclaimed Marxism, the people were not socialist but out-and-out capitalists. By nature the Chinese seem to be the most capitalistic of all peoples; their genetic code must have a gene which other people lack. Now that the government permits private business ventures, the people are responding whole-heartedly at doing what they know best—making a profit. Poor Karl Marx!
>
> —Rev. Seumas O'Reilly, former missionary, returning to China after decades away

including several other *madchen* in uniform with severe expressions and scary bouffants.

"Is it a cult?" I suddenly whisper to Mei. All of the waiters and waitresses are acting like indoctrinated converts. Or perhaps, after so many years, they are merely addicted to the stuff they push. It seems that all of them are unnaturally preserved, with taut skin, a stunning profusion of hair and wildly bright eyes. I feel like we're dining in *The Village of the Damned*, that sci-fi flick where all the children have eyes that glow with an inner, alien light. I keep an eye on Mei to make sure she doesn't ingest too much cobra, lest she take on the same eerie glow. Now I fear that I'll catch her hissing each time we make love. Call this the Revenge of the Snake People.

"Can you guess how long I've been here?" the head snake goddess asks ominously. "Twenty year!" This grandmother doesn't look a single shred of skin over thirty-five. And she nods fervently when I ask if she regularly tastes of the serpent.

"One day, I'd like to open my own snake restaurant," she confirms. "With reforms, we have good pay and are able to travel abroad." But there's no place like home when it comes to snake.

"I'll bet you don't envy people abroad after a meal like this," observes our irradiated hostess. Willing to hear only one reply, the number one snake lady asks, "Don't you think Chinese people really know how to eat?"

I grunt my approval while munching on a morsel of cat. But in the morning, I wake with relief at having survived this final ingestion, relief at having survived China one more time. And it's only once we've arrived at the station for the train to Hong Kong that I really feel Canton's connection to the rest of the motherland's needy mass. Inadvertently, the town's greatest tourist sight has become an unstoppable deluge of blue-clad peasants with bed rolls, this stampede of poverty-arriving undocumented and unblessed to the new economic zones which stretch the borders of China's economy to bursting. But we've soon boarded our non-stop express from underdevelopment. Crossing this most abrupt of the world's borders, it felt like everything had gone from dim bulb to bright, as though the wattage of the world had experienced a sudden power surge. No doubt the transition grows less shocking every day. But perhaps it was best to come out of China gradually—walking the surreptitious routes, floating down the Pearl River, throwing oneself into the sea and the fate that awaited in the outside world.

A half-hour out of Canton, I already miss the dumplings and the fish-flavored shredded pork. I already feel farther from China than I ever wanted to feel. But with Mei by my side, I will always have a handy way back. Perhaps we should have started our search elsewhere, for it is going to be hard to top the mainland's flavor and punch—if not service. It was an amazing comment in itself—about Chinese history, about the relative prosperity and ingenuity of the Chinese at home and overseas—that I should feel daring and heretical enough to suggest that the best Chinese food in the world might actually be found in China.

"You want Chinese restaurants?" asked the balding, shoulder-shrugging leader of an Israeli tour group in the seats ahead of us. "Come to Tel Aviv and try Moishe Peking. It's kosher!"

This is the strangest argument I've ever heard for convincing me to exercise my right of return. As for his impressions of my adopted homeland, the balding man bellows, "Suzhou! Shmoo-joe! Enough already! We saw the whole schmear!"

And we ate the whole schmear.

Award-winning writer John Krich is the author of two widely praised non-fiction books, Music in Every Room *and* El Beisbol, *as well as a novel about the private life of Fidel Castro,* A Totally Free Man. *This story was excerpted from his book,* Won Ton Lust: Adventures in Search of the World's Best Chinese Restaurant. *His travel and sports writing, reportage and fiction, have appeared in* Mother Jones, Vogue, Sports Illustrated, Village Voice, Image, Commentary, California, The New York Times, *and many other publications.*

YINJIE QIAN

Where Harmony Sings

*In Lijiang, the author encounters not just the remnants
of matriarchy among the Naxi,
but a sweet culture as well.*

IT WAS RAINING WHEN I LANDED IN LIJIANG, A SMALL TOWN
nestled in the Jade Dragon Mountain ranges in Yunnan, southwest China. At once, I smelled the fertile valley and alpine meadows; I felt the snowy mountains looming. And yet all was shrouded
behind a heavy, mysterious mist. I had long hoped to see this unspoiled land of beauty, to explore the fascinating, yet little-known
culture of the Naxi (Na-shee)—a people with obvious matriarchal
influence. Now with the rain, my plan seemed thwarted.

"Is the rain going to stop soon?" I asked the driver plaintively
the moment I hopped into the taxi.

"No one can predict," he said, smiling. "It's nature's blessing
whether rain or shine." He didn't seem to understand my disappointment.

We set off for Lijiang Old Town, a previously-isolated place,
now a World Heritage Site, whose main habitants are the Naxi—
a small group among China's fifty-five minority nationalities, who
have lived for centuries with the Bai, Yi, Tibetan, Pumi, and Han
(Chinese) on the Qinghai-Tibetan plateau located 7,000 feet
above sea level.

Music filled the taxi, monotonous and ancient. How strange that a taxi driver would like this, I thought, hoping he wouldn't fall asleep. My eyes moved to the meter on the dashboard. My mother had told me before I left Shanghai: "Make sure drivers turn on the meter." She was worried about me traveling alone to this remote region to which criminals and out-of-favor Mandarin officials were banished in ancient times, a place still considered "uncivilized" by most Han people, who constitute 95 percent of the Chinese population.

"My name is He," the driver volunteered. "It's one of the two major surnames among the Naxi."

I noticed that he had a full-moon face, quite tanned, with high cheekbones—a feature rare among the Han. "But you speak very good Chinese."

"Not very well," he replied modestly. "We learned it in school."

"Do you speak your own language?"

"Yes. But I can't write. Our written language is pictographs. Except for a handful of old men, most people don't know how to write it now."

"This 'He' is not a common name among us Han," I said. "We have a different one."

"I know. In the old days the Naxi had no family names. We went by first names. In the fourteenth century the emperor of the Ming Dynasty awarded our tribal chief the name 'Mu' for his loyalty. The chief then named all his slaves 'He'—the character that is written like a man in a straw hat carrying a basket on his back.

"I like my name," he continued. "It means harmony. We're peace-loving people. Over the centuries, we've lived in harmony with the surrounding tribes and the Han, despite all the differences. You will find a heavy mix of the Han, Tibetan, and other tribal influences in our culture. But unlike some ethnic groups that have totally acculturated to the Han, we've kept our own."

The rain was still falling. Strangely, I felt it wasn't annoying anymore. We drove through the new town—an urban sprawl with some awkward-looking concrete buildings, shops and modern hotels. After a few traffic lights, the driver pulled up at a stony square.

In front of me stood a huge granite monument on which was inscribed "World Heritage—UNESCO."

"Welcome to Lijiang Old Town," said the driver with a proud smile. "No vehicles are allowed in town. You need to walk to your hotel. It's not far, about five minutes." He showed me the direction.

"Thank you for giving me such a good orientation."

"You haven't seen Lijiang yet. The rain is to blame," he teased.

"But at least I've met one of its people." I waved goodbye.

In the rain, I rolled my bags through the narrow, winding, cobbled streets. The houses looked ancient, earthen-walled with gray slate roofs, reminiscent of Ming Dynasty architecture. Tiny bridges connecting each house, some stone-carved, others just a piece of plain board, spanned the gurgling canals that crisscrossed into the heart of the town. A windmill spun cheerfully in a nearby stream lined with weeping willows. The red lanterns glowed, creating a warm ambiance. I felt an instant attachment to this place. It reminded me of some aging water towns in southeast China, though the wood tracery, boldly colored, carved with intricate mythological figures, suggested a strong Naxi influence. There was something else different. What was it? I wasn't sure.

My hotel was a wooden, two-story inn with an open-air corridor leading to a courtyard where orchids in earthenware pots were in full bloom.

"*Ar la la,*" a Naxi young woman greeted me warmly in her own language, then followed with the Chinese, "*Ni hao.*" She wore the traditional outfit: a white apron around her waist and a cape tied to her back. She quickly found my name in the computer and handed me the key.

"I'll help you with your luggage." She picked up the bags and went ahead of me through the narrow passage. From behind I saw the colorful, embroidered circles sewn onto her cape—seven of them. It is said that they symbolize the stars. To me, they looked like her pretty smiling face.

I left my bags and walked out to find a place to eat. It was quite late, but the town was still busy. Tourists were bargaining for souvenirs; restaurants were full of diners babbling in various tongues; disheveled backpackers roamed through the maze of alleys. I turned into a quiet lane and found a little noodle shop. It was not crowded. I picked a table by the window. The table was at my knees and the stool was even lower. A Naxi woman, plain and down-to-earth looking, emerged from the kitchen smiling, wiping her hands on her soiled black apron; the sheepskin cape on her back was worn. She pointed to the board by the kitchen door where the menu was written and asked kindly what I wanted to eat.

After a long day of switching flights, I wanted something warm and soft to please my grumbling stomach. I picked *Guoqiao mixian* (literally "across-the-bridge rice noodles"). In a few minutes, the woman came with a bowl of angel-haired rice noodles, a plate with sliced raw meat, and another with spinach, chives, bean sprouts, and chili peppers. Then she brought me the broth in a big bowl, and, explaining like a patient mother, said, "You first put the meat in the hot broth. Let it cook for a few seconds, then throw in the noodles and vegetables, and mix them together."

"For the Naxi, a fat woman is beautiful. The fatter you are, the better," Norman, our local guide, said. I noted that the older women had round faces, rosy cheeks, and their bodies looked solidly strong. The younger women were taller and thinner than their mothers and grandmothers. On the spot I decided that Naxi women have the most beautiful smiles in the world.

—Chris Card Fuller,
"In the Neighborhood of
Shangri-La"

I quickly made myself a bowl of noodle soup with red peppers floating on top. By the time I got about halfway down, my eyes were watery, my nose was running, and I had to stick out my tongue to get cool air. But the soup was delicious.

"Why is it called *Guoqiao mixian*?" I asked when the woman brought me the tea.

"It's an old story," she said while wiping the table. "A long time ago, a man was studying for the Imperial Examination. Every day his wife walked several miles and crossed a bridge to bring him noodle soup. She continued doing this until he passed the exam and became a Mandarin scholar. Later all Naxi women made the soup for their men. This is how it became popular."

"I've learned that Naxi men were much into literature and music," I said. "But they didn't have much say in the family. A woman had power over her husband. Is the matriarchal tradition still strong?" I was curious, having come from the patriarchal Han society in which a woman's role was trivialized.

"Yes, women are still in charge of the family. We do everything—we run the family business, handle money, go to the market, work in the fields and barns; we wash, clean, and cook. Naxi men don't do any of these things. You don't see them in the kitchen or at the marketplace. They spend most time reading or playing music."

"Don't you ever complain that you do so much?"

"Never," she shook her head. "It's not good. It destroys the harmony in the family. Would you rather have arguments or music at home? The old way has been around for ages. I find it fine."

I told her I had my father's calligraphy on the wall at home, which said, "Books and music bring harmony to the home."

She smiled approvingly, and I asked her about their marriage customs.

"Most Naxi practice monogamy," she said. "But the Mosuo, a sub-tribe of the Naxi, still keep the old tradition. When the *axia*—a Mosuo word for lovers—are in love, the man comes to the woman's place every night and leaves at dawn to go home to work for his family. They stay like this as long as they want without having to be legally married. If they split up, or the man gets kicked out, the children they have together belong to the woman and are raised by her family. He doesn't have any financial responsibility for his children. Then both can find a new *axia* and start another relationship."

I was a bit surprised that this *axia* system existed. In the traditional Han culture, with its deeply rooted Confucian influence, this would be condemned.

It was late. I thanked the woman and rose to leave. She disappeared into the kitchen, and came out with a brown paper bag, thrusting it into my hands. "It's *baba* (flat wheat bread)," she said. "For your snack."

In the rain, I held the bag close to me. It felt warm despite the damp chill in the air. The rain fell on the stone-flagged street, on the bridges, and dimpled the surface of the water flowing quietly in the streams. The ancient lanes, dark and bewildering, seemed to hold many stories—happy, nostalgic, and mysterious. I felt a sudden unknown force pulling me deep into the labyrinth. The stories in the shadows began to unfold before me—beautiful, intriguing.

I found myself in the town again the next morning. The air was fresh and crisp. The sun was a little pale behind the clouds. Bougainvillea—red and hot pink, impatient to show their passion—peeked from behind the earthen walls. Lush, green willow trees swayed gently in the morning breeze. The town had come to life. Naxi women with hoes on their shoulders or loaded baskets on their backs marched to the market. Naxi men loitered with bird cages in hand and rosy-cheeked children in colorful traditional outfits skipped on their way to school.

I followed the women to the market. If a visitor complained about seeing more tourists than Naxi women in town, then the market was the right place to be. Here was a world of them. They brought the fresh produce that grew in their yards—beans, soy, nuts, corn, vegetables, fruit. And they bought things they needed for the household. Occasionally, I saw some Yi or Bai women in traditional dress, often adorned with heavy metal pieces on their necks and elaborate head wraps. Compared to them, Naxi women in their dark-bluish outfits looked homely and unembellished. The Mao-style hats they wore made them even less attractive. Most of them were well-built with broad shoulders and big feet; their skin was dark, roughened by the blazing sun of the plateau. I walked around and watched. I found them to be the happiest of people. They were warm and cheerful. The heavy loads on their backs didn't seem to add any grudge or displeasure to their faces. They laughed and joked; they shared their *baba* for breakfast; they showed each other things they had bought for their husbands and children. If, by their matriarchal tradition, they had to be the "captain" at home, the marketplace seemed to be their playground, a place where they rediscovered their girlish innocence. I bought some bananas from a smiling woman. They were sweet and delicious.

At a Naxi culture museum near Yuquan Park, I met a young lady who offered to give me a tour. She told me her name was He Wen. "I'm part Naxi, part Han," she said. "Interracial marriage is common here."

We went to the first exhibit room, where a teacher was telling a group of school children about Dongbawen, Naxi's written pictographic language. On the wall were charts comparing Dongbawen with ancient Chinese and Egyptian hieroglyphics.

"Teacher, I want to learn Dongbawen," one girl said. "They're beautiful, like pictures. I know this is the sun, a river, a tree, a hill..."

"I don't," a boy argued. "It takes forever to write. I want to learn English and computers."

I was amused. I asked Wen if Dongbawen was being taught. She didn't reply directly. Instead, she showed me some thread-bound books in a glass case. They looked extremely old, their pages turned a coffee-brownish.

"These are Dongba classics," she said. "A valuable anthology of Naxi culture and religion. They were all hand written in Dongbawen by Naxi shamans. These men are learned; we call them Dongba. They perform rituals and record events and scriptures into the Dongba classics." She told me she was taking lessons with an old Naxi shaman. "Sadly, not many of these learned men are left. But the classics need to be studied. They're too precious to be left forgotten."

In the next room I found exhibits on the Naxi religion—its rituals and festivals, scrolls and pictures of frescoes suggesting the strong influence of Taoism, Buddhism, and Tibetan Lamaism on the Naxi culture. One introductory panel indicated that there once had been more than sixty temples, lamaseries, even churches in the Lijiang area. I told Wen that I didn't know much about the religion, and had always associated it with voodoo. "You're not the only one," she said understandingly. "Compared to Buddhism, Taoism, or Lamaism, ours is not a strict religion. It doesn't teach doctrines. It doesn't worship a specific god. We don't have temples. All rituals and festivals are held outdoors in open fields or by the water, where we have direct contact with nature. More appropriately, we're nature worshippers. We worship heaven, ancestors, and every living thing in nature—mountains, rivers, trees, and animals. We believe the world is in peace if we keep a

---

———— ✳ ————

We attended a performance at the Dongba Palace to learn more about Naxi shamans who have preserved their pictographic language.

The interior reminded me of Chiwong Gompa in Phaplu, Nepal, and it was hard to discern where Tibetan influence ended and Naxi tradition began. As the musicians played, the shaman opened the ceremony by blaring on animal horns. I couldn't help but think of the Mani Rimdu ritual which we'd attended in Phaplu. Mani Rimdu brought pilgrims and locals together for an event they understood: Good vanquishing Evil. I was surprised at the similarity between the Dongba spirit dance and the Tantric magicians' vestments and dances we admired during Mani Rimdu. However, tonight's performance in Lijiang was meant for tourists. In trying to make Dongba culture accessible to outsiders, would it succumb to "folklorification"?

—Chris Card Fuller,
"In the Neighborhood of
Shangri-La"

harmonious relationship with nature. If we abuse nature, the harmony is broken and disasters will occur."

I remembered what the Naxi driver had said about nature. I felt ashamed of my folk—the "civilized" Han, who had destroyed so much of our environment in the past. I began to understand and appreciate the Naxi belief system.

We finished the tour and came out into the courtyard, where the ground was paved with beautiful pebbles in the shape of a Bagua Diagram. Wen suggested I walk around it, clockwise, three times. "You'll be blessed."

I took a shortcut through the park back to town. The mist had dispersed. A few white clouds, thin as a cicada's wings, were swirling around the snow-clad Jade Dragon Mountain. Shy like a young maiden, the unconquered peak slowly revealed her beauty—stunning, shimmering under the blue sky, as if the clouds were the veils she had tossed away, the arched marble bridge the jade hairpin she had left behind. The placid lake, rimmed by emerald-green trees, flowed peacefully at the foot of the mountain into numerous rivulets to nurture the town, and its people. It was a paradisiacal land of sheer beauty and harmony! Why were the Naxi so blissful? I suddenly realized that the Naxi revered nature and in turn, nature delivered its promise, beautiful and bountiful.

That evening I went to a concert of ancient Naxi music. The hall, remodeled from a courtyard inside a simple-looking house, was festively decorated, and full of tourists, both Chinese and foreign. I took my seat, actually a long bench with a dozen of us sitting in one row, elbow to elbow. Shortly, the musicians walked on stage, unhurriedly, with their ancient instruments. Most were old men, bald, or with inch-long white goatees, in long robes topped with shiny satin vests. I thought of sages from ancient times.

Then Xuan Ke, the spectacled host, appeared. He told the audience, in both Chinese and English, that he was a musician. He had been put in jail for twenty years, but his love for music was never diminished. In 1981, after he was released, he got these people together in the single hope of reviving the ancient music from the Han and Tang dynasties that had disappeared in most parts of China due to war and upheaval.

"I feel an immediate urgency," Mr. Xuan said. "I'm almost seventy and the oldest one here is eighty-nine. Every year we lose about two people." He pointed to the beam above the stage with pictures of those who had died. "If we don't do anything, the music that only the Naxi have been able to keep alive for hundreds of years will die with us." His voice was low.

"Over the years, we grew and added new blood," he continued. "People from all over the world have come to hear our music. We've also performed in some European countries. I remain hopeful that our ancient music—our legacy—will be preserved and understood without national and cultural boundaries."

With the applause from the audience, the orchestra started to play. Slowly the melody flowed, sacred and peaceful. It filled the heart, it touched the soul, it infiltrated every inch of one's existence. I closed my eyes. I felt as if I had been carried away to a place of serenity and peace, a land where nature and man existed in perfect unity, a world free from woes and chaos, a realm in which I felt close to the Divine.

> Bell and drum on the south river bank:
> Home! I wake startled from a dream.
> Drifting clouds—so the world shifts;
> Lone moon—such is the light of my mind.
> Rain drenches down as from a tilted basin;
> Poems flow out like water spilled.
> The two rivers vie to send me off;
> Beyond treetops I see the slant of a bridge.
> —Su Shi (1037-1101)

The audience was captivated, immersed in the immeasurable richness of the music. Then a cell phone rang—the most disturbing noise of the modern era! Worse, the man who'd received the call started to talk, oblivious to the furious looks around him. Mr. Xuan stood up, his face red with anger. "Please turn off your cell phone or leave. No dissonant chords are allowed here." We all applauded. The music resumed—again, celestial and harmonious.

The concert ended and I walked out. A few stars sparkled in the deep night sky. The air was invigorating. The music was still lingering, inspiring. I thought about the beautiful people I had met, the simple, industrious Naxi women, their smiles, their beliefs; the fascinating culture, the snow mountain and the lake. I walked around, asking myself a question that had been in the back of my mind for days: What made this town unique?

Suddenly, I found the clue: There was no wall! The Han built the wall around the country, in each town, to fence us in. The Naxi didn't. With their open hearts to embrace nature, and to accept differences, the Naxi were able to create a culture colorful, rich, and prismatic.

On the stream nearby floated some flickering candles in lotus-shaped little boats. A Naxi said it was their ritual to pray for blessings on their town and their people. I lit one candle and made a little wish.

Yinjie Qian grew up in China. A high school teacher in Boca Raton, Florida and a novice travel writer whose stories have appeared in the Sun Sentinel, Philadelphia Inquirer, Chicago Sun-Times, *and other newspapers, she is learning to write in her second language, a prohibited language she risked her life to learn during the Cultural Revolution. This story is dedicated to her late father, who inspired her to dream amid the nightmares and to hope when despair seemed to know no bounds.*

JACQUELINE C. YAU

King Kong in Shanghai

If the cup fits, wear it.

I AM FIVE-FOOT, FOUR-INCHES AND 125 POUNDS. I HAVE A long, slim face, wide shoulders, long arms and legs, short waist, skinny ankles, average breasts, and a medium-sized butt. I'm about a size 8. I'm not your garden variety, extremely slim and petite Asian-American woman. O.K., hardly noteworthy in the United States but in China…I might as well be King Kong. I am HUGE. I am a deviant. I'm an alien squared because I actually resemble someone who belongs to the same race living in China, but I'm shaped very differently. Nothing fits me except the occasional XXL.

I need a dress and I'm in China for another three months. I only brought functional wear, thinking that no one cares about fashion here. Silly me. I missed China's fast forward into consumerism in the four years since my last visit. I also surprise myself. I discover I want to look more feminine while I am in China. My good friend, Shirley, takes me to downtown Shanghai, to dressmaker row, to a *cheongsam* dressmaker she knows. The dresses stun the senses in copper, iridescent blue, bright green, searing red, sumptuous eggplant—all luxuriant silk fabrics shot with gold threads and Asian patterns. I try to squeeze into a ready-made dress. Nope. Here in China, I'm lush and voluptuous.

The dressmaker, a small fireball of a woman, charges over from the other side of the shop and takes over my dress selection, clucking and emitting a slew of Shanghainese and Mandarin phrases. She doesn't quite believe that I can't fit into any of the off-the-rack dresses. I look smaller than I am and taller than I am. My body is an optical illusion. People constantly misjudge my shape, size, weight, and age. She tries to stuff and zip me into a custom dress they are making for an Italian woman half my size. I think that Italian women and Chinese women must come from the same genetic stock judging from this dress—tiny people stock.

My Mandarin comprehension suffers a total breakdown when the excited shop staff surrounds me buzzing in two dialects, a deafening cacophony. The dressmaker summoned the entire staff out onto the shop floor to look at me. Two other girls from the back room, the dressmaker, the cashier, and now, a gathering horde of customers who just came in, gawk at me, the human burrito. This is a society of people who stare. I am a circus attraction. Passersby linger, looking in from the floor-to-ceiling picture windows behind me, no doubt wondering what is going on inside.

Hands touch me, prod me, poke me, as the dressmaker and her staff try to figure out why I can't fit into any of the dresses she has hanging on the dress racks. My body is a Tickle-Me Elmo toy to them. They confer. Finally, the dressmaker calms down enough to say in choppy English, "You have body of Eastern European woman. You need custom dress." They have never seen anything like this in a Chinese woman before. I don't think that this is a compliment but they look at me in awe. I have visions of Soviet Bloc Olympians pumped full of steroids. That's me?

The dressmaker further states in a loud voice, "Your bra is no good...flimsy." I cringe internally. So now both my body and my underwear are under scrutiny. She measures me but tells me I will need to get re-measured after I come back wearing the correct bra. O.K. I can buy a new bra. No big deal. Lingerie has arrived in China. The dressmaker asserts that women are like flowers that need to be artfully arranged. I need structure, stiffness, and uplift to show off my lush Eastern European figure and their workmanship.

I marvel at the sacrifices women make to look good, including myself, even in China.

As I walk from the dressmaker's shop, down a couple of blocks to where the big department stores are, I notice that a full-scale war is in progress to persuade women that dressing pretty inside will make them feel great on the outside. Billboards lining the streets, on the sides of sleek new buildings, and all along the subway line, show beautiful glossy-haired Chinese women in skimpy lacy bras and underwear. Quite a change from the standard-issue shapeless silk or cotton waist-high briefs and undershirts of the past.

Against the backdrop of colorful advertisements for shampoos, contact lenses, lotions, and toothpaste, stylishly dressed and made-up young professional women walk purposefully past me, clutching knock-off Prada and Chanel purses. Amazing. They look no different than young, optimistic, and ambitious young women in other major cities around the world. I, on the other hand, look decidedly rumpled and not sleek in my faded jean shorts, 1986 5K fun run t-shirt, denim floppy hat, white athletic socks, and jogging shoes.

Given my "special" build, I skip the regular Chinese department stores and go to one that looks more Westernized to seek out that perfect bra. The store possesses a simple interior décor, cleaner lines, dramatic colors, better merchandising, and a wide selection of imported Western goods that probably were made in China. On the third floor, I see a small selection of lacy bras, neatly arranged on tastefully spaced islands of metal racks. Three ladies dressed in matching powder-blue suits, neatly combed black hair, and carefully applied makeup approach me and ask if I need assistance.

Wow! Service. Customer service in China? Things have changed. Ah, that's right. This is a Japanese department store where service reigns supreme. In Chinglish, a mixture of English and street Mandarin, I tell the ladies what I am looking for.

I suffer a moment of indecision as I wait for the ladies to find some bras for me. I'm not going that far in my pursuit of beauty, am I? After all, I'm not disfiguring myself. Have I embarked on that slippery slope of beauty where one thing leads to another until my body is a jigsaw puzzle of tummy tucks, face-lifts, and liposuction marks? Is this how an addiction starts—first it's a made-to-order dress, then a bra to lift, a tube of lipstick to enhance, a blush and eyeliner to brighten, and then a shot of Botox to smooth? It's ironic that I feel insecure about my looks in China, my ancestral home, and feel the need for the trappings of the fashion industry.

I'm just getting a dress and a bra. That's it, I tell myself. Don't stress. Thankfully, the ladies quickly choose a few bras and pull me out of my panicked reverie. The young woman with her hair neatly pulled back in a ponytail shows me to a very small space to the right of the bra racks. Before I can close the door, the saleswoman pushes in after me and closes the door behind us. What is she doing? In my surprise, I can't say a word. This must be standard practice. I guess I'll let her stay. Perhaps she thinks I'll steal the bra and she needs to watch me. Who knows? I take off my shirt and bra and lay them down to the right of me, on a chair. As I look back towards the mirror after taking my own bra off, I feel a hand on my breast. Her hand is on my breast!

I feel the coolness of her palm cup the curve at the bottom of my left breast. Heat sears my cheeks in embarrassment. I am absolutely

A priceless moment on Shanghai's Bund occurred after I walked into a local sex shop. As the author of a book on human sexuality I had to see what the state of Chinese thinking was in regard to the public display of sexual aids. It was exactly the same as any sex shop in the U.S.: male and female rubber body parts of all sizes and colors, and other exotic paraphernalia to quicken jaded appetites and disappointed hearts. What I loved though was that the attendants wore white doctor's lab coats as if they were administering some sort of beneficial medicine. Like their equally serious counterparts in the U.S., they did not appreciate my uproarious laughter. Where, I thought, was the thinking of Chairman Mao in all of this?

—Sean O'Reilly, "Oh Mao, Where Art Thou?"

dumbfounded and weirdly turned on at the same time. She pulls upward and stuffs me into the cup of the bra, holds me there while deftly doing the same with my right breast. She instructs me to hold myself up as she closes the clasp on the back.

A bra has never fit me so well. She compliments me on my figure. After an ego-bruising time at the dressmaker shop, my confidence is restored by her praise. Perhaps having an Eastern European build has its advantages in this country of slim people and new imported lingerie modeled on Western women. I don't even need any adjustments to my bra. I try another one on. This time, I politely decline her assistance as she reaches for my breast again. Hard to do when there's barely enough space to reach my arms in back of me.

I end up buying four bras, two of each kind. It's the most I have ever spent on bras. She assures me that this French label is of the highest quality. I believe her. I quickly make my purchase, thank her and the rest of the sales ladies. They must see the redness of my cheeks as I walk quickly away. I don't pause. I go down the escalator, down to the first floor, and out the door before I allow myself to think too deeply about what just happened. I laugh hysterically, dispelling the nervous energy and embarrassment built up inside me, causing a few people who passed me to whip back their heads to see what they missed.

How odd is it that I have to travel more than twelve thousand miles to find out certain truths about myself? I actually care that I'm huge in this country of smaller people (basketball star Yao Ming notwithstanding). I feel dowdy in fashionable Shanghai. And I want to look good. The hard part is admitting to myself that I feel that way and that's O.K. I shake my head slightly and mull over this revelation about myself. Then I smile as I walk back to the dressmaker to begin the prodding all over again, this time with the right bra.

Jacqueline C. Yau ate her first bowl of noodles on the road when she was three, traveling with her parents from California to Vancouver. Thus began a lifelong love of pasta and travel. When Jacqueline is not curled up in a chair reading romance and adventure stories, she's sampling new cuisines, ricocheting down hiking trails, indulging her curiosity, or laughing with family and friends. Her alter ego brings home the bacon as a strategic marketing consultant, drawing on her experiences as an internet keyword evangelist, brand manager, social entrepreneur, access cable TV host, and news reporter.

Emperor Qin's Army

They've been awaiting orders for twenty-five centuries.

THE ARMY STANDS IN PLACE, NEARLY 7,000 STRONG. ARRAYED in battle formation, unmoving; not even blinking; they are a juggernaut about to pounce. Each face is unique; a study in concentration of warriors ready to die.

The commanding general and his aides ride chariots behind armor-shrouded horses. Legions of archers, lancers, and foot soldiers surround them. A sense of doom pervades the air. War is about to be unleashed.

Most amazingly, this army lived 2,500 years ago.

We have braved the summer monsoons of central China, traveling to Xi'an in a pelting downpour. I welcome the cooling rain after the sweltering humidity of Beijing, knowing three dozen people have died in the floods. This is the normal state of affairs for China in summer. We spend most of an afternoon sitting next to an underwater highway, watching military engineers attempt to pump away an inland sea of rainwater. Our driver passes the day chain-smoking Marlboros and cursing the weather. I tell him we will wait all day if necessary. He smiles through a cloud of smoke. We are here to see the Terra Cotta Army of Emperor Qin.

In 259 B.C. China was a series of feuding states commanded by local warlords all calling themselves "King." That year, the wife of the "King" of Qin province bore a son, Zhao Zheng. When the boy was thirteen his father died and he ascended the local throne, changing his name to Ying Zheng. Being too young to govern, his mother administered the affairs of state until the boy reached the age of twenty-two. At that time he began a series of military conquests to unite the various provinces. In 221 B.C. at the age of thirty-nine he had defeated the six ruling warlords and united the country, declaring himself to be, "Qin Shi Huang Di," First Emperor of Qin.

Today he is known as Emperor Qin, and the modern state of China claims its name from him

Emperor Qin suffered a lifelong fear of death. He constantly searched for an elixir to guarantee his immortality. Having failed to find one, he decided to assure himself an easy passage into the hereafter by taking his legions with him. He amassed an army of artisans almost as large as his military. He commanded them to create a life-size clay duplicate of every soldier in his service. One by one his soldiers modeled for the sculptors. As each statue was finished, it was fired in a kiln, painted, and mounted in a giant pit, exactly where that man would stand in formation on a battlefield. When they finished, the emperor had a terra cotta duplicate of his entire army.

Qin died at the age of fifty. The next emperor ordered all of Qin's concubines who had not born him children put to death and interred with him. The thousands of artisans who created this wonder were also put under the sword to assure it remained a secret to the outer world.

For 2,400 years, the army stood silent and unknown, covered in its tomb next to the emperor himself.

Then, in 1974 a poor farmer named Yang Jun Peng dug a well for his village. Breaking into a dark cavern he found small pieces of metal and shards of terra cotta. At first he was disgusted at not finding water and tossed the pieces away. A village elder realized the importance of his find and notified local authorities. Four months later a massive excavation began. No one was prepared for what they would find.

Two thousand years of earthquakes, floods, and a fire had taken its toll. Most of the army was in small pieces. Still the sheer size of the discovery dictated a massive effort on the government's part. Museum curators and restorers were dispatched to begin assembling the world's largest jigsaw puzzle.

By 1979 more than 1,000 warriors had been reassembled, plus 300 horses and dozens of chariots. A massive museum complex was constructed to house the army and its restoration. In 1987, UNESCO declared the area a World Heritage Site.

The army finally lowers the water enough for us to creep through, and we slip and slide into the parking lot. I see two buses unloading their cargo of saffron-robed monks. As each one disembarks, they immediately open identical white umbrellas. Arm in arm they scurry into the building like a moving garden of mushrooms. I follow them inside snapping their photos and amusing them greatly.

The first look at the army is overwhelming. They occupy an enormous pit inside a building the size of an airline hangar. It is dark inside, for daylight can damage these delicate pieces.

Most of the warriors are over six feet tall; some are close to seven. These soldiers were recruited from northern Mongolian stock and were formidable in size. The statues tower over modern-day Chinese. The

> I feel as warm as the evening, the sweat like a mist on my skin. I am thinking of how my former life and what I called a self has flaked off like dead skin. Afternoons when I ride into the city, through its seven mile wall, under the old archers' towers into the back streets of Xi'an, I can leave everything to chance. Engulfed by the Chinese, I do not want to be anywhere else in the world.
>
> —J. D. Brown, *Digging to China*

detail is astonishing: Each piece of armor is articulated. Mustaches, beards, hairstyles, even fingernails are rendered with exacting craftsmanship. Archers wear silk scarves to swivel their necks without rubbing them raw on leather gauntlets. Boot soles have ripples. Thongs wrap around leggings so they will not catch the brush while on the march. Hair is tied to one side, allowing the clear draw of an arrow from back quivers. Horsemen have spurs and infantrymen wear body armor. Horses wear leather jerkins to ward off arrows and blinders to keep them moving forward. If a piece of equipment existed in the actual army, it was faithfully recreated.

Row after row stand in silent formation, waiting for orders. It is more than daunting to stare into faces that lived and fought more than two millennia ago. Every statue is unique. Each is the death mask of its owner. No one speaks here. Partly out of reverence, but even more, it is the unconscious longing to hear the order for battle to be called, as if at any moment the march will begin. This army is alive.

The army recently numbered 7,000, along with several hundred horses. Ground piercing radar has detected shards still underground that when finally excavated will produce an army in excess of 100,000 soldiers.

Sadly the Chinese government has neither the funds nor experienced personnel to finish this task in our lifetime. At the time of my visit, excavation and restoration was crawling along at two days a week with a tiny handful of people on the job, mostly student volunteers working under the tutelage of local university personnel.

My wife and I spend most of a day with the army. Flash photography is not allowed so I use a tiny tripod. Braced against the railing, I take time exposures. Soldiers stare at me through the viewfinder and I think of the history that passed while this army has stood in place. They were assembled long before Christ walked the earth, and long after I am gone they will guard their emperor.

We leave the museum with regrets, for it is not easy to break from its spell.

Near the exit I notice a small man sitting at a table. He is drinking a Coke and smiling at all who pass him. At first I take him for an official greeter, an honored job in such places. Then his image pops into my mind.

I have seen him in books. It is Mr. Yang Jun Peng, the discoverer of the site that has become China's single largest tourist attraction. More people come to see this army now than visit the Great Wall, and most people walk right by without realizing he has been declared a living national treasure. His job is to sign books and pose for photos, but today, none of his countrymen recognize him.

He is visibly pleased when I approach. We share no common language, but I smile and bow. He puts his arm around me and my wife snaps our photo together. I have given him great face, and a crowd begins to gather. He smiles broadly at the recognition and begins to sign books for his admirers. I slip out the door, and he gives me a final bow.

There is a brilliant sunset outside, and for a moment, I think I hear the commander calling his troops to arms.

James Michael Dorsey is a photojournalist, painter, and avid sea kayaker who makes annual trips to Canada and Mexico to photograph whales. He is a director of the Los Angeles Adventurer's Club, a public speaker on the subject of close encounters with whales, and a volunteer photographer for the National Wildlife Federation and the Cetacean Society International. His work has been published in The Christian Science Monitor, Sea Kayaker Magazine, *and* Travelers' Tales Alaska.

Dubbing Over the City

Hong Kong: Act II, Scene I

THE FIRST TIME I SAW JACKIE CHAN, HE WAS WEARING A white undershirt and white pants with black suspenders, and he was sitting on a chair by a circus tent. The humid Hong Kong summer sunshine streaked through his slightly tinted hair. He looked tired and serene—a muscular little angel called upon to do his fair share of saving the world.

Four other *gweilos* (foreigners) and I were waiting around, seeing if we would get hired as extras for a big party scene where Jackie would do a few stunts over our heads, without a net of course. We were in the back lot of the Shaw Brothers' studios, where mogul Run Run Shaw nearly single-handedly invented the "Hollywood of the East," built on a hill in Clear Water Bay with views of Hebe Haven and the New Territories beyond. Scores of small islets surrounded it with a checkered sea of varying clarity and pollution levels. It was the side of Hong Kong that few tourists see: the vivid green hills full of hiking trails and poisonous snakes, hiding round cement grave sites with lacquered photos of the deceased who would enjoy good *feng shui* for being buried with a hillside view.

While waiting for an answer regarding employment, I wandered the empty, decaying sets of Chinese streets, rickshaws, herbalist stores, and temples. These were the dusty lanes and rickety sets where Bruce Lee starred in his first films in the '60s. I tapped a wall painted like stone. It was hollow. I picked up a fake turnip, and it was the weight of a piece of paper. The smell of pressed geese or stinky tofu was absent, but somehow the place felt and looked more real than the Hong Kong I was currently experiencing outside—the faraway, ultra-modern, shiny steel metropolis that defied gravity while dollars and yen flowed through its cold veins. I wanted my own personal fantasy of Hong Kong to somehow coalesce with the reality of it. Nearly every place in the world enjoys these two parallel worlds—the fantasy of what the place is "supposed" to be, and the perpetually different reality of what it actually is. That summer I tried in vain to marry the two, but Hong Kong wouldn't let me.

We *gweilos* didn't get hired that day, but it wouldn't be the last time I set eyes on Jackie Chan. The Hong Kong film industry needed *gweilos*. We were the "background artists" who lent an international feel to a set, as well as often being cast as the villains in Chinese movies. *Gweilo,* a generally accepted Cantonese term for foreign person, literally translates as "ghost-man." Seeing a ghost is extremely unlucky in Chinese superstition,

> M y acquaintance with Hong Kong and with things Chinese now extends over a quarter of a century and nothing has been a cause to me of more anxiety throughout that period than the fact that the Chinese and the European communities of Hong Kong, although in daily contact with each other, nevertheless move in different worlds, neither having any real comprehension of the mode of life or ways of thought of the other. This is a most regrettable misunderstanding which retards the social, moral, intellectual, and even the commercial and material progress of the colony.
>
> —Governor Cecil Clementi
> (1936)

with a meaning akin to this: you or someone you know might die. Hence the common translation as "foreign devil." Either way, it's not good—but oddly enough, no one really takes offense to its usage. As a *gweilo* who was spending a few months killing time in sweltering Hong Kong, I thought it would fun to get in the movies. The former British colony is the third largest movie producer in the world after Bombay and Hollywood, cranking out more than six hundred films a year. Amazingly enough, the post-1997 Chinese government has not cracked down on film content, as long as it's not too blatantly political. It never is, or was. Like a mosquito feeding off an elephant, Hong Kong still does not want to disturb the sleeping giant of China.

Hong Kong has always been a strange international capitalistic zone, unabashedly intent on turning a buck. And long before the "handover" in 1997, that behemoth of a civilization that lay beyond the colony's borders was Hong Kong's meal ticket. But, instead of Hong Kong becoming more like "mainland" China, China began to mimic her once lost colony, setting up little Hong Kongs ("Special Economic Zones") throughout the Middle Kingdom—so that Shenzhen, Shanghai, even Beijing began to act more like Hong Kong than Hong Kong herself.

I longed for the days when I had briefly beheld the colony as a twelve-year-old. That was the Hong Kong of yore, the Hong Kong of wooden junks with burgundy sails, of fisherman beating ancient drums to

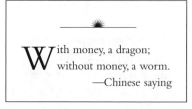

With money, a dragon; without money, a worm.
—Chinese saying

scare fish into nets, of dirty sweatshops with prematurely aged women hunched over machines. You could almost see Suzy Wong turning tricks. Perhaps it seemed even more fantastical through a prepubescent's eyes. More than a decade later, I would find myself wandering around monolithic shopping malls of glass and steel, buying Gap clothes and watching Hollywood sequels, passing by McDonald's and generic young people who looked like they could be found in any city in the world. Where was the city I had left behind in my memories and dreams, the world of Suzy Wong and Bruce Lee? In my consciousness, this other Hollywood Hong Kong was more real than the modern city before me, devoid of junks and rickshaws. Did reality always have to trump fantasy?

And so I began playing a number of bit parts that summer. I was Mr. Wong who taught Chinese manners on a local English kid's show. I was the "man on the street" who just adores a particular brand of razor in a commercial. And I finally did get a chance to be in a Jackie Chan film, too—I got to wear a Speedo and throw a ball back and forth to two bikini-clad girls in the background behind him. We were next to a swimming pool with huge lights and cords dangling into puddles everywhere, and we hadn't signed any releases.

It was a classic breakneck Hong Kong experience, but at least I got to meet my hero Jackie and watch him try to converse in English with us (we nodded and smiled, having no idea what was coming out of his mouth). We witnessed him orchestrating some kicks in front of women in the traditional slit-up-the-thigh Qi Pao dresses (which were never seen in Hong Kong outside of movies). I was satisfied—this is what Hong Kong was supposed to be like: kung-fu fighters and exotic *femmes fatales* everywhere. I was so happy to be a part of the myth making, recreating the city of my daydreams.

Then, I got my first big break, or so I thought. It was my first speaking part in a Chinese-language film—conversing in French and serving a table of upscale Chinese yuppies in a comedy entitled *Tom, Dick, and Harry.* Thank God I had a (albeit weak) year of high school French under my belt. It was a long involved scene where the main character finds out he has actually been taking French classes when he thought he had been learning English, since he is able to communicate perfectly with me, the French waiter. I studied my lines diligently—I wanted my French to be perfect. The shooting began at a restaurant around midnight, and I wore a tuxedo and tried to dazzle my co-stars sitting around the table.

"*Et pour vous, monsieur? What would you like for dinner?*" I said with the camera rolling and the crew listening. It came out well, but I wasn't sure if I had the right cadence and intonation. I figured someone watching who understood French would see right through me.

I got a little flustered. "Can we do it again, please? I don't think I said it right." I was trying to sound like a perfectionist who only wanted to make the best possible product.

"Sure," the director complied, slightly puzzled. I figured it was because Hong Kong films were shot lickety split with few retakes, but I wanted to show how professional I was.

I did the scene several times, handing out menus to the actors, asking each one in French what they would like to eat, and conversing with the main character. The filming dragged on into four in the morning, but I kept practicing my lines as we did coverage, filming close-ups and wide shots. I was surprised that the other actors would flub a line and just keep talking. It seemed all anyone cared about was getting every shot in, regardless of the dialogue.

Finally, I was to film my last close-up of the morning. I was tired, and my high school French began to show it. I apologized every time I said "*tous*" instead of "*vous*" and asked for retakes. The director politely consented every time, glancing at his watch.

It wasn't until my scene was over that one of the other actors came up to me. Her English was impeccable, with a crisp British flavor to it. Her makeup looked fresh and she didn't seem tired at all from the night's work. She smiled and told me, "Your French was good, you didn't need to worry."

"I just wanted it to be perfect," I replied.

"Is this the first film you've done in Hong Kong?"

"Well, my first speaking part."

"Did you notice how there were no microphones?"

I stopped dead in my tracks. She continued, "All your lines will be dubbed over in the studio later. You could have been speaking Swahili for all they care."

Sure enough, I dragged a friend to see *Tom, Dick, and Harry* without telling him of the great surprise in store—my big scene.

Well, the scene came and went and he didn't even notice me—I was up there for perhaps twenty seconds tops. The actress was right, I could have been speaking Serbo-Croatian since there was no way to tell my if lip movements matched with my words anyway. It was just another illusion of place for me to let go of, another dubbing over of my own hollow fantasies with Hong Kong's ever-present and much more interesting reality.

Matthew Link is editor-in-chief of Out Traveler *magazine, and contributor to* Newsweek Travel *and* MSNBC.com Travel. *He was destined to be a travel writer, having grown up on his father's fifty-two-foot sailboat during his teenage years, cruising around Southeast Asia and the Pacific. He has at various times called Hong Kong, the Philippines, Micronesia, Papua New Guinea, and New Zealand home. His last stint was on the Big Island of Hawaii for five years, where he wrote and published his own guidebook to the islands, the* Rainbow Handbook Hawaii. *Matthew has also produced award-winning documentaries that have shown in international film festivals and on PBS stations, and he is also an avid kayaker, hiker, snowboarder, and skin diver.*

Stepping Stone to Shangri-La

Caught between Mr. Rock and a mythical place
in Sichuan and Yunnan.

SHANGRI-LA: A REMOTE PARADISE WHERE THE AGING PROCESS has slowed down, where people do not succumb to disease. A place where knowledge is exalted, and where gold mines take care of any cash-flow problems. Shangri-La lies in the fertile Blue Moon Valley, a realm bordering the frontiers of Tibet. A monastery with mixed Chinese and Tibetan features is perched on the flanks of a towering pyramidal snowcap: a monastery with central heating, stocking a superb collection of books, music and Chinese art—and one that allows the luxury of ample time for their contemplation.

The High Lama of Shangri-La is an expert on the passage of time: this wizened Capuchin monk, originally from Luxembourg, stumbled into the valley more than two hundred years ago, and is still alive to tell the tale. The escort for new recruits is a smooth-talking Chinese gentleman in a silk-embroidered gown called Chang. The people of the valley are stocky Tibetans in sheepskins, fur hats and yak-skin boots.

There's a definite Chinese touch in the décor of Shangri-La, from blue Sung ceramics to green porcelain baths. Chinese cuisine is served—probably augmented by medicinal herbs from the valley—and Chinese attendants are among the staff. And this, of

155

course, is all fiction. Shangri-La is an impossible composite that sprang from the imagination of British writer James Hilton—creator of the novel *Lost Horizon* first published in 1933.

No sooner did Hilton create this paradise than he lost control of it. He was quickly summoned to Hollywood to assist in making a movie version of *Lost Horizon*, released in 1937—a blockbuster that spread the fame of Shangri-La far and wide. Were Hilton alive today, he would be astonished at the uses the Shangri-La logo has been put to—from beach resorts to a hotel chain.

Hilton claimed in his book that Shangri-La would not be found on any map, but that has not prevented mountain realms from Ladakh to Bhutan from staking claims. For more than seventy years, debate has raged over the exact location, citing the author as being inspired by a real model. The Chinese have been rather slow off the mark, but they've done so in spectacular style. In 2002, Zhongdian County in northwest Yunnan was renamed Shangri-La County by official decree from Beijing. The previous year, the county seat of Zhongdian opened Deqin Shangri-La Airport, with a runway that can handle Boeing jets.

I asked the man in the fur hat about the poem by Li Bai, the one about traveling to Sichuan. I'd always thought of Sichuan as the heart of China. The province is surrounded by mountains and in Li Bai's time, the journey there was treacherous:

> …May I ask if you expect
> to return, traveling so far
> west?
> Terrifying road, inaccessible
> mountain peaks lie ahead…
> The road to Shu is hard,
> harder than climbing to
> the heavens,
> Sideways, I look westward
> and heave a long sigh.

I was an outsider, the poem reminded me. But maybe that was all right after all. Getting to the heart of China had never been easy.

—Jennifer Walden,
"The Road to Sichuan"

The two events are connected: this promoting of Shangri-La paradise is a ploy to attract tourism—mainly Chinese tourists from the east.

The photogenic and highly marketable attractions are: a soaring pyramidal snow-capped peak, a monastery milling with burgundy-robed monks, and smiling local folk in colorful ethnic garb. Trouble is, lots of places at the edges of the Tibetan plateau possess those attributes—but never in one spot, although glossy brochures make it appear that way. And the brochures and books shy away from anything modern in pictures: you won't spot a single bus or motorcycle, or karaoke bar—which certainly exist in the region. In western Sichuan and upper Yunnan, dogfights have broken out between a dozen places vying for the Shangri-La crown. So bitter have disputes become that another solution has been proposed: the creation of "China Shangri-La Ecological Tourist Zone," embracing all the contenders from the highlands of Sichuan and Yunnan—thus keeping them logo-happy. That zone is a chunk of territory approaching the size of Switzerland.

Intrigued by the hype, I set off to see the contenders for myself—well, three of them anyway. Shangri-La fever draws me to the highlands of western Sichuan and upper Yunnan. For the first leg of the journey, I team up with two feisty Australians, Tony and Peta. We take a series of buses, rattling over a high alpine route from Chengdu, headed for the remote town of Daocheng, the gateway to the Konkaling range—passing through a sparsely populated region that is home to yak herders who live in triple-storied stone farmhouses.

Then there's Sun. We meet by accident, Sun and I. A passenger window near the front of the bus shatters somehow, and as cold air blasts in, Sun moves to the back to claim the vacant seat that I've been hogging to gain more legroom. At first, I am annoyed by this intrusion, but it turns out Sun has a good command of English, and he and his companions are all headed for Konkaling. They are young, affluent professionals from the east coast—bankers, hotel managers—who have joined forces along the way.

This is perfect—if we tag along, they will lend legitimacy to our quest (access rules are different for Chinese and foreigners) and provide a ready-made crew for cost-cutting in hiring jeeps. They can handle language problems: the guidebooks run out here and we're not sure how to reach our final destination—the sacred peaks of Konkaling.

In Daocheng, when we sight a guesthouse called Blue Moon Valley, we know we're onto something...mythical. Indeed, the local tour office offers brochures and photo books in Chinese and English about the Dreamland of Shangri-La. The glossy literature is vague and somewhat skewed about the connections of Daocheng to Shangri-La. One book rambles on about Joseph Lark—by which is meant American explorer Joseph Rock, referred to elsewhere in Chinese touring literature as "Doctor Lock" and "The Rocker."

In fact, all the Shangri-La claims in southwest China go back to Joseph Rock. That much quickly becomes clear to me: I am following in the footsteps of Doctor Rock. Failing to find any other descriptions of this area in his advance reading, Tony is reduced to carrying a copy of the July 1931 *National Geographic* that contains Rock's article about his expedition to the Konkaling range—a whopping sixty-five pages of text and photos (the vain Doctor Rock initially demanded an entire issue devoted to his story).

This eccentric Austrian-American plant hunter arrived in southwest China in 1922. He stayed on an off until 1949, when he was booted out by the incoming Communist government. For nearly three decades, he explored the uncharted ranges and rugged terrain of southwest China, collecting rare fauna and flora, indulging in photography, and documenting the lives of the Tibetan and Naxi ethnic groups. Along the way he produced ten articles for *National Geographic*, some of which may have inspired James Hilton. The link has never been proved: when two American researchers caught up with aging actress Jane Wyatt, the last surviving member of the movie *Lost Horizon*, she told them she'd met Hilton and that he *hinted* his inspiration derived *in part* from Rock's articles. However, Hilton used a number of different sources, and Rock wrote about several lofty mountain regions in China's southwest. Not trained as a geographer, Rock rashly claimed one of these titanic peaks, Minya Konka, to be the highest in the world (he was off by about a mile).

In any case, Yading Nature Reserve is where the real Shangri-La can be found, we're assured by the tour office in Daocheng. We discover a wonderful Tibetan-style B&B to stay in—a castellated structure on the edge of town where we can recover from the awful bus rides and marshal our forces for the road ahead. Rummaging through his backpack on the rooftop of our castle, Tony curses, facing the ultimate Australian nightmare: "I've left the Vegemite back in Chengdu!"

The next morning Tony has better reasons to curse. It is pelting snow, throwing all our plans into disarray, as the road to Yading is not passable by jeep. Great—stranded in Shangri-La! But at noon, the snow suddenly stops and the skies miraculously clear. We pile into two jeeps and head for the hills. A lengthy kidney-jarring ride brings us to the fortress-like monastery of Gongaling, with more than three hundred monks—the same one that pops up in the Shangri-La brochures from Sichuan. After a lunch stop here, we push on to a tented camp outside Yading village. The splendors of Konkaling are within reach.

Yading Nature Reserve occupies close to 400 square miles of rugged terrain: gushing streams, luxuriant forests of larch, pine, cypress, fir, and oak, and majestic snowcaps with cascading glaciers and odd-colored glacial lakes. And this day, the beauty is magnified because everything is blanketed in fresh snow.

We rent ponies for the nine-mile ride to a tented camp near the base of the sacred peaks. Turns out to be a wise choice, because underfoot is all slush and mud. Horsing around in Shangri-La: we move in a long caravan of Shangri-La seekers, dismounting occasionally at photo opportunity spots. Joseph Rock would have marveled at the high-tech equipment of the Chinese tourists—their digital cameras, video cameras, and knock-off North Face jackets. I guess if you are from the polluted urban core of Shanghai or

Nanjing, then Yading indeed appears to be a slice of paradise. The phenomenon seen in action here is of wealthy Chinese tourists visiting the far-flung exotic corners of their realm. Photography is essential to prove they've bagged the trophy destination.

Rock was the first Westerner to lay eyes on this region, and the very first person to photograph these peaks: he lugged heavy glass plates around and developed pictures on the spot in tents in primitive conditions. Rock was a pioneer in the use of natural color photography, taking pictures not only of landscapes but of the tribespeople he encountered and their customs. A number of explorers had tried to penetrate the region but failed, due to brutal weather conditions, but mainly due to the threat of bandits—who were in the habit of robbing pilgrims coming to pay homage to the peaks. These bandits included 400 monks from Konkaling Gompa (Snow Mountain Monastery) who used to rob pilgrims blind and then return to their quiet meditations—apparently not a contradiction in these parts.

In mid-1928, the resourceful Dr. Rock enlisted the help of the King of Muli (a.k.a. the Head Lama of Muli Monastery), who dispatched stern missives to the bandit chiefs telling them to back off—at least long enough for Rock to photograph the area and gather enough information for a *National Geographic* article. The former kingdom of Muli is itself another Shangri-La candidate, and the subject of an earlier article by Rock.

Rock rode into the Konkaling region with a posse of Naxi and Tibetan bodyguards, armed to the hilt. The expedition visited twice during the monsoon season when torrential rain left the peaks obscured by cloud. When the clouds finally parted for Rock, the panorama knocked him out: "In the cloudless sky before me rose the peerless pyramid of Jambeyang, the finest mountain my eyes ever beheld." Rock was pumping up the prose for *National Geographic*; there are plenty of peaks that rival Jambeyang in the Himalayas.

Still, Jambeyang—just under 20,000 feet high—is a conical classic, with razor-edged snow precipices leading to the summit.

For mountaineers, it presents a tantalizing challenge—it has never been scaled, though expedition attempts have been launched. From a tented camp at Luorong, we have an afternoon to admire stupendous panoramas of Jambeyang and Chanadorje, two of the sacred peaks.

Snow scotches plans of making a full circuit of the sacred peaks, but next morning we hike higher to a magical lake where, it is said, the future can be divined. Along the trail, I strike up a conversation with a guide from another party.

"Oh no, this is not Shangri-La," he informs me. "Everybody knows that is in Deqin, in Yunnan." Where, it turns out, he is from—by more than coincidence.

"But how do you know?" I ask.

"It's a secret," he responds with a wink.

Deqin is next on my Shangri-La list. I bid my Australian friends goodbye—they are returning to Chengdu to pursue other travel plans. But three of my Chinese comrades, including Sun, are on the same trajectory, so we hire a jeep in Daocheng. On the map, Deqin looks like a short hop west of Daocheng. But these are remote mountain regions: getting there requires two full days of winding and switchbacking on rough roads. The route crests several high passes—including one of 15,400 feet. The high-altitude indicators here are the hairy yaks roaming the high pastures. This has to be one of the most beautiful road trips in southwest China: rambling past stone farmhouses, and then dipping back through dense forest ablaze with autumn color. By now, we have crossed the line—crossed into Yunnan Province—and reached the gates of paradise, according to the Yunnan spin doctors.

Welcome to Shangri-La! proclaims the map of the town of Zhongdian, the capital of Shangri-La County. Nobody with marbles intact could mistake Zhongdian for Shangri-La: it's a bland Chinese city full of concrete and karaoke. But Zhongdian is being spruced up with construction of fresh neo-Tibetan architectural monstrosities in preparation for its role as the gateway to Shangri-La—whose features are widely scattered around the county.

A number of businesses in Zhongdian blithely use the Shangri-La logo without rhyme or reason: Shangri-La On-line Tea Bar, Shangri-La Bus Ticket Agency. And you can purchase a bottle of Shangri-La Red, a wine made in Yunnan and supposedly based on a recipe concocted by Jesuit missionaries. Or smoke Shangri-La-brand cigarettes, also made in Yunnan. There was, after all, some smoking going on in *Lost Horizon*, which noted that the valley of Shangri-La grew a fine brand of tobacco.

To bolster their claim to paradise, authorities in Zhongdian un-veiled in 2001 some irrefutable evidence: an ancient flush toilet—imported, used, and finally abandoned by foreign missionaries. The mythical Shangri-La has state-of-the-art plumbing—gold in the valley pays for such luxuries to be imported by horse caravan. But unless the seat is made of solid gold, I can't imagine tourists lining up to look at a flush toilet. Lining up to *use* the device, yes, but not to look; they could do that anytime in the privacy of their own homes. Free love and flush toilets were some of the anomalies of Shangri-La. As for Zhongdian, well, there is a free love of sorts at the karaoke bar on the sixth floor of the Holy Palace Hotel. This is a disco with popping lights, and a radiating rabbit-warren of pri-vate karaoke booths stocked with hostesses who are supposed to croon along.

Deep chanting resonates from the main prayer hall at Songzanlin, a monastic citadel just north of Zhongdian. With more than seven hundred monks, it's the largest monastery in Yunnan, and a place that could easily have sprung from the pages of *Lost Horizon*—except for one glaring detail. The monastery is a great cluster of buildings stacked together in the middle of rolling farm-land—not glued to the side of a towering snowcap.

The snowcap collaged into brochures in these parts is in fact 125 miles north, near the small frontier town of Deqin. Sited at around 11,000 feet, Deqin lies at the end of the line in Yunnan—it is right up by the border of the Tibet Autonomous Region; the locals are mostly ethnic Tibetan.

At dawn, the peaks near Deqin are lit up like candles, one after another, by the rising sun. It's an awesome spectacle. Nestled among the dozen 20,000-foot snowcaps is Mount Kawagebo, Yunnan's highest peak—and one that has never been climbed. This conical peak dominates the vista. Far below, you can see the Mekong River coursing and villages dotting the landscape. The bewitching vista, with icy pyramidal peak, and green valley and river far below, could easily serve as cover shot for James Hilton's novel.

That potential is not lost on Chinese tourists, who pour out of buses at the viewpoint of Feilaisi and start a strange dance. For some, it is the Dance of the Tripod—jostling to get the best position for dramatic sunrise lighting over the peaks. Others gather at an array of white wayside shrines and murmur mantras, throw rice in the air at juniper hearths, and tie on prayer flags. The rituals are part of "Tibet Chic": Chinese tourists think it is a badge of cool to follow such practices. But there are no Tibetans in sight. Probably the last people to realize they are living in the heart of Shangri-La are the ethnic Tibetans of this area. The word "Shangri-La" was made up by James Hilton. It has no meaning in Tibetan except that "La" means mountain pass.

I notice that Sun has not followed the rituals at the shrines and I call him on it, but he is very vague. He is signaling *this is a taboo topic, don't want to talk about it, move on to the next subject please.* Having traveled with three Chinese companions for a few weeks now, I am testing the waters. To me, this is a new kind of liberty— being able to travel like this with young Chinese who are educated and wealthy. They are a new breed, an entrepreneur class. They have surprised me with their confidence and knowledge. And I in turn have surprised them in a few matters, too. Like the technique of bypassing the language barrier by walking straight into a restaurant kitchen, loading up a wok with the vegetables I want and telling the cook to chop and stir-fry—and that dish arrives well before those ordered by the Chinese menu-decoders.

Across the other side of the valley, tourists hike up to the toe of the glacier cascading from Mount Kawagebo—a place touted as lying at the very heart of Shangri-La. Halfway up the steep route,

a fellow hiker's cell phone goes off. Totally winded from the up-
hill and the altitude she stops to take a call from Shanghai, wheez-
ing and panting. "It's my mother!" she cackles.

Coming down to earth: starting the grand descent off the
Tibetan plateau. Down, down, down from Deqin to the ancient
town of Lijiang, in southern Yunnan. Lijiang is a another candidate for Shangri-La, but very different from the other two because
the major ethnic presence is not Tibetan but Naxi, a Tibetan-
related group.

In Daocheng and Zhongdian, businesses are mostly run by
Chinese, and the ethnic groups are marginalized. But in Lijiang's
Old Quarter, everything is capably run by Naxi women in exquisite costume—embroidered white chemise, maroon velvet
waistcoat, and ruffled white skirt. This points to another unusual
facet of Lijiang: Naxi society is matrilineal. Though a compro-
mised version of matriarchy is practiced today, Naxi women still
make the family decisions, control the finances and do much of the
labor in the house or in the fields, while men idle time away with
poetry, music, and calligraphy. In an ethnic sense, Lijiang is the best
Shangri-La candidate; in a religious sense, it is the worst—with no
large temple or group of monks (the Naxi follow a handful of old
Dongba wizards).

Architecturally, however, Lijiang's Old Quarter is without par: a
splendid labyrinth of weathered Naxi wooden shophouses and
guesthouses with tiled roofs that is a World Heritage Site. Twisting
through it are cobblestone alleys, stone bridges and scores of canals.
Sensibly, this zone is closed to motor traffic and is a very pleasant
place to stroll through, though besieged at times by Chinese
marching in group-tours. By day, the tourists flock to the key
sights of the Old Quarter to indulge in shopping. By night, the
place is thronged with Chinese flocking to eat at cozy restaurants,
and to see performances of Naxi music and dance. The Naxis lay
claim to the oldest dance score in the world—and the world's oldest orchestra. And (a touch of Shangri-La?) the world's oldest musicians. Many are in their 80s, because these octogenarians are the

only ones who can recall the music. During the Cultural Revolution, the music and culture of the Naxis was banned.

Xuan Ke, a Naxi musicologist, spent twenty-one years in jail for the crime of trying to preserve Naxi culture— and is now hailed as a hero for reviving it. That's not all he revived. Xuan Ke is credited with starting the Shangri-La craze in southwest China. After reading Hilton's book, he declared that the place was definitely where his mother lived— which was Deqin. On second thoughts, he also decided that the book reminded him of his hometown, Lijiang. Then the Joseph Rock link to James Hilton was forged, and a campaign to rename Zhongdian as Shangri-La was launched. And so it went.

> The sheer bulk of time in isolation has made China a world unto itself—a world forever in the dark, forever tearing itself to pieces, which is also the secret of continuity. It's a continuity punctuated with violence, always subject to a sudden shift to the opposite extreme.
>
> —J. D. Brown, *Digging to China*

Joseph Rock was the world authority on the Naxi, spending all his spare time documenting their culture and language. Naxi writing is based on a thousand-year-old pictographic script derived from shamans. This alone was enough to keep Rock busy for a number of years: he compiled the definitive Naxi dictionary. His studies of Naxi culture are highly ironic when you consider that Rock hated women, and the Naxis are matrilineal. Rock actually hated lots of things: he hated *National Geographic* editors for rewriting his prose, and he hated missionaries (not a good sign if Rock is the prototype for an adventurer in Shangri-La).

But he loved Lijiang. The reason he settled close to Lijiang was his quest for plants. In the late nineteenth and early twentieth centuries, southwest China was a magnet for plant hunters, keen to discover new ornamental species and medicinal plants—for export to eager growers in the West. Self-trained botanist Rock (the "Doctor" title appears to have been self-endowed) had boundless reserves of energy; he sent thousands of plant specimens and seed batches from China to the West. Two plants were even named after him.

Prime hunting grounds were on the slopes of Jade Dragon Snow Mountain, about eighteen miles from Lijiang. High-altitude locales like this are likened to "islands in the sky," preserving a rich biodiversity. The mountain's microclimate hosts a huge range of flora, depending on altitude. There are 50 specimens of azalea, 60 kinds of primrose, 5 species of camellia—the list goes on. There are estimated to be more than 600 medicinal herbs in the Lijiang area. The local remedy for high blood pressure, for instance, is wild snow tea, a rare kind grown on mountain slopes, while leaves from the Yunnan Rhodiola plant are used to make tea for altitude sickness.

Today, getting to the upper reaches of Jade Dragon Snow Mountain is a snap: the buses unload Chinese tourists at the foot of the 18,360-foot peak. From there, the highest cable car in Asia (nearly two miles long) whips them rapidly up to a viewing platform at 15,000 feet. The wiser tourists have rented down parkas and small canisters of oxygen. The less wise lurch and slip around unsteadily in suits and platform shoes. For most, it's a thrilling encounter with snow and ice.

This is the peak that functioned as the model for Shangri-La in Lijiang's claim. Lijiang's Naxi Museum houses a special Shangri-La Salon explaining the town's tenuous links to the legend, naturally channeled via Dr. Rock. But it is at Rock's former villa, in the nearby village of Yuhu, where I finally catch up with the man. The courtyard-style Naxi villa has been converted into an on-site museum, with a modest display of his photos, his gear and his rifles. Upstairs is a small room which served as backdrop for Rock's self-portrait, appearing in a *National Geographic* story. Though it looks exotic in the article, in reality it is disturbingly ordinary. The bed is made of wooden planks; above it hang glass photographic plates.

A monochrome print displayed in the villa shows Rock impeccably dressed in the silk and brocade of a Mandarin, while another shows him draped in a Tibetan sheepskin cloak, with fox-fur hat and Tibetan boots. Yet another shows him in a dapper suit, which he sometimes wore to a regal reception from a local official or fief-dom ruler—arriving in style in a sedan chair, with an armed escort. Rock reveled in his celebrity status in these parts: he was a short-tempered reclusive loner, but in this remote part of China, he was in his element—his wanderlust and sense of adventure were more than sated.

A short distance away, I come across a large billboard pointing the way to Rock's villa. The Chinese script may be more coherent, but the English on the billboard reads:

FOLLOW ROCKER'S STEP TO SHANGRI-LA

Having done that for the past month, I feel no closer to solving the riddle of Shangri-La: there's an awful lot of garbled hype and hokum attached to the various claims. The novel is, after all, fiction. In any case, the quest has led me to some beautiful mountain ranges: Shangri-La sentinels or not, they are definitely stunning. Did Hilton draw on Rock's adventures to craft the Utopian legend of Shangri-La? The answer to that question lies with James Hilton alone—and he can't be consulted because he passed away in 1954 (Joseph Rock died in 1962). So it will most likely remain a mystery—like Shangri-La itself.

Michael Buckley has traveled the length and breadth of the Middle Kingdom. He started out by seeing far more of the place than he ever wanted to in the course of researching and writing the first edition of Lonely Planet's China, *way back in the 1980s. On later forays, he has switched his focus to Tibet, and to remote minority border areas of China. He is the author of* Tibet: the Bradt Travel Guide, *and* Heartlands: Travels in the Tibetan World, *and he has contributed stories to several Travelers' Tales titles.*

PART THREE

GOING YOUR OWN WAY

JASON OVERDORF

★ ★ ★

Physical Culture

Boxing, karaoke, prostitution—one-stop shopping
in the new China.

WHEN HE OPENED THE BISON BOXING CLUB IN BEIJING, Li Zhu, a thirty-five-year-old entrepreneur, planned to become China's first fight promoter. Chinese athletes were notoriously ill paid, so it would be easy to find boxers who would fight for cash. Li counted on the Chinese love of gambling to pack the house. He also built a fight gym in the back of the club, and installed body-building equipment in an attempt to cash in on a fitness craze that culminated in 1995 with a government-sponsored National Physical Fitness Program.

The plan was a good one, but like many entrepreneurs in China, Li failed to take into account the numerous intangibles and un-written rules of the country's changing economy. The first hurdle was crowd control. Drunken gamblers watching a fight tend to start fights of their own. The Bison hired a security force of twenty-five men who wore motorcycle helmets and carried nightsticks to dis-courage extracurriculars. On top of the rent and staffing costs, the club also had to grease the palms of the police and the *hei shehui* (black society) to prevent them from shutting down the gambling, and there was an incessant flow of minor officials and friends of the club who expected free admission and free drinks.

The most unexpected cost turned out to be the fighters. China banned boxing in the 1950s after a death in the ring. In 1986 the Chinese government reinstated Olympic-style boxing, with its emphasis on safety and sportsmanship. Although the state-supported Olympic feeder system paid boxers the equivalent of only $12 to $25 a month, the same boxers demanded that Li Zhu pay them thirty to forty times that for a single match.

But Li refused to go down easily. He was no reformed bureaucrat. A martial-arts enthusiast, he claimed to have made his grubstake as a bodyguard in New York's Chinatown. Back in China he put the money to work "importing cars"—smuggling them, he implied—and in a few years branched out into other businesses that, although legal, required a certain flexibility: nightclubs, liquor, and real estate. So, adhering to Deng Xiaoping's famous advice, "It doesn't matter if the cat is black or white, so long as it catches mice," Li transformed the Bison into a mongrel that combined boxing with China's usual one-two:

B asketball is everywhere in China, more prevalent than Coke and more powerful than Mao. Even though NBA games are often broadcast here at three A.M., people are watching, and learning. Once, in the remote mountains of western Sichuan, while riding a horse along a glacial ridge, I met a young girl also riding along the path. We tried to communicate, but the only words of English she spoke were "Michael Jordan." That spoke volumes. Another time at Qinghua University, several old men came out to play. I never figured out if they were professors or not, but I did see at least one of them practicing Tai Chi, warming up before the game. They were the Taoist Three-Point Masters, ninety-year-old men with long white beards spotting up on the arc and launching bombs that swished almost every time, cracking gap-toothed smiles while I stood amazed.

—Jeff Booth,
"Basketball in Beijing"

karaoke and prostitution. He gave up on the gambling, dismissed the costly security guards, and replaced them with "chicken-girls."

That was the Bison Club I discovered when, at the age of twenty-eight, I decided I wanted to learn to box. It was my last year in Beijing, where I'd been working for Ogilvy & Mather Advertising, writing corporate propaganda and, later, a market-research study of what we called "the new middle class." After one frustrated attempt, I located the club in the embassy district, next to a factory that made People's Liberation Army overcoats and belts.

The Day-Glo graffiti outside the revamped Bison Club read "I won't tol•er•ance your im•pu•dence!" The syllable indicators painted right into the words suggested that the artist had recourse to a dictionary. Nearby he had spray-painted "Thun•der" and "Mor•al•ize," and a caricature of a bodybuilder who proclaimed in a speech bubble, "Bison Very Good!"

Inside, the black walls were covered with more luminous ex-hortations: "OUTBURST!" "DEFY!" "HATRED!" "MANIA!" "GO CRAZY!" A dozen or so sing-along "hostesses" sat at the bar, cracking sunflower seeds with their teeth and spitting the shells onto the floor. The TV played a Wang Fei concert video, and one of the working girls, packed into a floor-length white dress, dreamily sang along. In the daylight the club was deserted; the spectators' gallery overlooking the ring and the private singing-and-groping rooms on either side sat empty. Li Zhu, giving me the tour, told me that the club still held exhibition matches on Fridays, but most nights the ring doubled as a dance floor, and had the disco ball to prove it.

The Bison still taught boxing. The club's coach, Dongzi, was a former professional who fought for the Beijing municipal team in the late 1980s. He was built like a sprinter, with a fighter's nose. In just a few minutes he taught me what he called "the A-B-C": the defensive stance, the left jab, and the straight right hand. "Not bad" was his highest form of praise, "not pretty" his strongest condem-nation. He spoke in a steady patter of trainer's metaphors:

"You have to use the momentum of your body. Your body is your TNT."

"Your fist is the bullet, but your arm isn't the gun. Your hips are your gun."

"Watch yourself in the mirror. Watch your body, not your face! This is a gym, not a beauty parlor."

Although he was already teaching three or four other beginners and training an ex-pro who had fought for the industrial team Locomotive, Dongzi was apprehensive about teaching me, a Westerner. "I will be a very diligent teacher," he said, "so that one day, when you return to America and tell them that you learned to box here, China will not lose face."

Dongzi's vow of diligence became a recurring theme throughout my training. New students inevitably asked me what country I came from, and upon hearing that I was American, would exclaim, "American boxing is very good!" (No other language underscores the banality of everyday conversation like Chinese.) On cue, Dongzi would respond with the vow, which he always expressed with gravity.

Though he was partly responsible for railroading me into a bumbling interview with China Central Television's sports channel, Dongzi protected me from many of the indignities of being a *laowai*—a word that translates as "venerable foreigner" but is used as a synonym for "buffoon" or "rube." When, after I had a rudimentary grasp of the fundamentals, the club's managers began pressuring me to perform in an exhibition match, it was Dongzi who provided me with a series of face-saving excuses: I worked overtime, I had a mild injury, I had a date, and so on. My real reason for avoiding a match was that my opponent was sure to be Gao Qiang. One of the retired professional boxers who frequented the Bison Club, Gao Qiang was always trying to lure me into a thumping. I was certain that he would be unable to resist humbling me under the lights, especially with the crowd chanting, "China! China! China!"

Whether I fought or not, the club's managers reasoned, if they buddied up to me, my foreign friends would pave a path from the Hilton Hotel to their sing-and-grope rooms. They were always after me to sample the wares, offering free drinks and access to their hospitality rooms—I'd only have to tip the girl, they assured me. I told them I'd consider the offer, and declined the drinks. I was familiar enough with Beijing manners to know that once I'd accepted one, my hosts would make sure I didn't leave until I had to be carried out. Instead I placated them by making myself ill on the cigarettes they constantly proffered.

Nevertheless, in the end Wang, the night manager (meaning he handled the girls and the karaoke bar, not the gym), wore me down, and I agreed to attend one of the Friday night exhibitions— not to fight, not to bring friends, not to accept any of the Homeric catalogue of "courtesy girl" discounts, but simply to watch the match. "Excellent," Manager Wang said. "This Friday we will have genuine professionals."

When I showed up that Friday, bartenders, security men, and hostesses were all running around shouting into radios, trying to locate replacements for the "professionals," who had backed out. Nobody told me that, of course. To help them save face I pretended not to notice the panic surrounding us—a denial of reality that was quintessentially Chinese. Manager Wang did his best to distract me from the fiasco. He bought me a beer and set me up with a beautiful, calculating girl named Ju Ling, who draped herself over me but before long declared in a strong provincial accent that talking with me was "one part listening, one part guessing."

Finally they lined up the fighters, and Li Zhu announced that they were ready to begin. Ju Ling took me upstairs to the gallery overlooking the ring. We watched the other girls work the room below, finding their regular clients and escorting them up the spiral staircases that led to their seats. The johns were all businessmen from Hong Kong or Taiwan. The management turned away locals, because, as Li Zhu told me later, he didn't like to see brawling every night. Soon the gallery was full of businessmen and prostitutes, cuddling like teenagers. On one of the walls Day-Glo proclaimed: "COME ON GIRL, HAVE ENOUGH WINE FOR DRINKING! CRAZY!"

The match was a farce. I recognized one of the combatants, Old Lu, from the club's boxing class. A balding fireplug, he was nick-named "The Panda" by the ring announcer. By no means was Old

Lu a professional boxer; he was the proprietor of a roadside snack
stand that sold ice cream and shrimp-flavored chips, and he looked
drunk. His opponent, Cao Yu, had graduated from the boxing class
some time ago and was also a head taller and forty pounds heavier.

The businessmen shouted for Old Lu to charge in close and "*jia
you*" ("give it gas"). They sounded like big brothers trying to get a
little brother to fool with hornets. During the breaks one of the
hostesses climbed into the ring with a round card and strutted across
a few times. The DJ fired up the club music and colored lights.

The exhibition ended when Old Lu was hit with a love pat
and went down. Mr. Beijing 1996, the club's bodybuilding instructor and referee, lurched into the center of the ring and
stopped the fight.

"It's fixed," Dongzi explained. Later he warned me that Ju Ling
and the other hostesses were chicken-girls. He translated to make
certain I understood: "How do you say? Hookas?"

I assured him that my motives were purely anthropological. "I
know," I told him. "I just wanted to find out more about their way
of life."

"Don't find out too much," he said, "or I'll stop coaching you."

Dongzi's protectiveness was charming but absurd. That year I
was living illegally in Beijing's most notorious foreigners' ghetto, a
filthy enclave of crumbling alley houses and soot-stained, anonymous apartment buildings called Maizi Dian—"the Wheat Shop."
It was one of the few neighborhoods where the police overlooked
migrants without Beijing residence permits, so half the town's
prostitutes lived there, a short walk from the Hard Rock Cafe and
the "big boss" karaoke bars on the main road—monoliths flaunt-
ing the new Chinese aesthetic: Ionic columns, million-watt light
displays, and plaster-of-Paris knockoffs of Michelangelo's *David*.
The usual set of down-and-out-in-Beijing-and-Bangkok foreigners lived there too, "local hires" dodging restrictions that forced ex-
patriates to live in designated enclaves where the rent ran $1,500
to $12,000 a month. As a "local hire," a kind of second-class *laowai*,
I received no housing allowance, and on my salary I couldn't afford even the cheapest legal apartment.

A score of all-night barbershops and massage parlors lay between my compound and the main street. Whenever I went out for dinner, touts accosted me: "Massagie? Massagie?" I walked everywhere with purpose, because otherwise a furtive character would step into stride with me and begin whispering about a barbershop just around the corner where the girls were beautiful and cheap and where you could *da pao* (set off a bang) for only $25.

That the Public Security Bureau tacitly allowed prostitution was clear from the nonsense of its periodic crackdowns. Instead of closing the brothels themselves, Public Security preferred to cordon off the neighborhoods where the prostitutes lived and issue fines to people who had no residence permits. The officers had to make a show of doing something. The Strike Hard campaign against crime and corruption that the Chinese Communist Party had revived in 1996 was in full swing. But it was proving no more effective than an earlier campaign to force government officials to drive domestic "integrity

---

It was quiet walking up the length of Beijing Lu in Kunming in the evening sun. Were that broad street in America or Australia you might imagine sweaty redneck contingents going bananas behind the closed doors of dark bars, but this was China and seemed at first a far quieter and more conservative place. I was, however, wrong. I heard the bar before I saw it. By the time I reached the door it was deafening. "Oi! Oi! Oi!"

It took only a few beers to get in the mood and join the throbbing mass of people in front of the stage. It seemed to be the thing to do to get as drunk as possible and throw yourself around without any consideration for your own, or anyone else's safety. Who was I to argue? By 11:30 I wasn't feeling the pain anymore and things began to wind down and I thought it was probably just as well or I'd be in trouble. The night, though, was not over.

—Joseph Gelfer,
"Getting Down in the PRC"

cars" instead of the usual Mercedes-Benzes. When Public Security made its predictable raids before the city's political events (meetings of the National People's Congress, President Clinton's visit to China, the anniversary of the June 4 protests in Tiananmen Square), the few *laowai* bivouacked illegally in Maizi Dian spent the night elsewhere.

Li Zhu resented the Strike Hard campaign because he thought it gave the men he paid off, who could now say there was added pressure to close down the club, more leverage in negotiating bribes. He often complained that the club lost money and that it didn't make sense for him to keep it open. He claimed he persisted only because he loved boxing—he trained with the class between mysterious trips to his liquor factory in the south—and because he wanted "a place like this" for his own use. He waved his hand at the rusted Universal weight machines when he said "a place like this." I tried to imagine what he meant, how he reconciled his vision of a world-class fight club with the absurdity of the Bison's English graffiti and the prostitutes crooning saccharine Hong Kong pop.

The boxers went along with his face-saving fantasy, conspiring to ignore the hostesses, who arrived every evening around eight o'clock and marched haughtily through the gym to the drab barracks room in back where they changed into their work attire. Oddly, there were no off-color remarks, no whistles of appreciation, no lessons in comparative anatomy from any of the men. As far as I could tell, I was the only one who ogled. The boxers never acknowledged the prostitutes, except to remark with a kind of pride, "I bet there's no place like this in America."

Then one day, while Li Zhu was away on business, the girls didn't show up. None of us thought anything of it at first, until the two kid bartenders who had staged a comic slap-fight boxing match at the club's Chinese New Year party also stopped coming to work, and the karaoke bar closed down. Soon Manager Wang was gone too. The "auntie" who took membership cards and dispensed locker keys could tell us nothing about where everyone had gone. For a few days johns wandered back to the fight gym, where someone would inform them that the karaoke bar was closed. Word spread, and it wasn't long before the Bison Boxing Club had become just that—a boxing, karate, and bodybuilding gym, and nothing more.

I began to worry that Li Zhu had been telling the truth about the club's financial woes. I was glad to be rid of the johns, who liked to make wise remarks about me for the benefit of their companions, but I missed the nightly procession of girls.

Then, one Saturday morning, I arrived at the club to find Li Zhu back in town to handpick a beefed-up security force. Ever since the club had dispensed with gambling in favor of prostitution, its only security guard had been Old Zhang, a gray-haired gentleman whose principal qualification for the job was a well-fitting army-surplus uniform. He lived with his family in a shack next to the club's iron gate. Guard duty entailed waking up in the middle of the night when clients banged on the bars and letting them in. Today a section of the gym had been roped off, and Li was seated at a scorer's table next to it with his own harmless-looking bodyguard. About thirty young men between the ages of sixteen and twenty-five were smoking, stretching, or otherwise preparing to audition. They were demobilized People's Liberation Army soldiers, too fresh-faced to be frightening. Even so, this try-out seemed like an ominous development.

Li Zhu assured me that there was no reason to worry. He was evasive about his reason for hiring the new guards, though he did admit that he had closed the karaoke bar and dismissed the girls because there had been threats of some kind. He wanted the guards there mostly for appearances, he claimed. Only after I pressed him did he admit that some other karaoke-bar owners would be happier if the Bison closed down entirely. He hadn't paid the right people, or he hadn't paid them enough, or they just wanted to run him out. Still, he joked, nobody would be so stupid as to start trouble with the Bison, which was, after all, not only a karaoke bar but also, he proudly reminded me, a fight gym.

On Monday the young men Li Zhu selected moved into the prostitutes' vacant barracks and set up a field kitchen on the concrete pad beneath the front steps. When Li Zhu turned up to review the troops, they sprang into servile orderliness, scrambling into a line and standing at a semblance of attention while Li Zhu paced up and down in front of them in an imported track suit, declaiming in high rhetorical style. The rest of the time they dozed on the lobby couches or on their bunks in the back room. Apparently my big nose and blond hair afforded me some rank with this bunch, because when, between naps, they patrolled the entrance, they would snap to attention and greet me with a somewhat facetious salute.

This routine lasted three weeks before Li Zhu decided that the thugs who were trying to run him out of business were a lesser evil than his own forces, who were doing it involuntarily. The Bison might have made money, but not with two dozen young soldiers to feed and no girls to turn a profit. That night Li Zhu rejoined the sparring sessions and announced that he had taken on new business partners. I interpreted this to mean that his rivals were taking over the club.

Li Zhu admitted that he would no longer take an active role in running the Bison, but assured us that he would still come around to spar now and then. Later, at what seemed like a farewell banquet at a nearby restaurant, Li tried to save face. He explained away the club's failure with his well-rehearsed fantasies: he had failed to make a profit because he had been more concerned with improving Olympic boxing in China; all he had wanted was to provide a service for the community. With the girls gone, even his nonsense about Olympic boxing seemed less outrageous than usual. The new business partners, Li said, planned to remodel the karaoke bar and go after a better class of clients.

I was nearing the end of my time in China, and Li Zhu's final, inevitable failure was the first proof I saw that no matter how soon I returned, nothing would be the same. Manager Wang never came back. Presumably, the new partners fired him. Soon he was replaced with a grinning sycophant, whom I resolved to dislike. Four pimps installed themselves in the front offices. They brought in a new string of girls every week—a practice that would stimulate repeat business, Li Zhu said.

The new manager cornered me one day and explained that when the renovations were finished, the club would hold a grand re-opening party to welcome back its loyal customers. For the festivities they had hired singers and exotic dancers—real professionals, he assured me. They had even planned a fashion show, a soft-core substitute for striptease, which was not tolerated by the authorities—even in a brothel. There would also be boxing.

Now the reason for the sales pitch surfaced: the new management wanted me to box at the show. The manager went to great pains to persuade me that it would be "very interesting"—a phrase the Chinese use to describe things that are not interesting but humiliating, dangerous, laughable, or all of the above. I was reluctant to participate in the farce, but after almost a year of training I had become something of a club mascot, promoted in status from "the foreigner" to "*our* foreigner." The boxers were all keen to give me a grand send-off. It would also be good for me to have experience "under the lights," Dongzi said, and besides, the fight was fixed, so nobody would get hurt. Wang Zhe, my usual sparring partner, volunteered as my opponent, and my pro debut was on.

In the dressing room before the fight Dongzi issued peremptory instructions. In the first round Wang Zhe would lead and I would counterpunch. In the second round we would reverse roles. The third round would be up to us to improvise, but, he cautioned us, "*Bie luan da*"—"Don't get crazy."

Either because they had seen pro boxing only on television or simply because the public-address system was there, the managers decided that international standards demanded a deafening play-by-play. As I bullied Wang Zhe around the ring, the announcer wryly observed, "Wang Zhe is in a little better condition than his opponent." This was an understatement: I outweighed him by twenty pounds.

Li Zhu came to my corner during the first break. He was dissatisfied with the script. "We don't want anyone to get hurt," he said, his tone suggesting that an injury would be very good for business indeed. Then he suggested that I make a *whffft!* noise with my mouth whenever I threw a punch. He seemed to think that would make the conflict seem more genuine, though it was obvious to me that it would do the opposite.

I have little doubt that that night's spectators were treated to the dullest boxing match of all time. By the end the greasier portion of the crowd had turned its attention to groping the hostesses, perking up only when one of the go-go dancers strutted across the ring with the round card. My supporters were entertaining themselves with their own sarcastic commentary. Nonetheless, by the time the third round, mercifully, ended, and I was announced the winner (it was my good-bye party, after all), my efforts to look competent and make *whffft!* noises convincingly had left me exhausted.

The deafening public-address system told me to stay in the ring, and then Dongzi stepped through the ropes with the microphone. Whether owing to an innate affinity or as a side effect of their love for karaoke, the Chinese are great with microphones. It is as though the mindless rhetoric of the game-show host or the tour guide were a property of the device itself, not of the person using it. Dongzi deftly explained that the celebration also marked the end of my stay in China. The club wanted to present me with a parting gift, a Bison Club t-shirt signed by all the boxers and the entire staff.

Then Dongzi gave me the mike, and I commenced rambling in foreigner's Chinese. It was at least as bad, my friends told me, as what one of them called "the I love youse, because youse love me speech" at the end of *Rocky IV.*

Later Dongzi eased up next to me and slipped me 200 yuan—about $25. "Leader Li wants you to have this," he said, "for the fight." I couldn't help thinking that it was just what the girls received to *da pao.*

Jason Overdorf lived in Beijing for three years and traveled extensively in China. He is a former executive editor of the Harvard China Review.

CARLA KING

✦ ✦ ✦

China by Motorcycle

She did it her way.

No, I was not broadsided by a big bad diesel-dripping coal-flinging blue Chinese truck. I did not slide off the Silk Route into the Wei River along with the pieces of the shale cliff that knocked chunks out of the soft new asphalt. I did not catch a rare Asian flu, and I did not fall in love with a goatherd or decide to shave my head and become a Buddhist nun.

I've been flying under the radar. The traffic cops are more frightened of me than I am of them, and they don't ask me for my papers, which is a good thing because I don't have any.

After six weeks in China I still cannot identify a hotel building. The word for hotel is a string of characters too long for me to recognize. Like the word for restaurant and the word for motorcycle parts shop.

I've decided that it's too difficult to do alone, this kind of traveling—the maps aren't quite right, the roads turn into deserts or riverbeds and they leave me exhausted, dehydrated, in a permanent state of low-level panic, like a fever that won't quite go away. Then the bike loses an electrical connection, or I fail to realize that a road is closed, or darkness has come earlier than expected. It never ends, but this is what I've found works best: stop worrying and go

with it. Put yourself at the mercy of the place you land and someone will always save you from considering the whole place a hell-
hole, the whole race a collection of dead-eyed gaping idiots.

This sounds a little unfair, but let me tell you, the first time I
stopped in a remote country village I thought it must be the place
they kept all the retarded people. They approached, walking slowly,
blank-faced and wooden as daytime living dead—mechanically
placing sunflower seeds between their teeth. They spat out the
shells; some landed on their chins and stayed there in the dribble
while they gaped. More gathered, and the air thickened. A hand
darted in to work the clutch lever. Another tested the brake lever.
The crowd murmured in approval, and someone entered the cir-
cle to bounce on the seat spring.

This happened in every village, so I stopped in only the small-
est of them, and made sure there were lots of old people around.
The elderly protected me. I ate quietly in their shops while they
shooed the crowds away. It was not until I returned home that I
found out that the problem was iodine deficiency and inbreeding.
The Chinese are not allowed to move without government permission, so in small villages they intermarry, and intermarry again.
It is Appalachia on the other side of the world.

My fortieth birthday passed, a schizophrenic experience involving sledgehammers, coal trucks, and a kilometer-long series of
Buddhist caves that blew my mind.

The thirty-minute ride to the caves was pure hell. Like playing
dodge ball on a motorcycle. Coal trucks dropped skull-sized lumps
in every direction to explode onto the road or onto cars or onto
me. The broken bits were whooshed by the heavy traffic to the
ditches where old women and children collected the largest
chunks in burlap bags to use or to sell.

By the time I reached the caves my face and clothes were dusted
with coal soot. Still, well-dressed Chinese tourists insisted I pose for
photos with them. They ran around excitedly, quickly glanced inside the caves, shouted to one another, flicked their cigarettes on the

ground and left within an hour. I hadn't even begun to look around when I was captured by five young Chinese women. They plied me with a snack wrapped in a corn-husk package, a sweet sticky triangle of rice hiding a pitted date. They watched me eat, wiped my face with tissues, powdered my nose and brushed my hair. They chattered and passed around lipstick and a mirror. We took photos. Then they disappeared, leaving me on the wide white sidewalk, wondering where to start.

I spent five hours there, in the Yungang Buddhist Caves, trying to absorb the historic and spiritual importance of the place while Chinese vacationers whirled around, laughing as if it were an amusement park. Here at one of four major Buddhist cave groups in China, I experienced more raw spiritual power than I have felt anywhere else in the world, and I wondered how they could miss it. In the last cave, far from the madness of the central caves with their ice cream vendors and circus camels and astrologers, I was overcome by the stench of urine. Would anyone in Europe piss in the vestibule of a cathedral?

"*Zhaodai zenmeyang?*" said the man in the train compartment. "Are you used to life here? Are you being taken care of?"

I had answered this question many times. People seemed anxious to hear that I found the living standard high enough. "I'm used to it," I usually responded, mainly because that was about all I knew how to say in Chinese. But this time I heard the question differently; "I'm used to the living conditions," I said to the man in my compartment. "But one thing I'm not used to is a bunch of leaders trying to control what I do." As soon as I said this, there was a long silence.

—Jennifer Walden,
"The Road to Sichuan"

I revisited each cave. Coal dust from the factory across the road collected on the thousands of tiny Buddhas. There are over fifty thousand of them, and they are suffocating.

★

Datong was the point of no return. Irretrievably far from Beijing and stuck with a bad piston in Inner Mongolia, I was eons from anything the Western world might call a city and certainly far from a hotel and hot water. Locals kindly dragged the motorcycle behind a little blue diesel motorcycle truck to the town mechanic, a very young man with a two-year-old daughter and a young wife named Lily. The child climbed into my lap to play with my set of accordion-fold postcards of San Francisco. They had never heard of San Francisco, but by the third day the whole town of fourteen people were all calling me Auntie, and there was a banquet in my honor during which I taught them to say "cheers" when drinking beer. It came out "cherws" and I am sure that this word will be absorbed into their vocabulary and used, with no knowledge of its origin, a century from now. The most difficult task of the evening was to consume all the glistening slices of fatback that flew from their bowls into mine by the amazingly accurate flicks of their chopsticks.

There was nothing to do for three hot Inner Mongolian afternoons, so Lily and I spent them napping on the *kang*, the heated platform they used as a bed. Her soft snore mingled with the roar of blue trucks going by, most of them blowing their horns. So many blue trucks. Big ones, little ones, every single one of them was blue and they would be blue all the way to the Tibetan plateau and back to Beijing. One blue truck after another raced along the smooth asphalt between potholes and breakdowns, carrying their designated loads like a line of dusty, determined ants from the same hill, one accepting the load of another when it became injured or died. Already I felt like a drone on these highways. I'd given some rides in the sidecar to the blue-suited drivers when their trucks broke down.

Even though we had no common language, Lily saved me from thinking of China as one large human ant colony. Lily's flat Han face and features were wide and round, her eyes black and slanted, her body slightly thick. She looked exactly like every other Han woman in my experience. But now I could see that her eyes shone brighter than most, and there was something else about her—I can't say exactly what—that would allow me to immediately pick her out of a crowd.

I was happy here, west of Baotou, in the middle of nowhere. The Inner Mongolian mountains created a protective wall to the south. To the north, land stretched on, forever flat. Days were lazy—taking care of the baby, writing in my journal, taking photos, and making Lily laugh by being completely inept at cooking in a wok and washing clothes by hand.

For three days I felt what life would be like here. An endless parade of blue trucks passing by on the highway, beeping at nothing. An endless parade of customers coming to have their motorcycles fixed. An endless series of cooking and cleaning and fetching water from the stream a half mile away. Filling the jugs. Washing the clothes. Preparing the *kang* for sleep. Waking and preparing the *kang* for day. Keeping the baby out of the garbage pile when the sheepherder came around to let his flock pick at the edibles.

The sheepherder was dressed in rags from his head to his cloth-wrapped feet. His staff was a long stick with a curved hollowed-out end that allowed him to scoop up rocks for hurling great distances, to frighten a stray back into the flock. Flies buzzed around him, though he smelled only like dust, like everything else.

I wrote in my journal and waited for the motorcycle parts to arrive from Baotou. The baby clutched the accordion-fold of San Francisco postcards in one hand, displaying the Golden Gate Bridge and the crookedest street in the world and Chinatown and Haight Street. Will she be illiterate like her mother? I thought perhaps, when I got home, I would send her books. But who would read to her? The illiterate learn to communicate using other methods—when Lily looked at me obvious intelligence shone in her bright eyes. What does she think about all day when she stands in the doorway watching the blue trucks go by? The government-run TV station broadcasts a soap opera about the troubles of the wealthy. Another show is an ongoing, highly produced historical saga, and the rest is propaganda. It is all propaganda. None of it has anything to do with Lily's life. Lily stands behind the colored strips of plastic in the doorway and watches the blue trucks go by. Sometimes her husband's customers come in for a cigarette and to gaze at the television while the little repairs to their motorcycles are made, but mostly they stand watching him, engrossed by the mystery of his craft.

By the map, I figured the highway by the Yellow River to be a main trade route with good roads, so on day four I was tearfully on my way, following this route west through Inner Mongolia. Everything became lush and green, the landscape a patchwork of fields tended carefully by peasants in rags and pointed woven hats. I was so happy buying produce from them, and they seemed happy to see me, but at Shapoto the desert suddenly appeared. I never saw it on the map but there it was.

The young man leaned close and spoke softly so none of the eavesdroppers draped over the back of the seats could hear. "It is the *tcherem* of every Chinese to live in America." I am pretty good at Chinglish but as I was trying to figure the translation of "*tcherem*" he wrote on a piece of paper, "dream."

Me, dumbstruck: "Oh, really?"

He leaned even closer, and as the train screeched into Guilin station, he spoke even more softly: "It is my *tcherem*, too."

—Dorothy Aksamit,
"The American Dream"

The desert is called the Tenger and the fine yellow sand is moving in on Shaanxi Province like the Sahara is moving in on Senegal, piling up in dunes right into the river. The Gobi sits just over the dry brown mountains to the north. For the first time I was really afraid. How far to the end? How long would it take to cross? The map didn't tell me, so I struck on.

The wheels of the motorcycle disturbed the ribbons of sand that snaked across the road. A lazy hot wind shoved at my right side and the sun glared as if it wished to fall from the sky and obliterate me.

The motorcycle engine overheated, forcing me to stop. I hid under the motorcycle cover from the sun and stinging sand, waited, and started again. There was no traffic for an hour and I wondered if a weather warning had been issued. Did the sign I passed twenty kilometers back read road closed due to dangerous weather conditions? Was there a radio broadcast that the truckers listened to? For an hour there wasn't a burro or even a single blue truck carrying coal to the next place. My skin burnt pink from sun and heat and I used the last of my bottle of watered-down tea to hurry the engine cooling.

A herd of camels appeared, shimmering in the heat waves in the hollow by a nearby dune. It could be a mirage, but if they were for real the camel herders would be Muslim men. So I fled, fearing Muslim men in general, with their strident disapproval of women without veils.

The heat rose in waves and the sand covered most of the road and it didn't seem quite real; in fact, I thought I might be in a dream trance, maybe even a state of shock. As I rode on, I thought I saw an ancient woman leading a burro through the storm. It might have been a mirage but she leapt off the road to land in the ditch. The burro only flicked its ear when I brushed it with my left-hand mirror.

The right side of the road was invisible, and so I continued down the middle, looking in the rearview mirror at the woman righteously shaking her hoe after me. Where was she going that she needed a hoe? There seemed to be no use for a hoe for a hundred miles.

The farther west I headed, the more bizarre the surroundings and the people. I picked up a hitchhiker on the way to Yinchuan, and then got stuck in what quickly became a nightmare experience in a factory town without women, where men crowded around to see the foreigner. I nearly fainted from heat and stress. But I needed a new clutch cable, and some adjustment to the timing.

I know. I don't have a good history with machines. I don't choose well. I chose local transport when I ought to have imported some fancy precision instrument made for all-terrain, all-weather motocrossing, one of those Paris-Dakar specials from Germany or Japan. But I chose a Chinese motorcycle to take me to these extremes, from fields to deserts to high mountains and back. It is a slow machine, but even so, the trip has been going too fast for my psyche. Perhaps one needs to walk in order to take it all in—the Yellow River, lush and green landscape one moment, nomadic Muslim camel herders at the edge of the desert the next, and not too much farther on, a stream of Tibetan monks falling prostrate every ten steps on their pilgrimage to the Labrang monastery. Rounding a corner I nearly hit three of them but they got up quickly, orange robes all aflutter, and kept walking. Around the next corner I had to brake hard for a herd of yaks led by a Tibetan woman swathed in brown wool.

After only an hour through pine-covered mountains the Tibetan plateau appeared. The air became thin and cold and even in the sunshine my fingernails froze blue. Can I tell you how I felt then, after having been through that horrible dry desert to find the pine-scented mountains so nearby? It was a relief that came from the gut, the realization that no plan was going to make any sense at all because I hadn't any idea, despite my guidebooks, what was coming next. The only thing to do was to surrender to the resignation that I was not in control, and to simply absorb whatever came next.

The solution? To get to the next place as if it were my only goal. This requires only a small effort. One can always get to the next place.

It consumed me, that thought of "getting to the next place" with its myriad complications that have more to do with instinctual survival than wit or intellect or planning. The path was difficult, but not impossible. This simple phrase—getting to the next place—took on great meaning during the six weeks that had just passed. It included all the complications of taking care of the very basics of life—food, clothing, shelter—plus a tolerance for bodily aches and a mind that looped in only upon itself. This busy mind has no time for mulling over the sacrifices one has made before one boards a jet plane to land on the other side of the world. Climbing the road to the Tibetan Plateau I reached Xiahe and found other tourists and a hotel room that had hot water between nine and ten at night. During the day I visited the monastery, shopped for trinkets, and met other foreigners. Here there were the luxurious moments to think about more than the fact that my thumbs no longer worked properly, about the long stretch of land I'd just crossed, and whether or not to continue the trip south to Burma. At a traveling speed that averaged twenty-five miles per hour because of bad roads and mechanical failures, I decided that no, I couldn't do it. Not by myself. I wanted only to return to my ivory tower on the other side of the world. It was a mistake to come alone. I was definitely on the wrong side of the world, and all the way back to Beijing I was grateful for every little thing because I was headed home home home!

Today, here on the other side of the world, ten thousand raindrops hit the earth, but there, then, I was grateful for the ping of cooling metal that meant the engine wouldn't overheat. When a stack of rattan containers appeared I was grateful for steamed buns and then I was grateful for somewhere to crouch for a moment in privacy. I was grateful for the gas station that sold the right kind of motor oil and that there were only three broken spokes on the sidecar tire from when I hit that last big pothole, and that the brakes were holding, that there was water to wash my hands and face, and that there was someone to indicate that there was a town with an inn a couple of hours up the road. A couple of hours later I was grateful that I had not been too exhausted to get there. When you travel you are almost never too exhausted, I remembered later, just before I went to sleep. Whenever there's no other alternative, you can do whatever it takes to do whatever you need to do.

In sleep my dreams were replays from events of the day: Peasants gather round to stare, so dumbly astonished that they cannot return my greeting. They gather round until there is no more air, and I can't move without bumping somebody's face with my elbow.

Why must they be so close to me! "Idiots," I mutter. "Move away!"
I shout, and push the ones nearest back so that I can crouch next
to the engine. They gather closer, delighted with my performance.

But, in my dreams there is
none of the anger I feel in
daytime and I forgive them. I
am the first foreigner they've
ever seen. I am the last foreigner they will ever see. The
only foreigner that they will
ever see is a pale-faced green-
eyed woman with wispy
blond hair who rides a big
Chinese motorcycle with
Beijing plates. The woman is
obviously something that has
dropped in from outer space.
In my night dream I don't
think of what I have done to
them by coming here and
simply passing through. I'm not responsible for what I've seen.
China is China. They've been closed off for a million years, so it is
not the fault of the people of the West, at least. Everything that's
wrong here is their own fault. I only got a look at it because I was
flying under the radar.

> When Moscow claimed in
> 1969 that China's north-
> ern frontier since the fourth
> century B.C. had been defined
> by the Great Wall and that areas
> north of the wall were not his-
> torically subject to Chinese
> sovereignty, a Chinese historian
> acidly commented, "Where, one
> may ask, were the frontiers of
> the *Russian* state in the fourth
> century B.C.?"
> —David Bonavia, *The Chinese*

Every traffic cop who pulled me over waved me on quickly, in
obvious panic, as soon as they saw the blond braid tumble from my
helmet. They waved me on before they had to be obligated to admit
that yes, they had seen a foreign woman on a Chinese motorcycle
and she didn't have the proper papers. What would they do with
me? There is no precedent. One of them saluted me repeatedly until
I tucked my braid back under my helmet and rode out of sight.

Were they following me, though? Sometimes I wondered. This
idea, along with other useless thoughts, followed me closely like an
overweight passenger.

"Now remember," one of the Americans advised on the day before I left Beijing, "don't get in an accident, because the Chinese will just stand there and watch you bleed to death. I saw plenty of blood. Truckers in a head-on collision and no one who knew what to do."

What if I died here?

There is something surreal about being so alone in the midst of so many people. One-point-two-billion people. For a long time I felt the fear, but in the middle of my trip it was suddenly replaced by freedom and I was able to let the road take me farther and farther away from the edges of country and the edges of issues and right smack into the middle of everything that was happening around me. In the middle, my head emptied itself of everything but the moment, and the moment contained the cabbage harvest and the sun shining brightly on the tips of green wheat. The moment contained a small forest and the scent of trees being felled, small delicate trees with white bark that looked too fragile to build with.

Most of the road was shaded with bigger trees, their trunks painted uniformly white to four feet up and trimmed with a thin band of red paint. This landscape decoration goes on for miles in China. Kublai Khan had once ordered trees to be planted by the roadside to give solace to travelers. It had become a Chinese habit. Solace was finally mine. Solace was everywhere. Peasants sawed laboriously, sending the fresh green dust into the air. Peasants pulled carts piled high with their green cabbages to market, smiling at the realization of the fruits of their labors. Peasants watered the green wheat. Peasants squatted on their heels and slurped noodles from steaming bowls. I was inside all this, through the forest and the village and then on a road that barely hung onto the sides of terraced mountains. A bee flew up my sleeve. I rubbed at the swelling place on my arm and kept going.

Here, in the shade, is the place I can say that I became a participant and not an observer, when I stopped bothering my mind with the problem of how to send my words away and the problem of the words I might retrieve. Here there was no place for the disturbing bouts of expectations and longings for home that were only exacerbated when seeking an Internet connection.

From now on the ride occupied all the mental space I was willing to spare. Food clothing shelter gas oil adjustments repairs. No room for disturbing thoughts. No room for worry, hope, disappointment, expectation, even joy. A resignation and a real emptiness came to take their place. The kind of emptiness that people go on meditation retreats to seek, using breathing and techniques and rituals that I know nothing about. I can access this space now, when I begin to think too much about how things might turn out, when thoughts just loop around without any possible positive result. What burdens I have placed upon myself! The gamut of emotions tossed around in my head like doomed ships tied together in a stormy sea, banging on each other until they sink, one by one, into depths, hopelessly irretrievable. In the middle I lost them all. Then I was finished. I wanted tea and slippers, and then home.

I had two more hard rides ahead. The first one was an obscure branch of the Silk Route by the Wei River. The road was closed but I couldn't read the sign. I wondered why I was all alone until five hours later I saw a huge scraper completely blocking the road. It would be there until the next day, they said, there was no way to get around it. Huge ditches on each side prevented a drive-around. I would have a ten-hour ride, maybe more, back and around to get to my destination. The men continued working. I walked up and down the road, through a small village, and found a place where, with help, I could get the bike down, around and halfway up. Couldn't they hitch a rope to me and drag me the rest of the way? No. They simply picked up the motorcycle, ten men, and hauled it onto the other side.

Alone again, I was lost in thoughts of Marco Polo and Kublai Khan on their hunting trips—this is where they would have come—until an electrical connection rattled loose. Tightening wires didn't help, the spare coil didn't help, the voltmeter showed everything was O.K. The truck that picked me up was the only one that ever passed by; it brought the workers home just before dusk. Kindly they dragged me to a town with a hairdresser who braided my hair so tight that my round eyes became slanted like hers, and three mechanics who only made the problem worse. But by the next day I was operational again and off to ride over a huge mountain that, again, wasn't on my map. Dirt road and switchbacks. Riverbeds and road construction. This was my life, day by day, so when I came to Baoji and a truly American-style freeway, I was in reverse culture shock. Xi'an was only a two-hour ride at sixty miles per hour down the road, and I made it to the outskirts of town just as the gearbox started rattling. No adjustment would make first or third gear work, so I cruised around town without them and started making arrangements for getting the damn machine on a train home. I had finally had enough.

The terra cotta warriors were a truly awesome sight but the tourism industry that surrounded them made me ashamed. I bought a grilled yam from a vendor who charged me ten times the fair price, and I had to literally wrestle the change from her hand. Westerners with fistfuls of play-money shopped and the Chinese took it, either slyly or aggressively. I wandered about in the middle of a thousand transactions, confused, feeling no affinity for the Westerners, who even to me seemed stupid, or for the Chinese, whom I'd traveled amongst for so long, who now seemed mean. I longed for a quiet peasant village, with people who had never seen a foreigner. Everything was different now. What arrogance, to have ever thought I could experience such a trip, and then return to my life unchanged.

Carla King is a San Francisco-based technology and travel writer who specializes in taking solo rides around the world on unreliable WWII motorcycles, sending dispatches from the road to her Motorcycle Misadventures website. These adventures are the basis for an upcoming anthology of the same name. You can read more of her work at www.MotorcycleMisadventures.com.

A Jew in Kaifeng

The song of the blood runs deep.

"You are Jewish? Oh—I know! Jewish people are very *clever.* For example...*Albert Einstein!*"

—Something I have heard, word for word,
dozens of times in China

KAIFENG WAS ONCE THE PROSPEROUS CAPITAL OF SEVEN Chinese dynasties. When I got there, it was nowhere near such splendor. It was poor and rundown. It was dusty and hot. It was in the messy midst of rebuilding itself: sidewalks uprooted, streets bare and muddy, and traffic skewed. It took effort to find the hotel, an old communist way station where I first came to grips with the realities of Chinese toilets, and where Chinese men of all ages stared at my hairy, circumcised, Western body in the public shower.

But Kaifeng also had its charms. The night market, right outside the hotel, offered such a dazzling rainbow of cheap, delicious things that I just *had* to try them all. The city's traditional Chinese storefronts had that vanishing old-world charm I thought I'd never see for real. Most of all, for me, there was the charm of being a *virgin*: I was traveling seriously for the first time, alone, and I barely knew the language or the culture.

I went for breakfast. Steamed dumplings, now and for all of eternity. I bought some by a little alley, from a friendly middle-aged woman. "Where are you from?" she asked.

"Israel," I broke my teeth pronouncing.

"Are you Jewish?"

"Yes."

She looked closer, and her face broke into a smile of childlike wonder. "Your eyes are so beautiful...." she said. Until then, she had no idea what a Jewish person looked like.

Maybe she didn't know about Kaifeng's history. One of the reasons I went there was to find Chinese Jews. The guidebook tells of seventeenth-century Jesuit priests who found a Jewish community in Kaifeng. It tells of the remains of a Chinese synagogue, of Chinese people who still put "Jew" on their IDs, and of a Jewish history research institute in the Kaifeng museum.

I'm neither religious nor a scholar, but I'm Jewish, and I wanted to see it. I mean, Chinese Jews! Would we have anything in common, I wondered. Would they be happy to meet me, a "real" Jew from the holy land?

At the place where the guidebook described synagogue ruins, I found a dump in which The People's Hospital No. 4 kept coal. Asking around did not help. My Chinese wasn't good enough, and many Chinese were inclined to give up quickly rather than risk confusion or embarrassment.

At a dried-up, under-funded city park, I stopped to admire an angelic baby girl. Her name was Xia Yu—Rain. She was a little scared of me, but her mother calmed her and told her I was a "foreigner uncle."

Xia Yu's mother didn't speak much English, but said Xia Yu's father did. They were waiting for him. When he came, I told him of my quest. Yes, he said after searching his memory, he knew a friend whose uncle was a Chinese Jew. Perhaps he could arrange a meeting. I took his number, and said goodbye to Xia Yu. To my delight, she blew me a kiss.

The meeting never took place. The next day, I took a bus to Kaifeng Museum, where (the book said) there were artifacts from the Kaifeng synagogue, and a Jewish history institute. It was hardly even a museum. It was a forgotten, decrepit building. It screamed: No Budget. The only other people except me were the cashier's friends, who played cards with him. I showed him the Chinese for "Jewish history institute." No good. He got another guy, who seemed to know more. This guy led me to a side yard, and pointed to a row of shuttered offices. I insisted, and kept using sentences with the word "Jewish" in them. Eventually it paid off. He made me buy *two* tickets, and took me inside.

It was the Ghost of Museum Past. The halls were silent, dim, and cool. The faded exhibits, many of them communist propaganda, were coated with dust. A middle-aged woman, probably a caretaker, kept a tiny Pekinese puppy with a bell around its neck. The man took me up four flights of steps to a padlocked lattice door, which led to a closed exhibit. The padlock was rusty.

The top room was in darkness. He threw the windows open. When the dust cleared, I looked around, and there they were. All that remains of the Jewish community that once lived in Kaifeng: A stone washbasin; a diagram of the synagogue, drawn by the Jesuits; and three large stone tablets, "steles" as the book calls them, carved with the community's history.

I stared at them for a long while. My discovery. To my surprise, suddenly I wanted to cry. I knew I was closer to those artifacts than the man who had let me in. They were *my* history, not his. But they were *there*, shut away where no one could see them. I felt the sorrow of waste, and, quieter and less familiar, the sorrow of my people.

He said I couldn't use my camera.

I didn't have to.

Raz Elmaleh has traveled in East Asia for two years. He can say "No chili, dammit!" in four different languages, and has no problems whatsoever with eastern-style squat toilets. His article on how to live cheaply and still date has been published in a Tokyo mini-mag, and he even got paid for it. Read his weblog at raztrip.blogspot.com.

JESSE BARKIN

✦ ✦ ✦

Guon Yen

Riptides of culture, sex, hope, and sadness
wash over each other in a Shanghai bar.

I PARTICULARLY LIKE THE IRONY OF THE CALLIGRAPHY GIRLS
in China, the ones who sidle up to you as you're walking down a
pedestrian mall like Shanghai's Nanjing Dong Lu and start chatting you up in English. They usually start with an interested-
sounding, "Where you from?" and from there engage you in a
conversation that leads you to believe that they want to learn
everything about you. Except that at some point they inform you
that they are art students at a nearby university and they're currently having an exhibition of student works and would you like
to come take a look? Which you should have seen coming, but you
don't because your rip-off defenses are momentarily overridden by
your desire for an actual non-commercial experience, a chance encounter with a native Chinese who just wants to talk. The irony
being that, unlike, say, the woman who approached me one time
on the street and enunciated a clear "We go your hotel room?"
these women who ask if you'd like to come with them to see their
etchings really, and only, want you to see their etchings.

I should have known better from the very first time I fell for it.
Pretty young women don't come up to me in the streets of San
Francisco and start chatting me up, so why would I think it should

happen in China? Even though I'm armed with what we're trained to believe everyone wants, the English language, I'm still just a short, spectacled forty-one-year-old man walking down the street. That's not to say that the English language doesn't have stature, because during my travels I did indeed meet a handful of Chinese who, wanting to practice their English, latched on to me once they learned that I wasn't German or French. And the power of English, as the calligraphy girls understand too well, is such that it doesn't just appeal to those who want to learn it, because I too found myself with the need to speak my native tongue.

Maybe it's a primal urge or mere loneliness, probably a combination, but in those stretches during my travels in Asia when I was by myself, when it hit me just how far away I was from my friends and cable TV, I found myself with a caffeine-like craving for English. And so I found myself hanging out at Starbucks in the mornings, if only to hear a local teenager struggle with such consummate English phrases as "vente cappuccino" while I wondered how they deal with the Starbucksian concept that "tall" actually means small. And it was that need for my mother tongue that led me to a young woman named Winnie, or at least, that's what it said on her black magic-marker nametag.

Winnie, I'd soon learn, came to Shanghai eight months before from Hunan province where her mom pieced together dresses for export after her dad was no longer able to work the rice paddies. Her real name was Guon Yen. She didn't choose her English name but was given it by her British boss at Goodfellas bar, he told her, because she reminded him of Winnie the Pooh. She had, of course, never heard of Winnie the Pooh, nor did she resemble the storybook bear in any way except perhaps in some metaphorical allusion to childhood. She had a broad nose and jet-black hair that framed her kitten-like face, and her smile shimmered with braces. I suppose she could have been as old as eighteen, but not much older.

Goodfellas is one of a handful of small pubs catering to expats on Julu Lu—with others scattered around town—all working on the same general principle. Their two most important features being to employ attractive, perky Chinese girls who speak English and like to chat up the customers, and to serve beer and drinks at moderate prices (translation: expensive for China but cheap for San Francisco). Some bars go for the hip crowd while others go more casual. Goodfellas has the look and feel of a neighborhood pub, with a dark-wood bar up front and pool table and dartboards in the back. What drew me most into Goodfellas on this particular Wednesday night was the music. I mean, how can anyone who went to high school in the '70s let pass by a chance to hear a DJ spinning Manfred Mann's Earth Band playing "Blinded by the Light."

It was about nine-thirty and there were maybe a dozen people in the bar, and that included the bartender, a DJ, and two bar girls, as they're often called. One of the bar girls, whose nametag said "Pamela," took my first drink order. She asked me my name and where I'm from—the usual—and Goodfellas was as I'd hoped.

It was nice to speak English after a day of walking and taking in the sights. With its phallic-symbol skyscrapers and overcrowded sidewalks littered with street vendors, Shanghai is a mess of an international city, one apparently intent on luring every multinational in the world to rent office space here. There are shimmering sixty-story office towers and storefronts selling Versace originals and Kate Spade handbags. But then you turn down a side street and you see people balancing wicker baskets of seeds over their shoulders on bamboo poles and you think you're back in the nineteenth century. Either way, all you see are Chinese faces, and they, as a rule, don't speak English. (All the storefronts in the business section of Shanghai are written both in English and Chinese, even though, as became abundantly evident, hardly anyone, including most of the clerks and wait staff, has any idea what that strange lettering outside says.) The Chinese whom I can converse with are invariably taking my food order or trying to get me to buy something, and even then their English is minimal. Fun as it is at first to be getting all this attention, a guy gets tired of being called "Hello Watch" or "Hello DVD" or even "Hello North Face" all day long. I chitchatted a little more with Pamela, finished my

After a long day of walking, the many advertisements for foot massage had their way with me. A hostess greeted me at a storefront door and brought me to a red lacquered waiting room that hinted at massages available for body parts other than feet. Discreet negotiating established that I did indeed want only my feet massaged. I was ushered into a dark room. An attractive young woman was selected by the matron in charge. As her blouse bulged, and her jeans revealed a trim backside, I invoked Chairman Mao (an unlikely patron) to protect me from the lascivious thoughts licking the edges of my consciousness.

After an excellent foot massage, I walked into the dusk to further explore Shanghai, finding wonderful tree-lined boulevards, and shops and bars of an astounding variety that seemed to radiate in all directions. I came upon two Irish pubs, and walking into one, sat in front of a giant TV showing American basketball via satellite, and raised a pint to the future of China.

—Sean O'Reilly, "Oh Mao, Where Art Thou?"

Happy Hour-priced beer, and was about to check out another bar on Julu Lu when a girl in blue jeans, beige sweater, and a mouth full of braces, floated over.

"You are from California," she said excitedly, and it took me a moment to realize that Pamela must have told her, that they must exchange information, that it's all part of the scheme. Except that, unlike Pamela, I quickly came to realize that Winnie really did care where I was from, that she really was interested.

After exchanging introductions—I told her my name and she said, "I know"—and after she told me that she has a friend who lives in what at first sounded like Pow Arto but eventually became Palo Alto, Winnie asked me if I was familiar with the song "Hotel California." She was talking about the classic Eagles song from the '70s, and I told her I was. She asked me if I knew what it was about, and I nodded. "Drugs," I said. She looked puzzled, and I was about to explain that when English-speakers say the word drugs that way they are usually talking about illegal drugs, like marijuana or cocaine, when she explained her confusion. She told me that she'd heard two theories, one being the drug one and the other being that the Eagles were referring to the race riots of the late '60s. She said that someone had told her that, and that maybe that's what it meant by the "back in 1969" lyrics. I told her that I'd never heard of that one, and that I was pretty sure it was drugs.

I soon learned that Winnie knew nearly every pop and rock song from the '70s and '80s—and suspected that she knew none from the ensuing, more recent two decades—and our conversation bounced from genre to genre. You'd think that most English-speaking guys over thirty are familiar with the music, and to a certain extent most are. But actually it's rare to find someone who actually knows the words, the contexts, the history, and I think she felt that we were kindred spirits, or at the very least that I was an interesting resource. I was filling in the blanks of her musical knowledge. At one point she was singing along with one-hit wonders Wild Cherry, only singing the famous lyric, "Play that funky music, bad boy." She had this puzzled look on her face that told me that she knew something wasn't quite right in her rendition. "Play that funky music, *white* boy," I said.

"*Wide* boy?"

No, I said, and while pointing my finger at my chest I emphasized, "WHITE boy." We both laughed.

We were talking about everything and then, stopping in mid-sentence, she nodded to someone over my shoulder, behind the bar, and she apologized sweetly and told me she'd be back in a moment. She scooted over to a barstool near the front where she took drink orders from the two guys in business suits who must have just entered the bar.

Winnie didn't return for a few minutes and I ordered a second beer from Pamela. She didn't speak English nearly as well as Winnie, which meant that even if we had lots in common our conversation was limited to the basics. We'd already exhausted the how-are-you and the where-are-you-from and my attention had begun to drift. Prince was rocking out over the speakers and I saw

Winnie dancing off in the middle distance. With her hips and arms moving to the beat—a puppeteer was pulling invisible strings and the same tug that raised the left hand to the sky jutted the right hip out to the side—she might have looked like a seductress if she didn't look so childlike. Instead, she came off as a G-rated go-go dancer, the kind that would be more likely to wind up in a Gidget beach movie than a Christina Aguilera video. I watched as Winnie fluttered from patron to patron, chatting up some more than others, going to and from the bar, taking filled and emptied glasses, while also finding time for a short, happy wiggle. Finally Winnie glided back over to my end of the bar.

By now our conversation had evolved into more than deconstructions of classic rock. I peppered her with questions about her background and family, not telling her that the best way to learn about people is to hear not only their stories, but in what they choose to tell you of their stories. Harry Chapin was crooning "Cat's in the Cradle," and I told her about the song, about the story of the absentee father who was always away from his son and how later his son wasn't there for him in his time of need. Winnie listened intently, her baby-fatted cheek next to mine as we tried to hear each other over the din. She asked me if I had a son, and I told her that I was married once but we didn't have any children and that I hoped to get married again and have a little boy or girl. And then, as she'd done all night, she retreated with a couple of back-up steps and was dancing and smiling again.

"I am so lucky!" she shouted above the music, her Siamese cat cheekbones pushing towards the ceiling.

"Because your father calls you his little pearl and holds you close?" I yelled.

Winnie nodded enthusiastically, confirming my guess. She had told me earlier that her given name, Yen, means a couple of things: a beautiful bird, and a pearl. Winnie had said she likes the bird interpretation, and, with a flapping motion, said, "a bird who can fly away and be free." But, I ventured, your dad likes the pearl? She nodded, and cupped her hands, held them close to her chest, as if rocking a baby chick. "He says I'm his precious beautiful pearl." I nodded and told her I thought she was a swan "because you have already flown away here to Shanghai." Winnie's eyes became thoughtful. "I don't know." Then she darted off to a table near the front door where three European-looking men were summoning her.

When she returned from her dance, I told Guon Yen that it must have been hard for her father to see her little pearl turn into a swan and fly away.

"He was the one who told me to go. We come from a small village. He says, 'Go, go, you can't learn anything here.'"

I told her that he sounds like a wonderful man. She gestured to her heart, but she is not smiling.

"Heart problems?"

Guon Yen shook her head no.

"Breathes."

I realized she was not gesturing to the heart but elsewhere.

"Lungs?"

She nodded. "Too much smoking," she said, and told me that last year he had to stop working and that his health was very bad.

"And your mother?"

"She works very, very hard in a factory that makes sweaters."

I conjured up an image of an older, beaten-down Guon Yen toiling on a machine designed to cause repetitive-stress injuries.

"She works too hard," she added. "She works all the time, and then comes home to take care of my father. I think my mother has a very hard life."

Disjointed as it was—what with her bopping off for a quick dance, and taking drink requests, and our mutual repeating required to understand what each of us were saying—I loved hearing Guon Yen's story. She said that she would go to school, maybe next year, but for now was working and getting used to her new, unwieldy hometown. She said that she was studying for her diploma, after which she could get into college. That she had originally wanted to enlist in the army—that most Chinese girls grow up wishing to join the army—but she was denied because of flat feet. "Some people have feet like this," she said, cupping her hand,

———— ✳ ————

When Julie and I arrived home from shopping, dragging Ikea bags and groceries from the taxi, I turned to see some Chinese laborers staring at us. And I realized we must have spent more in one afternoon than they make in, well, many days, to say the least. Then I remembered hearing a story of an old man who helps clean the international school where we teach: During Chinese New Year, there was a party and raffle for the Chinese staff, 300 yuan to the winning ticket-holder. A huge sum to be given in one go. This same old man—he usually sweeps the playground with a hand-made straw broom—heard his number called: 93. He ran to the stage with youthful glee on his weathered face, only to learn that, in his excitement and hope, he had transposed numbers. He had 39, not 93. He returned to his table, keeping his smile, but clearly embarrassed. This man is well-liked, and teachers at his table took up a collection and tried to give it to him. He would not accept. He adamantly refused.

—James Villers Jr.,
"Money and Face"

palms down. "Mine are like this," she said, and she opened her hand.

When I asked what she wanted to do when she gets older she shrugged, and of course smiled, and said she had no idea. I suggested that there must be great opportunities in Shanghai for someone who spoke English as well as she did—which was fairly fluent despite a thick accent. And that maybe she could talk to someone at one of the universities to see what was out there. Guon Yen shrugged again and smiled politely as if to say that's nice but I'm not worried or anything. Then she was off again. I watched her grab three mugs of beer from the bar and chastised myself because I knew that I must have sounded like a needling parent or a pesky guidance counselor. *Hell*, I thought, *I'm forty-one and don't know what I'm going to do when I grow up.*

I guess my mind was on Guon Yen because ordinarily I notice things like what happened next. A woman had taken the barstool next to me, and was sitting so close that when I swiveled around to grab my beer off the bar, my thigh inadvertently brushed against hers. I apologized, but the expression on her face suggested none was necessary. She was just smiling at me, kind of a friendly, silly smile that I decided was the smile of a Chinese who didn't speak English. Her face had the same round shape as Guon Yen's, and she was probably in her late twenties or early thirties. She had a beautiful pale complexion, marred only by acne on her forehead, and her eyes were the color of a river after a downpour.

"Where are you from?" she said.

Ah. The familiar refrain. "America. What's your name?"

"Nancy."

"What's your Chinese name?"

"Ling."

We exchanged a few more pleasantries before she ran out of English, and that was about it for conversation. I smiled again. She smiled back. After our third awkward silent smile I felt her putting her hand on my thigh. More smiles. Nothing much to say. Then I thought of something.

"Would you like a drink?" I said, gesturing with my half-filled beer.

She squeezed my thigh and gave me a look that said it's about time. She had a simple, confident air about her that I liked. When she told me that she wanted orange juice, I wondered whether she didn't drink alcohol, or whether it was the only drink she knew how to say in English. I waved to the bartender and ordered an orange juice.

"Is she with you?" the Caucasian man behind the counter asked me sternly, all the while keeping his steely eyes on Ling's face.

It was only then that I understood that she was a prostitute. I felt like I had been hit by a gigantic *duh!* thunderbolt. Why hadn't I seen this coming? And how many times was I going to fall for the old, "Where you from" routine?

I'm not sure what I should have felt at that moment, but I was puzzled by what I actually did feel. It was relief. I scanned my brain for a reason and the answer came to me when I noticed Guon Yen

standing at the bar behind Ling, waiting for the bartender, looking at me. Looking at us. What I realized was that Guon Yen was
not a prostitute, and in a very paternal way I was glad. I felt myself smile.

Following the bartender's lingering glare, I looked at Ling, who
was wincing. Although the entire episode of eyes opening and
closing took only an instant, and although the wince was designed as a defiant dagger directed at the bartender, I felt a chill because by the time she had opened her eyes she looked like a different person. It was as if a virus had invaded her body and replaced all her confidence with insecurity and fear. As if those four little words—Is she with you?—had stolen a piece of her spirit.

> Xi Ping understood me.
> When I told her I was
> considering giving up my job to
> go traveling around the country,
> she kissed my ear and whis-
> pered, "Wherever you go, you
> can always come back to me.
> My body is your sunset."
> —Ma Jian, *Red Dust: A Path
> Through China*

Because of the tone of the bartender's voice I also knew something else: that I held the key as to whether Ling could stay or go.
After all, his answer to my request for an orange juice wasn't to ask
Ling to leave the bar, but was directed to me in such a way that he
knew I understood what was going on here. What was going on
was that in the world of bars and bar girls, Goodfellas—located not
far from the American Embassy in one of the more expensive sections of the city—was, if I were to make an American analogy,
more like a Hooter's than a strip club. Management's scheme was
to tease and entice with pretty young women like Guon Yen, but
the objective was to sell beer and not sex. I didn't know why that
was Goodfellas' strategy, why they weren't more like some of the
bars in Southeast Asia where the women—every bit as sweet as
Guon Yen—sold anything the customer wanted. I wasn't familiar
enough with the turf to understand Shanghai's terrain as it related
to prostitution (except that I had a feeling that the Communist

government might not be as tolerant as, say, that of Thailand); maybe the police frown on this type of activity in so "respectable" an establishment. All I knew was that in this particular power play, two white men had sway over a Chinese woman, and for some reason the single American traveler held the trump card. That would have been bad enough anywhere in the world, but the fact that it was happening in Ling's own country made it all the more bitter.

Having lived in my body my entire I life, I knew that this was the kind of confrontational situation that I was never really good at. I'm the type who tends to avoid confrontation if at all possible. And since I wasn't considering having sex with Ling or any prostitute my course of action was clear.

"Yes," I said resolutely, saying exactly the opposite of what common sense had just dictated.

So what was I doing? Some part of me was standing up for Ling in some macho way that I don't particularly wish to be part of my psyche but nonetheless is. I mean, I loathed the attitude of the bartender who'd just made this woman sitting next to me feel like shit. And partly I was standing up for some oh-so American egalitarian principle that goes something like this: *Yes it's sad that women sell their bodies but who am I to tell them they can't? Who am I to tell a woman that it's better for her children to starve than for their mother to make whatever decision she feels she must to survive?* In the aggregate, and in a nutshell, I think the world's oldest profession has helped subjugate women from the beginning of civilization, and the modern-day stories in Asia of women (still) being sold into the sex trade are horrific. I wished I had been able to ask Ling about her upbringing, her dreams, and desires. I envisioned a cute little girl with straight black bangs, baby-smooth complexion, and clear brown eyes, who at some point in her childhood met with unfortunate circumstances.

If I was expecting a confrontation, I had miscalculated. The bartender shook his head, poured the drink, and took my money. I dragged the orange juice and rested it in front of Ling. Her furtive eyes first watched the bartender turn his back and start filling what

I suppose was Guon Yen's drink order, then darted around like she'd expected the Red Guard to slap on the handcuffs at any moment. Instead, she clasped my wrist with her hand and asked, "Your hotel room near here?"

Now would come the hard part, the part where I would say no after implicitly saying yes. The best course of action seemed to be to leave the bar with Ling and once outside tell her that I wasn't interested. At least that way she wouldn't lose anymore face than she already had. She could go on her way, find another bar, another foreign traveler. And I would go on my way as well. It was a good plan.

"Let's go," I said. I took her hand and walked brusquely out of the bar.

It was about eleven o'clock and taxicabs littered the curbs of the well-lit Julu Lu. An older man leaning against the first cab pushed himself up and straightened his cap. A gust of wind whisked Ling's straight hair across her face, and she zipped up her lambskin jacket. The man motioned for us to take his ride, but Ling took my arm and turned us away from the line of cabs and towards the busy corner the other way. I resisted. She stopped.

"I'm going to say goodbye now," I said.

"Maybe too many police." She obviously had been spooked by the bartender.

"I just wanted to get you out of the bar," I tried again. "I'm not going back to the hotel room with you."

"Not to hotel room?"

"No," I said. I didn't tell her any more, figuring that because of the language gap she wouldn't comprehend. I just shook my head for emphasis. She looked into my face for what seemed like a long time.

"It O.K.," she said.

And that was that. She said goodbye, squeezed my jacket at the wrist, and hurriedly walked towards the corner. I don't know what she understood. She may have just thought I was a guy who changed his mind, chickened out at the last moment. I figured that happens every now and then.

I thought about hopping in the taxi and heading back to my hotel but now that I looked again, I didn't like the expression on the cabbie's face. I thought that I had caught Ling's paranoia. Besides, it was early, and this was my last night in Shanghai. There were a few other bars on the street, including one with the oddly broken-English name Nice Time bar, and any one of them would do. But then my mind's eye saw Guon Yen's face, still standing at the bar, watching me. And I was flooded with what sure felt like guilt. Or maybe shame.

Guilt over what I couldn't pinpoint except that I was sure that I didn't want her to think of me as that kind of guy. That line of thinking probably was borne out of ego, self-consciousness, and insecurity, but it seemed a ridiculous thought all the way around. Why should it matter what someone I'll never see again in my life thinks about me, not to mention the probability that she'll never even give me another thought two days from now? But it did matter. I tried to convince myself that it mattered because I didn't want her to think stereotypically of American men, that we all come to China to get laid by prostitutes. But

> Chen Buo and I met in the typical way a local and a foreigner might, but there was nothing typical about our friendship. To begin with, there were not many female foreigners who had platonic relationships with Chinese men. Even friendships between Chinese men and women were quite rare. There was a definite stigma attached to foreign romantic relationships, although Chinese men dating foreign women had less stigma attached to them. I was once told that it is considered a trophy for the Chinese family if a foreign woman loves a Chinese man. It means he has made himself irresistible to her. His family gains face in this situation. In contrast, a Chinese woman would lose face if she were in a romantic relationship with a Caucasian man.
>
> —Daneal Charney,
> "My Chinese Family"

listening to the frantic butterflies in my stomach, I had a feeling it was more about my own insecurities. I think my insides were telling me that no matter what I did with Ling, the alchemy I'd felt with Guon Yen had been shattered. That what had seemed like such a perfect evening in Shanghai had been ruined. That I had ruined it.

I thought again about taking a cab back to my hotel room, but something inside told me that I needed to face the music.

James Brown's "Sugar and Spice" was blaring through the speakers and a haze of cigarette smoke that I hadn't noticed before helped camouflage me as I walked deliberately past the bar, hoping the bartender wouldn't spot me, and towards the dartboards in the back. I noticed for the first time that the place was considerably more crowded than when I'd first arrived, with all the barstools being taken and tufts of people scattered about. Two college-aged women were sitting at a table rifling through a street vender's collection of CDs and DVDs. Pamela was pushing towards the bar with a tray filled with empty pint glasses. Four suits and ties were playing pool. I didn't see Guon Yen anywhere, and ran out of real estate at the very back of the bar, near the men's room with the broken latch, where I found a piece of wall and leaned against an old poster of Jimi Hendrix. I found myself watching the pool table, contemplating the implications of the all-powerful white ball smacking around pawn-like balls of color.

"Can you tell me who sings this song?"

It was Guon Yen, whom I didn't see coming, and I could tell by her expression, delightfully the same as ever, that I was a complete idiot. Whatever machinations that had rattled my conscience weren't even at play with Guon Yen.

I told her that it was James Brown, and that anybody who wanted to know anything about American music has to know about the Godfather of Soul. We both listened to the refrain, which was punctuated by those amazing horns. *Sugar and spice/so good, so nice/ I got you ooh-ooh-ooh-ooh-ooh.*

"What does that mean, sugar and spice?"

"In America we have a saying, 'little girls are made of sugar and spice.' That means they are sweet, like candy, and spicy, like a red pepper, both at the same time.'"

Guon Yen laughed.

"Why are you laughing?"

"I think that's what *you* like," she said. "Sugar and spice."

I smiled back thinly, scouring her face for a hint of condescension or judgment. There was none, and I felt my cheeks push up into a fuller smile. I asked her if she had a boyfriend, saying it in my most fatherly tone, in a way that I hoped she wouldn't misconstrue as me asking her out.

"I think so."

"How long have you been dating?" I asked.

"Eight months."

"And you only think so?" I shouted because she already had backed up and was in mid-jiggle.

She ebbed closer and said in my ear, "He doesn't tell me he loves or if he likes me."

"But he shows it." I made sure there was no question mark at the end of the sentence. She smiled and backpedaled.

"I think so."

I asked her if she believes in love at first sight, a question I had to repeat before she understood what I meant. She said that she doesn't look at a person and fall for him, that she has to get to know him. That she wasn't even sure that she knew what love is, except that she was sure that she loved him. Guon Yen looked at me in a funny way as she backed out to her dance floor, as if to say it was a silly question for an older man, a man who should know better, to be asking.

"We are so young!" she shouted as she drifted away from me.

James Brown screeched, and Guon Yen's arms rotated, her hips twisting in tow. Then she smiled, made an apologetic shrug, and dashed off towards the bar. *I feel good / I knew that I would.* I felt myself smiling in that way that causes others to want in on the secret. I lingered another moment and then I straightened up and left the bar.

The next morning I took the 6:15 shuttle to Pudong International and was on my way out of China.

Jesse Barkin has been a staff reporter for the San Jose Mercury News, Los Angeles Daily News, *and the* Orange County Register. *He left his most-recent position as senior editor at* Wired News, *at the age of forty-one, to travel the world, to scare himself, and to learn. When not roaming the planet, he calls Southern California his home.*

PAMELA LOGAN

✦ ✦ ✦

Dancing with the Conqueror

Biking China's frontiers provides
a memorable encounter.

I HAD AN APPOINTMENT WITH THE KHAN.

No, not just any Khan, but the Khan, Khan of Khans. The one who led his Golden Horde out of the steppe, the one who stomped over passes, romped over deserts, and flew like a firestorm across central Asia all the way to eastern Europe. The Khan who built the greatest empire the world has ever seen. The Great Khan. Genghis Khan.

That Khan.

I and a few thousand other pilgrims were slowly converging on Ejin Horo Banner, whose name means "enclosure of the Emperor" in Mongolian. In the past, worshippers trekked to this spot on the back of sturdy Mongol horses. Times have changed and nowadays they use minibuses, Land Cruisers, and Beijing Jeeps.

All except me. I was coming by mountain bike.

O.K., so I was slightly demented to be crossing Inner Mongolia on a mountain bike in March. But I had biked in China before—mostly in the country's wide-open west—and was therefore in practice. This foray into Inner Mongolia was part of my long-term and distinctly unofficial project to explore China's exotic frontiers. In between my responsibilities as Director of Research for the

Hong Kong-based China Exploration & Research Society, I had managed to log more than six hundred miles in the provinces of Yunnan, Sichuan, Qinghai, and Xinjiang. Now I had a well-seasoned bike and yen to get even farther off the beaten track. Guidebooks had neglected Inner Mongolia so much that I knew it was a place with possibilities.

My destination was Genghis Khan's "mausoleum" —although almost no one believes his remains are really here. No matter. It's still a monument to their hero, and Mongolians come regardless. On the 23rd day of the third lunar month they come: in business suits and track suits, in lama's skirts and robes of azure silk. They carry wine to drink in the Khan's honor and slaughtered sheep to place on the altar before his crypt. Some bring nothing at all, but still they come.

The Great Sacrifice is held in spring, and spring is a miserable season on the Gobi. I had expected cold but didn't consider wind, and certainly didn't figure on blinding sandstorms dogging my path all along the way.

China's original Silk Road was active from the second century B.C. to the fourteenth century A.D. It led westward from the T'ang Dynasty capital at Ch'ang An to Tun-huang at the edge of the Taklimakan Desert and split at Kashgar into northern and southern routes. This is now Chinese Turkestan, which in ancient times was straddled by the province of Khotan. There is abundant evidence of an extraordinary mixing of Roman, Greek, Hindu, and Buddhist cultures in this area. Buddhist monasteries, shrines, and grottos were carved into the soft sandstone cliffs on the edge of the Taklimakan Desert. The buried cities of Khotan were rediscovered in 1900 by Sven Hedin and later by Aurel Stein. Who knows what other treasures lay beneath the desert sands?
    —Sean O'Reilly, "Reflections on Chinese History"

Luckily, I had plenty of time, and the few days of good weather were just enough.

What I was learning had turned upside down everything I expected of Mongolians. I expected to find a stern, exacting people—men in silent communion with the limitless steppe on which they live, women rearing their children in the image of their warrior forefathers. What I got was completely different.

"You must drink the wine," one of my new friends whispered to me at my first Mongolian party, "otherwise he'll keep singing all night!" We were in a yurt—one of those round, felt-covered tents that are the traditional dwelling of nomadic tribes across Central Asia. Nowadays they are rare in Inner Mongolia, but once they were a ubiquitous sight. This particular yurt was set on a sidewalk in the capital of Otog Banner where it functioned as a pub for local Mongolians.

The yurt's owner was standing before me, his outstretched hands holding a blue silk scarf and a bowl of clear liquid. He had just finished a loud and hearty stanza of traditional song. Lesson One: Mongolians love to sing, and to them, song and drink are inseparable.

I took the bowl in my hands, steeled myself, and poured cool liquid lava into my belly. "Wine" it certainly was not; from its industrial-strength bouquet and its 160-proof kick I guessed it must be *baijiu*—Chinese whiskey. I returned the bowl, it was refilled, and the singing-drinking exchange moved on to another pair of guests.

After a few rounds, the scarf and bowl came around to me. "Sing an American song!" they begged.

Let me tell you something about Mongolians: You can't—you just can't!—say no to these people. It doesn't work. They won't hear you. They believe that, more important than anything else including God, King, and Country, it's their mission on earth to make sure you have a good time. Besides, Mongolians won't believe that such a wretched, pitiable human being exists as one who can't sing, for Mongolians are born belting out tunes over the wide-open spaces of the steppe. I would have to show them that Americans are different.

I picked a blues song, thinking that its soulful strains would carry across the language and culture gap. As I opened my mouth

I saw a ring of happy, anticipatory faces. Then it came: "Swing low, sweet chariot..." I croaked, and the faces suddenly fell. In my hands was the whisky-filled bowl, offered to the man sitting opposite. He snatched it from me and downed the booze in one swig. I closed my mouth, to everyone's obvious relief, and handed the bowl and scarf to the woman sitting next to me.

That night I began an informal research project into Methods for Alcohol Avoidance at Mongolian Parties. Being female helps, but it's not enough. One trick is to wait until their attention is elsewhere, then jiggle the bowl so that the contents slosh out. Pleas of a sick stomach work for one or two rounds, as do requests for beer instead of whiskey. But it's not easy.

The next morning, feeling a little wobbly, I pedaled out of there and on to my next adventure.

The road north from Otog Town is rough—little more than gravel sprinkled haphazardly over the sand of the Gobi. It passes through the heart of the Ordos, which is a league (prefecture) of Inner Mongolia. The Ordos is hemmed by the Great Wall to the south and the Yellow River to the north; girt by such durable geographic boundaries, the Ordos has developed its own distinct brand of Mongolian culture.

During most of its long history, the Ordos has had the bad luck of being a fertile and strategic buffer between two bristling empires. For 2,000 years, Mongolians and Chinese politely took turns overrunning it. By the early twentieth century the Chinese had won, but incessant warring and a weak central government had taken their toll. The Ordos was a wretched, bandit-infested land wrung dry by rapacious feudal princes and corrupt, parasitic lamas.

That's all changed now. Since Mao Zedong's communists took over in 1949, the Ordos has been cleaned up. Bandits and warlords are gone, and lamas (who have only recently reappeared on the scene after a long period of repression) concern themselves only with religion. Mongolians and Chinese don't always love each other, but they manage to live peacefully side by side, and intermarriage is common.

Before I came to the Ordos, I blithely imagined that society here is divided into two neat halves: settled Chinese and nomadic Mongolians. But it isn't that simple. Lesson Two: Beware of ethnic generalizations in the Ordos. Nomadism is virtually extinct; everyone lives in permanent houses now; moreover in the last few decades many Mongolians have become educated, learned professions, and become city dwellers.

In the countryside, choice of livelihood is driven not by race, but by economics. Long ago many Chinese settled here hoping to put the steppe under the plow, but poor soil has made agriculture a dicey proposition. It's not uncommon, therefore, to find Chinese living as herdsmen just like their Mongolian neighbors. Influence works both ways, and some Mongolians have taken up farming.

The ecosystem of the Ordos is fragile and changing. Archaeological evidence shows that the Ordos was once much wetter and warmer than it is now, and its inhabitants may well have been among the first farmers in Asia. But around 1500 B.C. the land turned dry, becoming what Mongols call classic "*gobi*"—arid, sparsely vegetated, gravelly land that is useless for agriculture but good for grazing sheep, goats, horses, and camels.

Lately the Ordos' population has begun to outstrip the land's meager resources. Despite the truckloads of fertilizer that go into the Ordos every year, its soil is dying. And even where no plow has ever touched, overgrazing is destroying once-verdant pastures. Now the Ordos is on the verge of total desertification. The government is well aware of this problem; widespread tree-planting has reduced the fierce winds, slowing movement of sand dunes that threaten to bury what little useful pasture remains. Yet these non-native trees bring their own problems, and no one is sure what the long-term consequences will be. With a rising population and a dropping water table, the Ordos has difficult days ahead.

Desert is what I found under my tires as I rode north across Otog Banner on an unpaved track. A steady headwind battered me, and sometimes I had to dismount to push my bike through sand dunes that had drifted across the road. But I didn't mind. The day was fine, the distance not far, and a slower pace gave me more time to enjoy the desert.

By now, after more than a week in Inner Mongolia, I had met a lot of Mongolians, but I didn't start to feel like a Mongol until I was crossing the Gobi's vast empty spaces. Riding a horse is undoubtedly best, but pedaling a bike is pretty good. In springtime the Gobi Desert is an endless plain of sand sprouting with withered grass and leafless bushes as far as the eyes can see. No wonder Mongolians have such sharp eyes; everything in their world is far: a runaway horse, a grazing camel, a house perched on an ever-so-gentle rise, clouds dancing over the horizon. As time went on I came to sense subtle changes in the desert: its slope and texture, its faded green and brown pastels. A greener spot means underground water and this, to a herdsman, is good.

Halfway along, I came to a crossroads where a highway maintenance station was built in the middle of nothing. The Chinese who inhabited it invited me inside for lunch. While I sat eating their humble fare of stewed mutton and rice, outside the wind suddenly increased, and the sky went black.

"*Guafeng,*" muttered one of the men as he stood before the window. Lesson Three is the meaning of this all-important word: icy winds screeching from the north, lacerating airborne sand, and visibility shrinking to nothing. I settled down for a long siege.

Before long a lonesome wail surrounded the brick house, which was stoutly built with a thick windowless wall facing Siberia. Gradually the keening grew into a dull, surging roar, as if ocean waves and not mere air were threatening to hammer the house to dust. Outside, grit flew and trees flailed. I was glad to be indoors, and that kindness to travelers is an enduring tradition on the Gobi.

After a couple of hours the storm unexpectedly died down. Rested now, and charged with new energy, I set out with my bike again. After three hours of wallowing on the sandy road, at last I reached a small town huddled in the lee of a sandstone hill. As I pedaled into the outskirts, Buddhist monks in flowing crimson robes came out to greet me.

After 1949, monks almost disappeared in Inner Mongolia, but since the 1980s, when China's government decided to tolerate religion, Buddhism has been making a minor comeback. The cities hold few believers, but in the hinterland there are enough to support a few scattered monasteries. Xin Zhao, where I had just arrived, had about twenty monks, most of them old men. They were hard at work reviving their ancient traditions—virtually identical to those of Tibet—here in this lonely, windswept corner of desert.

As an honored (if unexpected) guest, I was put up in a room on the monastery grounds and given all the tea, millet, cheese, and noodles I could eat. By day I went to the temple—a simple brick building erected to replace the original destroyed during the Cultural Revolution—to listen to the monks chant. I studied the religious paintings and books stored in the monastery, so familiar to me from travels on the Tibetan plateau. From villagers I learned fragments of Ordos Mongolian, and worked on my Chinese, which virtually everyone there knew. When the sandstorms eased I went for walks in the hills.

At Xin Zhao I learned to eat Mongolian-style: pocket knife in one hand, a joint of sheep in the other, mutton-fat lubricating my fingers and lips as I quickly reduced the joint to dry bone. This simple

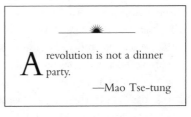

A revolution is not a dinner party.

—Mao Tse-tung

ritual made me feel part of the numberless nomadic tribes that have for millennia wandered Central Asia.

At Xin Zhao, time seemed to stand still, and before I knew it nearly a week had passed. The Spring Sacrifice of Genghis Khan was now fast approaching, and I hurried back on the road.

First traveling to the Ordos capital of Dongsheng, I then went south to Ejin Horo Banner, pedaling in the tracks of countless pilgrims. It was one of the Ordos' better roads, paved to accommodate tourists and others going to pay their respects to the Great Khan. Groves of hand-planted trees marked the borders of fields, for in the eastern Ordos many pastures have been given over to farming. After twenty-seven miles I knew I was getting close. Then, through a grove of willows, I spotted a high brick wall, and beyond it a triumphal blue-and-yellow dome rising from the summit of a hill: Genghis's great monument.

Legend has it that the Khan himself chose this spot to be his eternal home. They say that one day he was riding through the Ordos, accompanied by a contingent of mounted warriors, when he happened into a valley of extraordinary beauty. The Great Khan declared that it would be his final resting place, but when death actually came in summer of the year 1227, he was in the middle of a military campaign against the rebellious Tanguts in far-off northwest China. His lieutenants decided that the Khan's burial place and even his death itself must be a state secret. Accordingly, as the bearers carried his corpse in procession to a burial ground somewhere in northern Mongolia, they slew every living creature they met upon the road. The Khan was buried in a carefully concealed grave, which to this day lies undiscovered.

Sometime later, at Ejin Horo a cenotaph was erected in the Khan's honor, and the Seven Banners of the Ordos charged with the responsibility for its care. Originally the monument consisted of several great tents housing a crypt and assorted relics—bows, silver-plated saddles, swords—said to belong to the Khan. In 1955 the government replaced the tents with three permanent structures: domes decorated in Mongolian style. The interior has a gallery of huge murals that tell Genghis Khan's life story. In the climactic panel the burly, square-jawed conqueror appears sitting on a high throne, surrounded by representatives of all his conquered peoples; their faces span the rainbow that is Eurasia. Part museum and part shrine, the complex at Ejin Horo is an enduring place of worship for Mongolians.

The tiny town was buzzing with activity when I arrived. As if emerging from a long winter's hibernation, everyone was outside busily sweeping, polishing, and cleaning. The guest-house windows were being shined to perfection by housekeepers garbed in brilliant robes. And bus-loads of guests were arriving every hour. That night I was visited by a smiling trio of Mongols, emissaries of a group of teachers from Wushen Banner who were staying next door. They asked, would I like to come with them to a dance? At their words my head was filled with visions of colorful ethnic twirls and flourishes, an authentic Mongolian celebration. My answer was: Of course!

The teachers had a minibus to take us to the venue, which was outside the town. We pulled up to a building, and when I spotted a sign with the word "karaoke," suddenly my heart fell. So much for traditional ethnic dance, I thought. Inside the place was a twirling reflecting ball hanging from the ceiling, colored lights, and an enormous battered boom box. Someone started a tape, and the schmaltzified strains of "Thus Spake Zarathustra" blared out.

Couples formed and began two-stepping in time to the music, which briskly evolved into a John Phillips Sousa march. Soon the floor was full of shuffling pairs. A jazzed-up "Auld Lang Syne" came on, followed by "The Blue Danube." Then Otelai asked me to dance.

He was short and barrel-chested, strong as a bull, dressed in jeans and a much-worn denim jacket. He had untidy, razor-cut hair and a square face that seemed oddly familiar. "I'm called Otelai," he shouted into my ear in hoarse Chinese, afterwards saying no more.

The music came faster, and Otelai's feet sped up. Striding in perfect time to the music as he whirled me around the room, he made it impossible for me to miss a step for he was practically lifting me off the floor. Out of the corner of my eye I saw the teachers' prim, disdainful glances at the boorish usurper who was monopolizing their honored guest. He wasn't one of them, I realized. But who was he?

The music stopped, and Otelai went off to grab a slug of beer. But before I had even caught my breath he was back again, the next dance was starting, and he was begging for another turn. Without waiting for an answer, he took my hand; we were off and flying again.

Faster the music came, and the wild Mongolian dervish was spinning me with ever greater speed and abandon. Soon we were colliding with other couples and bumping into furniture. In the middle of the blur, I heard his voice in my ear: "Please excuse the Ordos—we're so poor and undeveloped."

I said, "That doesn't matter. You are still good people." At this his grip tightened and his hand became warmer. At 10:30 the party ended, and Otelai disappeared as mysteriously as he had come. The teachers and I piled back into the minibus and returned to our guest house at the Genghis Khan Monument.

The following day was the Great Spring Sacrifice. Each of the Seven Banners of the Ordos sent representatives to present sacrifices at the shrine of Genghis, and hundreds of ordinary people made their own small offerings. All day long, parties of reverent Mongolians were carrying sheep carcasses, silk scarves, brick tea, milk, and bottled liquor to give to their Khan. Kneeling, they sipped sacred wine and repeated the incantations of a tall, dour-faced priest. I'll never forget the solemn faces of a people who, even seven hundred years later, still worship their ancestral hero.

And I'll never forget when the ghost of Genghis Khan asked me to dance.

Pamela Logan received her doctorate in aerospace science from Stanford University before changing career paths. An interest in martial arts and photography led her to Tibet and resulted in her first book, Among Warriors: A Martial Artist in Tibet. *Returning to Tibet and taking an interest in ancient monasteries, she began leading international expeditions and established the Kham Aid Foundation to support monastery conservation work. She subsequently wrote* Tibetan Rescue: The Extraordinary Quest to Save the Sacred Art Treasures of Tibet. *Her life and work are chronicled at www.alumni.caltech.edu/~pamlogan/.index.html.*

J. D. BROWN

The Rubbing Master

There's more astonishing history in Xi'an
than the terra cotta army.

THE PROVINCIAL MUSEUM IS HOUSED IN THE OLD TEMPLE of Confucius, which dates from 1374 A.D. It contains the great treasures of Old China from the late and early dynasties all the way back to the Stone Age. Dusty, ill-lit, and poorly organized, it is my favorite museum on earth.

At its heart is Bei Lin—the Forest of Steles—the premier collection of engraved stone tablets in China. The largest single grove consists of the Confucian Classics, and occupies its own gallery: 114 double-sided stone blocks. Most of what has survived the successive incarnations of Xi'an had to be buried in the earth or cast into stone: the terra cotta warriors and royal tumuli; the pagodas and temple steles of the Han and T'ang; the pottery, the broken tiles, the bone.

This is the running text of those ruins; the Confucians deserve credit that it survives at all. They were the preservers, the collectors. From feudalism to socialism, China has remained a Confucian empire. Peasants may have prayed to ancestors and spirits far longer and in greater numbers, workers may have revered the patron and city gods with more zeal, but the scholars and bureaucrats have shaped China from the top. If Taoism or Buddhism or Christianity were necessary to address the wild and esoteric longings of the secret heart and mind, Confucianism took care of the rest, of what counted—the practical, the ethical, the material, the humdrum harmonies of family and society, the whole enmeshed hierarchy.

Confucius was a fifth century B.C. reactionary; he derived his wisdom from much older models. His teachings were concentrated on individual conduct and mass synchronization—the two are inseparable. His approach led to the elaboration of a ponderous state bureaucracy perpetuated by a rigorous system of examinations. The individual's every outward act was always under the microscope, a maze of lenses increasingly powerful and distant. By the time of his death in 479 B.C., Confucius had already been honored with the first temple built in his name. Two centuries later, his followers were numerous enough to feel the full wrath of Emperor Qin; their schools were closed, their books burned, their Sage denounced. A thousand temples to Confucius were to flourish after the first emperor died. The Imperial Examinations lasted well into the twentieth century; Confucian education and bureaucracy are still with us now.

The Temple of Confucius at Xi'an survived, however, only because its conversion to a museum came soon after the revolution, in 1952. Within its halls are bronzes and jades from the Zhou dynasty; plumbing pipes, a south-pointing chariot, and the world's first seismograph from the immediate successors of Emperor Qin; tricolored horses and scraps of silk from the days of the T'ang; and more than a thousand steles from every period, first gathered together in Xi'an in 1090 A.D.

The center of this stone library has always been the Confucian Classics, carved at Xi'an in 837 A.D.; like a bureaucracy of magical winches and cleats, it has anchored China to the center of its own world for centuries, and does so still.

To foreigners, however, the heart of the Forest of Steles is not the Confucian Classics, that petrified Encyclopedia Sinica, but a single tablet, the Nestorian Stele, which records the arrival of

Christianity in China in 635 A.D. and its progress in the capital during the seventh and eighth centuries.

The Nestorian tablet is nine feet tall, a yard wide, a foot thick, and weighs two tons. It is composed of limestone as black as a cast-iron lamppost and rests on a tortoise-shaped base. The rounded peak is finely carved: a cross floats in a lotus cloud with two flowering shrubs. Atop the cross is a massive pearl, held by a phantasmagorical figure described variously as a fish monster or crocodile. The cross has been set within a triangle. Immediately beneath is a matrix of nine characters, an inscription reading "The Monument Commemorating the Propagation of the Luminous Religion (Da Qin) in the Middle Kingdom."

> "I visited Europe a few years ago," Wang said. "And I was very impressed by all of the old buildings they have there. It is beautiful. We don't have that in China. We destroyed all of our old buildings. My hometown, Xi'an, is very historic. But there's nothing old. It's gone. The government was wrong."
> His statement was vague enough, but clearly critical of the bulldozing policies of the Cultural Revolution. It was the first negative comment I had heard since I arrived.
>
> —Jeff Vize, *Pigs in the Toilet (and Other Discoveries on the Road from Tokyo to Paris)*

The polyglot text is inscribed in long columns: 1,900 characters in Chinese, 50 words in Syrian, 72 names of Christian priests and functionaries in the old Estrangela script. The history it relates was composed in 781 A.D. by a local priest of the Da Qin monastery. His Chinese name is Ching-Ching; in Syrian, he is called Adam, pope of Zhinastan.

The story begins with an evocation of the Christian God, the "One who is true and firm, who, being Uncreated, is the Origin of Origins, who is ever Incomprehensible and Invisible, yet everywhere mysteriously existing to the Last of Lasts." The explication of doctrine on the Nestorian Stele employs phrases and concepts from a wide range of Chinese sources—Taoism, Buddhism, and the Confucian Classics—but the main thrust is clearly Christian.

The creation of the world recounted there recalls the account in *Genesis*; man is a fallen giant who in yielding to Satanic temptations suffers confusion and darkness; the Messiah who came to earth "took an oar in the Vessel of Mercy and ascended to the Palace of Light, whereby all rational beings were conveyed across the Gulf."

The priests and ministers of the Luminous Religion in China kept no slaves, accumulated no wealth, fasted frequently, worshipped seven times a day, and made a bloodless sacrifice once a week. They were bearded and bald. The first Nestorian missionary to reach the gates of the capital was Alopen. He was met by Duke Fang. The sutras he carried were translated, and the T'ang Emperor T'ai-Tsung studied the new faith in his "Forbidden Apartments." Convinced of its "correctness," the emperor issued an imperial decree. As copied out on the Nestorian Stele, it is a model of Chinese tolerance:

> The Way had not, at all times and in all places, the selfsame name; the Sage had not, at all times and in all places, the selfsame human body. Heaven caused a suitable religion to be instituted for every region and clime so that each one of the races of mankind might be saved. Bishop Alopen of the Kingdom of Da Qin [Christendom], bringing with him the sutras and images, has come from afar and presented them to our Capital. Having carefully examined the scope of his teaching, we find it to be mysteriously spiritual and of silent operation. Having observed its principal and most essential points, we reached the conclusion that they cover all that is most important in life. Their language is free from perplexing expressions; their principles are so simple that they remain as the fish would remain even after the nets were forgotten. This teaching is helpful to all creatures and beneficial to all men. So let it have free course throughout the Empire.

A Da Qin monastery was immediately built in the I-ning Ward of Xi'an; twenty-one priests were ordained there, and a portrait of the patron Emperor of Christianity in China was painted on its walls.

Succeeding emperors of the T'ang generally tolerated the Nestorians. Christian monasteries were built in every prefecture and province of the Middle Kingdom. With the ascension of the infamous Empress Wu, however, the Taoists were able to strike down their foreign rivals. For a generation, the altars of the Nestorian churches lay smashed. Not until 744 A.D., when a missionary named Chi-Ho reached Xi'an and converted the new emperor to the Nestorian Way, were the monasteries rebuilt. Then worshippers flocked to their Luminous Shrines which received royal tributes as great as "the highest peaks of the highest mountains in the south." They wore the shining feathers of the kingfisher and no longer looked or felt themselves foreign, but after a century in China, no one is left who is not very Chinese. Even the Jews who came here were absorbed utterly.

> I stood upon a hill in the ancestral burial ground, surrounded by a cluster of marble tombstones all sharing the same inscribed character for Ying, my family name. I, a member of the thirty-third generational Ying, knelt before the stone tablet of a seventh generational Ying. Six feet of dirt separated me from the distant-great grandfather who lived over a thousand years ago.
>
> —Chellis Ying, "The Chinese Way"

Royal favor rained upon the Christians for generations, and they gave their allegiance to the emperor. "The whole Universe receives life and light because of him," the Stele proclaims. And so the Nestorians settled themselves quietly and contentedly and firmly into the Chinese nation, worshipping at Xi'an for some 219 years until a single imperial edict, issued by Emperor

Wu-Tsung in 845 A.D., abruptly ended the progress of Christianity in China.

It is the reverse of the edict which welcomed the first Nestorians at the western gate two centuries earlier, and could have been penned by Chairman Mao:

> Wasting human labor (in building shrines); plundering the people's purse (to buy temple decorations); ignoring Imperial contributions (and decrees); neglecting both husband and wife (by requiring strange vigils)—no teaching is more pernicious.... How dare the insignificant Teaching of Western Lands compete with ours? Once established, these strange customs have been allowed to prevail far and wide, in a degenerate age, but now the people are soaked to the bone and the national spirit is unconsciously spoiled.

The masses were asked to help dispense justice: "We have finally decided to put an end to such conspicuous evils. Do ye, Our subjects, at home and abroad obey and conform to Our sincere will. If ye send in a Memorial suggesting how to exterminate these evils which have beset Us for many Dynasties, We shall do all We can to carry out the plan."

The plan of the people was simple—rehabilitation through labor: "As to those monks and nuns who teach the religions of foreign countries, we command that they return to secular life and cease to confuse our national customs and manners."

Eliminating all sources of spiritual pollution, China once again drew into itself: "More than a hundred thousand idle, lazy people and busybodies have been driven off, and numberless beautifully decorated useless temples have been completely swept away. Hereafter, purity of life shall rule Our people...."

The persecutions of 845 were extreme and thorough, a model of xenophobic action. By the end of the ninth century, it was said that only one Christian remained in China; the Nestorian Stele disappeared from the face of the earth.

✳

Eight centuries after the Great Persecutions, in about the year 1625, the Nestorian Stele was unearthed outside the city walls of Xi'an.

This discovery coincided with the reappearance of Christian missionaries in China. A few of them, primarily Jesuits, traveled through Xi'an during this period and saw the Nestorian Stele for themselves. The tablet was in superb condition, which suggests it had been buried since the end of the T'ang dynasty, like thousands of holy relics, for protection, then completely forgotten—as forgotten as the Christians of China.

The first rubbing of the Nestorian inscription was sent to Dr. Leon Li, a Chinese Christian living in Hangzhou; the first translation, into Latin, quickly followed. Meanwhile, the Stele was moved closer to Xi'an—to a Buddhist temple a mile outside the western gate. The Moslems razed this temple during the Islamic Revolt of 1862, but they did not touch the Nestorian Stele.

In the fall of 1907, workmen undertook to move it inside the city for the first time; the reason was the arrival of an art collector from the West. Rumor says he offered 3,000 taels for the stele and that he intended to ship it to the British Museum, where it would be placed beside the Rosetta Stone. The Governor of Shaanxi Province intervened; he ordered the stone to be hauled to the Temple of Confucius for safekeeping. A tortoise foundation was carved for it in the Forest of Steles. On October 2, 1907, the Nestorian Stele reached its present location.

The would-be purchaser of 1907 was actually a Dr. Frits Holm from Denmark. When he could not procure the original stele, he ordered a full-scale replica to be cut from limestone in Xi'an. Once cut, it had to be transported overland 350 miles in a special cart to what was then the nearest railway station, Chengchou. Red tape kept even the Nestorian Stele's replica in China for another year. On February 28, 1908, it was shipped from Shanghai and on June 16, it was deposited in the Metropolitan Museum of Art in New York City "as a loan." According to Dr.

Holm, the replica was an exquisite work in its own right, perhaps one of the last great steles crafted in China.

The Stele stands as much for the disappearance as for the arrival of Christianity in China. Francis Nichols, who saw the Nestorian monument in 1902, a few years before it was carried into the city proper, made the key observation in *Through Hidden Shensi* (1905):"Like every other foreign-born influence that has been left to itself to battle with the traditional conservatism of Shensi, the Christianity of the eighth century was simply dissolved in its environment as easily as the waters of a spring might lose themselves in the sands of the desert."

And within a few years, Nichols himself dissolved into the deserts of China, dying of pneumonia in southern Tibet eighteen months after he "left New York with the plan of penetrating Tibet to Lhasa, then still the mysterious and unvisited city." Nichols came within a hundred miles of Lhasa. He was my age exactly, thirty-six, when he died, and he found China pitiless.

I've been giving the Nestorian Stele plenty of thought this week, filing through old books. Rick Wacker's given me another translation of the Nestorian Stele. A friend has an oddball study he picked up in Japan. Nobody really cares what I discover, of course. They're just humoring me. Dr. Fu thinks I'm crazy. I've become a mole. Maybe that's what China means to make of me in the end.

Last night I reached some conclusions.

"Earlier in the year 1625," writes A. C. Moule, in *Christians in China Before the Year 1550* (1930), "perhaps about the beginning of March, trenches were being dug for the foundations of some building near the district town of Chou-chih, thirty or forty miles to the west of the city of His-an, when the workmen came upon a great slab of stone buried seven feet beneath the surface of the ground." It was the Nestorian Stele. According to the Chinese version, they were not digging a foundation but a grave that day. The governor's favorite child, a devout Buddhist, was about to be buried, and the child's spirit was believed to have guided the gravediggers to the holy monument.

Exactly where the Nestorian Stele was buried or where it stood in the eighth and ninth centuries, no one can say; but it was not within the walls of Xi'an. P. Y. Saeki, a Japanese scholar, has made the most detailed inquiry. He argues in *The Nestorian Documents and Relics in China* (1951) that the Stele first stood and was subsequently hidden in the ground southwest of Xi'an at Lou Guan Tai—specifically, on a middle slope in a place called Wu-chun, where in 756 A.D. the T'ang Emperor Su-tsung built a Nestorian monastery.

I don't doubt that Lou Guan Tai, by tradition the birthplace of Taoism in China, was also the location of a Nestorian monastery and, ultimately, the original site of the buried Stele. *The Topographical Book of Chou-chih*, written in 1563, certainly confirms the existence of a Nestorian monastery "in the middle of the hillside which forms a tableland of the Tower valley." Moreover, in the same place there also stood a pagoda, "an eight-cornered one, seventy- or eighty-feet-high, originally built by the imperial orders of Emperor T'ai-tsung," who welcomed the first Christian missionary to China. This is the leaning pagoda that I saw myself when I visited Lou Guan Tai. It predates the Nestorian Stele, to which it is intimately linked, by a full century.

In 1933, four Chinese scholars spent a night in the Taoist Temple at Lou Guan Tai. From there, according to Saeki, they happened to see below them "a Tower rising high into the sky at the foot of the hill." In the morning, they went down to it. A villager told them that the ruins around this pagoda had an old name—Da Qin Si. It was the Nestorian monastery—a temple complex of the Luminous Faith of Rome.

Not much was left, even in 1933; but an iron bell cast in 1444, which once hung from the western eaves of the monastery, contained an inscription confirming that the temple was built by order of the T'ang Emperor. The scholars also found a stone tablet describing a Throne of Buddha; in the eighteenth century, they point out, this monastery served as a Buddhist temple. In fact, the complex survived as long as it did only by undergoing various incarnations, serving as the vessel of successive religions after the

Nestorians disappeared, until there were no religions left. In this way, the pagoda might be said to represent the progress of all religions in China.

The chief remains of what was perhaps the first Christian monastery in China is the leaning pagoda at Lou Guan Tai. This is the only structure left. The scholars who visited there in 1933 were struck by its resemblance to the Great Wild Goose Pagoda in Xi'an. Farmers in the region believed that the Da Qin Pagoda was built of stone left over from the building of that most famous of all T'ang dynasty towers. Those scholars were also able to climb to the top despite the poor condition of the tower's interior. On the second story and the third, they saw clay images of Kuan-Yin, the Goddess of Mercy, in a style dating from the T'ang or Sung dynasty. On the seventh story, they made rubbings of the characters carved over the archways on the south and the west. These were later found to be Tibetan writings, including a six-character Lamaist charm.

All the faiths that once resided at Xi'an are entangled in the history of the Nestorian Stele, first erected in the shadow of this ruined tower of the T'ang; buried there in 845 A.D. when the Christians were expelled from their monasteries; forgotten after a few generations; rediscovered by the sheerest accident, in 1625, in the same way that, by happenstance, the First Emperor's treasures were returned to the surface in our time. What more do these loesslands conceal? Plenty, no doubt. Every block of this desolate plain is monumental.

A further odd note: On September 21, 1911, the Honorable Mrs. Gordon of Ireland caused a second replica of the Nestorian Stele to be placed upon the summit of Mt. Koya in Japan. It was on Mt. Koya that Kobo Daishi (Kang Hai), the pilgrim who came to Xi'an in 802, founded the monastery of Konga-buji upon his return to Japan in 816—and also where he preached the tenets of a new sect of Buddhism, Shingonbu. This became the largest Buddhist sect in Japan. The peak still attracts thousands of Japanese pilgrims each year. This is also the location of the Okuno-in Cemetery, where the dead by the thousands, emperors included, are buried in expectation of the coming of Miroku, a Buddhist Messiah. Within this messianic Buddhist cemetery—with its varied Xi'an connections—stands the reproduced Nestorian Stele, like a fetish.

There is only this to add: A certain pictorial stele at Xi'an is engraved with the journey of Emperor Hung Wu, founder of the Ming dynasty, up the holy peak of Hua Shan. Francis Nichols described this stele in these words:

> The picture of the sacred mountain, as it was indelibly stamped on Hung Wu's memory, was carved on a stone tablet in the yard of the temple at the base of the mountain. The white dotted line is the winding, difficult trail up the mountain-side. The figure of a man in the various stages of the ascent is Hung Wu in the garb of an ordinary pilgrim. The white spots represent the course of the rabbit which was the Emperor's guide in his dream-pilgrimage.

For me, history and heritage are what's important, and the city of Xi'an thinks so as well because it did take the time and the effort to preserve and reconstruct the city wall. Throughout the years, a number of bricks from the wall were looted for building projects and personal use. Some of those bricks became lost, some broken and unusable, but some were in surprisingly good condition. When the city decided to renovate the wall in 1984, it asked the residents of the city for those original bricks. The residents donated the usable ones back to the city, and as a reward their family names were carved on them and laid on the wall for all to see. But for those places that bricks cannot be found and replaced, concrete and new cement blocks lay next to the older bricks.

—Tina Zhang, "Biking the Xi'an City Wall"

It hasn't escaped my attention—holed up as I am in this vault with nothing but memory and cement—that it was on the slopes of Lou Guan Tai, returning

from the Da Qin Pagoda, that I chanced upon an old woman leading a rabbit by a string. No doubt it was the emperor's rabbit, sent
for me or at the very least, an odd coincidence of displacement
which, in the pagan mind, connects mountain to mountain, stone
to stone, making the ruins of these various religions one.

On my final visit to the Temple of Confucius and its Forest of
Steles, I enter at the south gate, a passage once reserved for the emperor and the number one scholar of the realm. I observe a rubbing master at work on a series of stone tablets.

The rubbing master is transcribing the stone carvings to inked
paper. Tamping with his wooden mallet until the tracing sheet is
firmly mounted, stripping off the scroll, then wrapping up his tools
with great care, he proceeds from commission to commission. I
merely follow. The tablets are jet black with rubbing ink, their in-
dented texts worn and defaced from centuries of copy. The process
has not changed in a thousand years, but demand has fallen off.
The mallets are often silent; most of the rubbings these days are
made in downtown Xi'an, a block north of the Friendship Store,
in a factory where metal forms of the original steles are used to
make impressions.

I move in tandem with the rubbing master. Twice a year, on the
fall and spring equinoxes, the Confucian gentlemen of old Xi'an
would slaughter a cow and sprinkle its hot blood on the altar that
once stood at the entrance to these grounds. During the Cultural
Revolution, their descendants passed by here in dunce caps, eyes
cast to the ground—Professor Zhong among them, perhaps. Those
fallen scholars might have had in mind their sage's dictum—to remain true to oneself in the era of a bad Prince—but there's a point
at which even a sage can't go on.

The rubbing master stops at the stele of Da Ma, the Buddhist
pilgrim to China. His hair in ringlets, his earlobes weighted down
with circular baubles, Da Ma contemplates a bowl of incense in the
shape of a cup of sake; instead of wearing his halo, he sits upon it.
Some say Da Ma introduced Buddhism to Japan; others say his

likeness is actually that of a Chinese Jew; a Jesuit missionary insists that Da Ma is Saint Thomas the Apostle in disguise. But all these identifications are pure piss-water. Good God, no apostle ever stood on this piece of earth, I'm sure of it.

Quite sure: Xi'an is too weighed down, too full of misery, to ever be a source of happiness. There's nothing on either side of the great screen now. Even on the other side there's only a blank stone without a single line of calligraphy on its face.

I hear the mallet in another room, pounding shoulder-high on a black plate.

J. D. Brown is the author of The Sudden Disappearance of Japan: Journeys Through a Hidden Land, *and* Digging to China: Down and Out in the Middle Kingdom, *which won a Lowell Thomas Travel Journalism Award, and from which this story was excerpted. He lives in Oregon.*

China's Unknown Gobi

On the Alashan Plateau, sand is both emperor and enemy.

GHOSTS LIVE HERE. THAT'S WHAT THE CHINESE SAY. THEY claim this place, a walled fortress abandoned in the fourteenth century and called Khara Khoto—Black City—is inhabited by demons and spirits. I understand why. Around me Khara Khoto is a haunting pile of drifted sand that partly covers its thirty-foot ramparts. Inside the city's walls lie ruins of a once vital kingdom. All that remains is shattered and tawny mud buildings crumbled long ago, scatterings of bleached bones unidentifiable with age, and smashed crockery pots and bowls. Granite millstones—their three-foot faces etched by lines seven centuries old—also sit half-buried in the sand.

In the slanting light of an October sunset the legend of the Black City's violent and bloody end spreads across the sand around me. The year was 1372, and the Mongol king Khara Bator—his people protected inside these walls, which were taken by Genghis Khan's Golden Horde in 1226—was witnessing the end of Mongolia's reign across Asia. Outside, the armies of China's ascendant Ming Dynasty were massing, and they'd employed the surrounding desert as their deadliest weapon. Diverting the Black River, the city's water source that flowed just outside the fortress, the Chinese denied Khara Khoto moisture for its gardens and wells. Then they simply waited.

As the Black City's thirst grew deadly, Khara Bator recognized his fate. Insane with fury, he murdered his family—then turned his sword upon himself. After his suicide Khara Bator's soldiers vainly continued inside Khara Khoto's fortress, weakening beneath the sun. When the Ming finally attacked, they slaughtered the remaining Mongols like livestock, leaving bodies unburied, the garrison sacked, and a stain of murder so dense on the sand it spawned the ghosts of today.

Walking from the walled city's center, I climb a sand dune inside Khara Khoto's fortifications to stand on the rampart's top. To the west the sun is touching the horizon. The day's tourists have gone, fearful of the ghosts and the hour-long drive across this rugged desert to the hotels of town.

Me? I'm staying.

In the night I'll walk the city's twelve-foot-thick outer walls—as much as 450 yards to a side—and doze beneath the stars. I'll listen to the stories of Wang Zegong, the seventy-year-old guard at Khara Khoto, who sleeps in a canvas tent outside these walls every night from April to December. He's witnessed the ghosts' doings: the fuel-less flames that burn for hours and rise ten feet into the night sky, the roving pool of light that arrives after midnight and that once led him miles into the desert, left him for lost, then—when he called out for help—returned and guided him back to his camp through the darkness.

"My favorite story is this," he tells me over a bowl of instant noodles. "One night I heard two logs colliding, again and again, outside my tent. *Bang! Bang! Bang!* So I got up, went outside, and there were two big firewood logs lying near each other on the sand, exactly where the noise had been coming from. They were logs from my firewood pile, which is on the other side of my tent. I had not moved them. They had not been there when I went to sleep—but they were there now."

If there are ghosts here, I want to know them. During my travels I've encountered many things on the verge of being haunted:

Ali told us about the djins, spirits of the desert. Travelers sometimes reported beckoning voices beyond the campfire's glow, just over a dune. They went out to investigate. Their tracks vanished and they were never heard from again. Twice in the deep desert, Ali's father had heard them. He believed. We huddled closer and piled more sticks on the fire.

Tusun pulled a small tape recorder from his bag and blew off the sand. The quality was bad, the recording scratchy. It was a famous imam reciting the Koran in Mecca. Ali and Abdul Rahim lay on their stomachs on the sand, hands propped under bearded chins. They listened intently for the feel of the words; their eyes seemed to wring meaning from the slowly turning reels of tape.

As the embers of the fire died and faded, the imam's wavering chant reverberated across our patch of dunes and into the empty desert night, frightening off the prowling djins that we all knew were out there.

—Ryan Murdock, "The Worst Desert in the World"

institutions and ways of life being abandoned by a China equally reverential of its past and hungry for its future. But actual ghosts?

So after dinner with Wang Zegong, I grab my headlamp and return inside Khara Khoto's walls. There I sit and wait for ghosts. Above me in the darkness, the bright pinprick of Venus slips toward the western horizon as constellations emerge. During the night a cold October wind rises to whip the corners of the ruins. But the ghosts never come. It is only me, sitting inside the ancient walls of a ruined city in the dark, pondering mankind's endless dance across these sands with time, events, and rain.

The Gobi isn't the world's largest desert (that's the Sahara) or its driest (the Atacama) or its most dramatically diverse with life (the Namib). Instead, it is Earth's northernmost desert and the least-populated environment outside the polar caps. And it possesses a record of human habitation that is among the longest on Earth. Straddling the boundaries of China and Mongolia, and at 500,000 square miles nearly twice the size of Texas, the Gobi is a place where often less than three inches of rain falls a year. In fact "Gobi" is a Mongolian word that means "waterless place." Geologists have tagged the word with a slightly more specific meaning. To them the word Gobi is shorthand for "gravel desert." And at this rocky, gale-scoured desert's heart, in the reaches of northern China, is the Alashan Plateau, a place so remote and sparsely inhabited it has scarcely figured in China's long history. Today it remains rarely visited owing to its status as a missile-testing zone for the Chinese military.

One recent fall, thanks to the goodwill of the Chinese Academy of Sciences and its Institute of Desert Research in Lanzhou—photographer George Steinmetz and I were given unprecedented access to the Alashan. During eight weeks of exploring by camel, on foot, by rail, and by road, we looked for human traces on the desert's surface. The Gobi expands and contracts, allowing people to press civilization inside during its wetter intervals, only to be driven out when the desert expands once again. Throughout these cycles, however, resourceful Mongol herdsmen, the descendants of Genghis Khan, have clung to the hard earth. To better understand the remnants of Mongol culture inside China was one of our aims. Today the desert is spreading, and for China's 1.26 billion people this is one of their gravest problems, so we also wanted to learn from the Alashan how the entire Gobi steals thousands of acres of farmland every year.

But as we begin, we're aiming beyond the Alashan's edges into its center. There, we've been told, we'll find the world's largest dunes: sand mountains that often top 1,200 vertical feet. Many are separated by valleys holding spring-fed lakes. This 17,000-square-mile zone of megadunes—the Badain Jaran, sometimes called the Miraculous Lakes—is unique in the world. Only one other Western group has ventured inside in modern memory, a 1995 expedition led by the German geologists Dieter Jakel and Jurgen Hofmann.

After a week of travel by aircraft and four-wheel drive, we arrive at the end-of-the-road town of Yabrai Yanchang to collect our string of twenty two-humped Bactrian camels and five horses. "Where we are going, we will need these camels," says our guide, Yue Jirigele, with a smile that reveals a gold-capped front tooth. Yue, forty-six, is a sturdy six feet tall, with a tanned and wind-creased face. He is a Mongol herdsman and the area's former mayor. He asks us to use his familiar name, Lao Ji. He shares some sweet, hard bread with us and says he lives amid the big dunes about twenty miles away. He has five children, ages eight to twenty-two.

Like all children attaining primary-school age in this isolated place, they spend the academic year at boarding schools outside the Badain Jaran and return home each summer. The best students among them are then allowed to continue beyond a government-mandated ninth grade to higher learning outside the Gobi. Lao Ji's oldest daughter, he's proud to add, is in college in Beijing—studying English.

"Did he himself leave the dunes to study?" I ask as we walk.

"No," Lao Ji says. "The new education policies in this part of China started with my children's generation. I was schooled at home—in the *ger* [Mongolian for yurt]—but not enough. I think it's good my children are being educated. My wife and I miss them, but education is the future...." He gestures toward his pack animals. "Not this."

For two days we press on, leading our loaded camels into yellow dunes that slowly—imperceptibly almost—rise taller. We camp near a few of the spring lakes, their water made salty by chlorides leached from the sand and left in high concentrations by evaporation. By the third day—carrying a canteen of water taken from beyond the Badain Jaran's edge—I've trudged up and down several steep dune passes that rise 800 to 1,000 feet. Sand is never easy walking, and climbing each dune's pitched face is exhausting. Sweat stings my eyes and soaks my shirt. Then, standing atop a dune on our third day, I turn to stare back at our progress and discover we've entered a vast sand mountainscape. Like a treeless Tirol, the sand mountains are draped in a dozen shades of saturated yellow beneath a clear blue sky.

Standing in the pass with me is Dong Zhibao, one of two Ph.D.s on the expedition from the Institute of Desert Research. A friendly, lighthearted geomorphologist of thirty-five, he plans to study these 1,200-foot dunes and publish a paper on his findings. "What we are seeing here, these megadunes," Dong says, "is the result of very specific factors. Things that could only happen here."

Dong reaches down and lifts a handful of clean yellow sand. "These sand grains are coarse and very uniform in size," he continues. "This allows spaces to be created between them, spaces capable of trapping drops of water, which allows plants to grow."

Over time, as the plant roots stabilize the sand, each plant helps fix the dune, while blown sand and newer dunes roll over the tops of existing megadunes. These new dunes are then held in place by the plants beneath, and revegetation begins on the new top layer.

Like a bed thick with quilts of Velcro, the megadunes have seen successive fresh covers for millions of years. "At the interior of each megadune," says Dong, "you may have a dune four to forty million years old—though a precise age has yet to be determined. But no matter how old the base of a megadune is, its top layer, its newest feature, may be only one year old. It's a complex process. Layer on layer on layer, requiring time and the area's characteristic mix of sand and rain."

On the afternoon of our third day we crest the top of another megadune pass, and below us sits a bowl-shaped valley. At the valley's northern end, fringed in rich green grasses and reeds, there's a small lake so saturated with salt-loving bacteria that its color is glittering vermilion. Sheep and goats drift across the dune hillsides, eating the sagebrush-like artemisia that grows on them. Camels and a few horses graze near the lakeshore. And at the far end of the lake, all alone, sits a pair of small square blockhouses.

We trudge down the dune, surprising the lady who lives in the valley. Her name, Lao Ji tells us, is Diudiu, and she's seventy-two. She was born to a semi-nomadic Mongolian family near here. She never had children, and her husband died in 1974, leaving her as the last of her family.

Birds appeared to be riding the currents above the snowy summit; I continued on as effortlessly as hot air rising. And sure enough the updrafts had swept the desert floor clean, and my seagulls, seemingly in pursuit of higher truth, turned out to be swirling debris, yesterday's newspapers flapping their pages. Had I known that the beacon for the great beyond was a lodestone for litter, and that I was not looking at birds but garbage—well, I would have gone back to my beer before I reached this point of no return, high in the grainy saddle, looking out upon mile after mile of rolling swells, cresting to an altitude of a thousand feet or more. And so I continued to climb the cascading incline, until reaching the summit, about 1,500 feet. How do you measure a mountain of shifting sand? I looked upon the Jade Gate, and gazing upon the phantasmagoria of the phantom Lake of Lop and across the infinitude of the Taklimakan Desert, I had some feeling for the fools who passed this way before me.

—Antonio Cammarata,
*Unraveling on the Old Silk Road:
Hitchhiking China and Beyond*

With the same hospitality we'll find across the entire Badain Jaran, Diudiu sets up for visitors. She goes inside her house and fills a tea kettle with water from a small cistern, then walks outside to a mirrored solar collector the size of a TV satellite dish. At the dish's center, where the rays of the sun will be focused, Diudiu snaps the kettle into an iron fitting, then she pivots the dish to face the afternoon sun. In seconds the kettle is smoking. Within three minutes, the water is boiling furiously. "I sold hair from my camels and sheep to buy this on the outside," she says, turning the mirrored face of the dish from the sun to retrieve the kettle. "It keeps me from having fire going all day."

Diudiu invites me inside her house. A wide earthen platform for sleeping and sitting occupies the back wall. The other walls are lined with wooden pantries and lockers; the boxes hold bags of rice and dried meat, a few potatoes and wild onions in baskets, and some extra clothes. In a corner a stack of folded blankets waits for winter. There's a small hole in the roof for the chimney of Diudiu's potbellied Mongolian stove, which is now outdoors for summer cooking.

She sprinkles dried tea into the kettle's hot water, then pulls out drinking bowls and a bowl of rock sugar. "Come and drink," she says, motioning for me to sit.

Diudiu is four feet tall and dressed in loose trousers and a button-front jacket, both of blue cotton. Her black hair is covered with a bandanna, her dark eyes sharp and quick. She has a wide Mongolian face—broad planes of cheekbones—which has weathered into a map of wrinkles.

I gesture toward a cliff swallow's nest that clings to the interior front wall, above the door. Diudiu smiles. "I like birds in the house," she says. "They're good company."

Spending the next few days with Diudiu, I will see that she possesses everything she needs. Though winter can get cold, as cold as -30 degrees Fahrenheit, she is prepared and experienced against it. Outside the house there's a sheep and goat pen whose four-foot-tall walls are made of camel dung wetted and pressed into bricks. In winter these bricks, which burn hot, warm her house and provide cooking fire. She also eats four or five sheep each winter, deep-freezing what she doesn't need by hanging the butchered carcass in a shady spot outdoors.

Following an hour or so of visiting, Diudiu goes outside. She fires up her stove and boils a pot of rice. In a wok she stir-fries potatoes and wild onions. Then she walks into her house, opens one of two large ceramic cisterns, and dips an eight-ounce plastic water bottle inside. "Rice wine," she says. "Have some?"

Diudiu produces some thimble-size glasses and pours the wine. Luckily the cups are small, since the wine is powerful and goes down like kerosene. One of these cisterns, she says, is fully fermented. The other is in the process of fermenting, so there's always a supply of wine. "I drink one of these bottles a day," she says. "It's my recreation."

Slipping back outside, Diudiu checks the rice. Night is starting to fall. The first stars peek out. She lifts the food, carrying it inside the house to her small table. "See? I have everything," she says. "I don't understand the outside world. I know only eating, drinking, tending animals. This is what my parents did. Their parents. The young people today, once they leave the Badain Jaran, they never return. I don't blame them. The old life of herding is coming to an end. Work in cities is the future. But for me, I will live in this place until I die."

During two weeks in the Badain Jaran, I will meet several solitary men and women—most are sixty- to seventy-year-old herders—an aging population still living a tradition that stretches back to a time before Genghis Khan. But I also pass as many abandoned encampments as occupied ones. During my visit, in fact, I will find only two people younger than Lao Ji's forty-six years. One, a government official and radio operator at a small outpost near the desert's remote center, is thirty-six years old; he talks longingly of leaving, the way a man dying of thirst speaks of water. The other young person, a three-year-old child, the afterthought of a middle-aged herding family, is still too young to be sent away to school "outside." Other than that, the youth of the Alashan, it appears, never return home after going off to school. Everyone I speak with agrees: The future is not among these unforgiving dunes and valleys.

But as the people of the Badain Jaran work and dream of escaping the desert, Chinese scientists are puzzling out how to stanch the desert's steady growth. According to the Institute of Desert Research, land degradation costs the nation 6.7 billion dollars a year and affects the lives of 400 million people. Current estimates say that 950 square miles of land becomes desert every year—a 58 percent increase since the 1950s—much of it land that formerly supported crops and livestock. In a nation of more than a billion people, all of whom have adequate amounts of food but many of whom need better nutrition, such enormous losses are potentially devastating.

"Most desertification is due to increasing human population," says Wang Tao, acting director of the institute. "Increasing the number of people in an area places incremental pressure on land through farming, construction, road building, and other human activity. Add to this increasing water use and slight fluctuations in larger weather systems, and depletion of soil nutrients and desertification quickly become problems demanding great consideration."

Since 1956, beyond their laboratories and offices in Lanzhou, the institute has operated a research station a half day's drive away in the little town of Shapotou, along the Yellow River and about 250 miles southeast of the Badain Jaran dunes. At the research station scientists and visiting colleagues experiment with different ways to stem drying and erosion by wind and water. They also develop new crops suitable for the desert, look into ways to preserve soil richness in China and beyond, and use a wind tunnel and banks of optical-scanning computers to study the movement of blown sand.

A few days after we emerge from the dunes of the Badain Jaran—saying a sad goodbye to Lao Ji and his camel train—I visit the station with the geomorphologist Dong Zhibao. The station itself covers more than a square mile on the side of a steeply pitched dune that traces the Yellow River's northern bank. Today the station is a tilting garden plot in what must be one of the world's most dramatic locations. To our southwest, across the river, the rocky peaks of the Tibetan Plateau jut into a cloudless sky; and just beyond the northern edge of the complex, separated by a railroad line bordered with vegetation, spread the dunes of the Tengger Desert, another district of the Alashan.

In Chinese, *shapotou* means "steep dune slope." And initially, Dong says, the research station was placed here on a temporary basis to study the desert's dangerous relationship with the railroad. Dunes would blow across the tracks, halting trains and interrupting commerce. Within weeks, though, scientists had conjured an inexpensive remedy. They arranged grids of straw in roughly one-by-one-yard checkerboards along the rail lines; then they drove the straw into the sand, leaving the stalks standing four to six inches above the ground, which created a low windbreak. This slows blown sand grains at the rail tracks, allowing plants to gain a foothold and fix the dunes.

Owing to its success at halting the desert here, the Chinese government decided to make the temporary base a permanent post. Since then the research station has forged partnerships with the United Nations and countries as disparate as Japan and Israel to explore erosion and desertification. Inside the labs, greenhouses, garden plots, and erosion test zones, nineteen full-time personnel and a phalanx of visiting scientists push desert study forward. "We do a lot here," says Dong as we walk past greenhouses growing new hybrid strains of arid-soil melons. Ahead is a mile-long "reintroduction garden," where the station tests varieties of trees, shrubs, and annual grasses for desert suitability.

Dong pauses to touch the leaves of a ten-foot-tall European poplar. "Vegetation is probably the best and least expensive way of controlling dune movement and wind erosion," he says. "But you have to find out which plants can survive in which environments. Take these poplars. They're resistant to wind, salty soils, and salty groundwater. That makes them very suitable for deserts and windbreaks."

Despite the garden's being initially set on sandy desert, the soil is now loamy dirt: a result of using silty Yellow River water for irrigation. The water may sink into the earth or evaporate, but the silt has stayed behind.

"This place is proof you can make a desert bloom," Dong remarks. "But we are careful, making sure we test and approve many different varieties of plants and grasses. If you only O.K. a few species for use, you are vulnerable to blights or parasites that could destroy everything again and return useful land to desert. Plant biodiversity is insurance against that."

We keep walking. A robust vineyard and orchard blanket a hillside within the station's brick walls. To the west are experimental rice fields. "Growing rice in the desert isn't advised, too wasteful in water," says Dong. On some sandy black hillsides they are testing new petroleum-based sprays for sand fixing. "It's still too expensive for general application," he says. "And not very environmentally sound."

Ahead, inside a steel fence topped by barbed wire, is the station's Drip Irrigation Center. A joint Chinese-Israeli project, it has developed a stingy, drop-by-drop irrigation system using hoses punctured with tiny holes every few feet to irrigate desert-friendly fruits and vegetables.

As we step through the gate, the center's curator, Zhao Jinlong—a sixtyish man wearing dusty gardener's clothes—meets us. While the other gardens seemed lush, they are paled by the fruits and vegetables inside this fence: watermelons, apples, green onions, cucumbers, corn, hot peppers, honeydews, bell peppers, radishes, carrots, cabbage, soybeans, pears, tomatoes, squash, spinach, cilantro.

"I turn on the irrigation three and a half hours a day," Zhao says. "And by planting seeds just beneath the perforations in these hoses, we save 90 percent of water used each day. Usual irrigation, with canals and ditches, is very inefficient. Evaporation. Runoff. A large percentage of irrigation water never reaches where it is directed." The center's drip system uses 800 gallons a day, a saving of roughly 7,200 gallons. Conventional irrigation, Zhao says, also makes land prone to erosion. "So though it requires larger initial investments, drip irrigation is clearly a much less expensive way to farm for the long term."

Dong reaches down and plucks a few tomatoes from a nearby bush. He hands me one. It is wet and saturated with tomato taste, far tastier and meatier than tomatoes I buy in the United States. "Because drip irrigation is so consistent, the quality of produce is very high," he says. "Over time, look for these techniques to be implemented in China's arid regions and beyond."

Dong steps away, popping some ripe apples from a drip-irrigated tree. "Here," he says, handing me a large, red, shiny apple as I finish the tomato. "You are eating the future."

To see what may be China's most desertified place, Steinmetz and I head north to the desiccated city of Ejin Qi, hard against the

Mongolian border and near the shores of two dry lakes. According to Dong and Qiao Maoyuan, director of water resources for Ejin Qi, about 1.5 inches of precipitation falls on the area each year, while evaporation occurs at a rate of about 150 inches a year. "So as you can see," says Dong, "this area of the desert has significant water-related problems."

To get to Ejin Qi is a demanding 400-mile overland trip: three days across dry desert valleys and through jagged mountain passes. Unlike the Badain Jaran and Tengger deserts to our south, the northern part of the Alashan has been raked by relentless winds off the steppe to the north, leaving exposed rock everywhere. There is little water, so few herdsman live here. Despite long hours behind the wheel, we are lucky to find one lonely encampment a day. Only when we get within about 50 miles of Ejin Qi do we encounter dunes again, great rolling pillows of sand. Here the sand covers roads and devours telephone and electric lines as it blows south from the deserts of Mongolia toward the megadunes of the Badain Jaran.

In Ejin Qi we find a city of 14,000 that is vital and new and full of young people. There are fresh tile sidewalks and pin-neat shops. There is work in construction, in engine repair, in making and selling goods and clothing. In the cafés and restaurants and movie theaters everyone, it seems, is carrying a cellular telephone.

Ejin Qi has always been surrounded by desert, but a drought in recent years has brought such diminishing returns to farming that civic leaders have now gone capitalist, turning a raptor's eye toward a new, tourism-based economy. Our visit happens to coincide with the area's first cultural heritage festival, a tourist-minded event honoring the native Mongolians who settled the area and are now a minority as China's Han majority floods in. As the four-day celebration unfurls, it too is active and bright and well put-together, with traditional Mongolian dances, demonstrations of Mongolia's traditional wrestling, horsemanship, and archery. There is food: bubbling mutton kebabs seared over red-hot braziers. There is drink: hot tea and Coke, strong rice wine, and the ever-present tall green bottles of warm Chinese beer. In the lilting and clipped tones of the Mongolian language, songs are sung—usually about the toughness of the Mongolian horse— often accompanied by dancing troupes of Mongolian men and women dressed in traditional red robes bound by sashes around their waists. The festivities all take place in a pavilion beneath towering, golden-leaved poplars.

While I enjoy the festival, the locals are thrilled with its effect on the town. The hotels and restaurants are full, and, caught up in the party, natives and visitors alike spend money freely. Ironically the only people in Ejin Qi not attending are the area's few remaining farmers: Mongolians whose fields are close enough to underground water sources to irrigate crops from wells.

At one farm near the festival pavilion, inside a shady grove of poplars, a thirty-seven-year-old Mongolian woman named De Qiqige and her husband and seventeen-year-old son occupy the *ger* where she was born. Dressed in gray trousers and a white sweater, she invites Dong, Steinmetz, and me inside for a cup of tea. While theirs is a traditional Mongolian house, it is not one Lao Ji would recognize back in the Badain Jaran. The satellite television on one wall is flashing a Jackie Chan movie. In the kitchen area is a gas stove and electric appliances.

"We live between two worlds these days," De Qiqige says. "I love many of the modern things, but some things this new population is bringing, I do not like. At all."

The drought in this part of the Alashan, she says, began in 1982. "They were diverting the rivers upstream for irrigation, and one day there was simply no more water in the river. It dried up." De Qiqige sips her tea. In the years since she was a child, the grasses have disappeared, she says. Their land cannot support the 300 sheep and goats it used to. Now they have only 200 animals, and government officials have suggested her family cut the herd to 100 or less.

"The government is talking about relocating us, too. Away from this place where my father lived his entire life, away from where I was born. I have no argument with the people upriver who have taken the water. They get their water before me. They are trying to make the best farm they can. But my land is dying. The river is dry. The livestock are weak. Soon we will be gone. Like Khara Khoto we will be destroyed after being weakened by thirst. I'll show you."

Putting down her tea, De Qiqige leaves the *ger*. She begins walking up a hillside behind her house; the hill's powdery dirt makes puffs beneath her shoes. We come over the hilltop. Ahead of us, a small tractor is pushing dirt around an equally dusty field. I can barely see the machine through the gritty clouds. "That is my husband," De Qiqige says. "He is preparing this ground for next year. We are digging a new well in the middle of this field, to irrigate it. It will cost all of our savings to do this. If we have a bad harvest next year, we could lose everything."

De Qiqige's husband won't talk. He's too busy, he says. But I sense desperation; I can see it in his eyes. I also realize I'm standing inside the Institute of Desert Research's statistics: 400 million Chinese affected by encroaching desert each year, 950 square miles of land gone.

"So this is desertification?" I ask Dong.

As he did back in the Badain Jaran, Dong stops walking and reaches down. He picks up a handful of powdery dirt and lets it sift through his fingers. "This is it," he says. "No nutrients. Nothing to bind this soil together. This is land falling into desert. Very bad."

Ahead of us, at the far side of the field, the river lies empty. We walk to its bank, then look down to see sand where water should be. Trees line the shoreline, their leaves red and gold at the height of autumn's color. I step nearer the edge of the steeply cut bank, which plummets a dozen feet to the dry river's floor.

"There you are." De Qiqige says. "We are becoming Khara Khoto."

Where fish should be swimming, a six-inch lizard—colored the same pale brown as the dry riverbed—scrambles across the sand. It pauses, curling its tail into a tight loop, then darts beneath a flat rock.

Donovan Webster's work has appeared in major American publications including The New Yorker, The New York Times, Smithsonian, *and* National Geographic. *He is the author of* Aftermath: Cleaning Up a Century of World War, *and he lives with his wife and family outside Charlottesville, Virginia.*

PATRICK JENNINGS

✯ ✯ ✯

The Wheat Was Ripe
and It Was Sunday

*In Shanxi Province, the seasons
reveal life to the visitor.*

Since entering northern China more than two months ago I've been watching the countryside shed its winter gray cloak to reveal the green, green springtime color. The winter wheat progressed from scattered seedlings to a lush carpet of long grass. Then the grain itself began to plump, changing the texture of the fields. This past week the grassy green gradually began browning and yesterday it seemed everywhere the landscape had been lightly toasted to a honey hue. Harvest was imminent.

Today, cycling away from Huo Zhou with the sun breaking through the previous day's smoggy shroud and the worst of the smokestack forest withdrawing, I am treated to something special. In the fields peasants stoop to sever wheat stalks with short sickle strokes. Stalks are bundled and stacked on all manner of vehicle on two, three, or four wheels pulled by horsepower, manpower, or mulepower.

Cycling through this scene reminds me of a favorite short story by Sinclair Ross, "Coronet at Night." The story's first line reads, "The wheat was ripe and it was Sunday." Ross was a Canadian contemporary of John Steinbeck who, like Steinbeck, wrote extensively about the plight of dust-bowl era plains life, though his were the Canadian plains.

In "Coronet at Night," Ross explores conflict between the practicalities of farm life and the imposition of "civilizing" structures on human interaction. The story's opening line perfectly expresses this conflict which manifests in the struggle between the pragmatic father and the upright mother to influence their son's understanding of the world. The father wins the short-term battle, sending the young son into town (a rite of passage) on a Sunday to find laborers. But the son brings back an unemployed and destitute musician, useless as a farm hand but whose lilting coronet, issuing from the hand's barracks that night, leaves a lasting impression on the boy, and even the father. There must be a place for this impractical beauty amongst all the necessity.

And so I wonder while rolling and crackling through the prone wheat what day this is and am pleased to discover from my wristwatch that it is, indeed, Sunday. A smile, and a quick acknowledgment that life on the Canadian prairies early in the twentieth century, in appearance so different, the underlying essentials remain the same, and still do, and always will.

In Chapter 1 of the *Analects*, Confucius said, "If you would govern a state of a thousand chariots [a small-to-middle-size state], you must pay strict attention to business, be true to your word, be economical in expenditure and love the people. You should use them according to the seasons." Using the people "according to the seasons" refers to the unwise practice of some tyrants who pressed the farmers into public works labor when the harvest was in.

And while I'm thinking about all this, the tremendous loads of wheat shimmy their way to some available strip of highway and are there dumped along the roadside. Pitchforks break and spread the bundles across the throughway's width so that coal trucks and buses and Volkswagen Santanas drive through, crackling the husks like blister wrap underfoot.

A few simple threshers perform this same function on the larger fields, preening the wheat kernels from their housing much more quickly. But more efficiently? Perhaps not in a country where human sweat can be had so cheaply.

And so the peasants wield their pitchforks again, lifting sun-bleached stalks and their liberated husks from the honey hued wheat-fruit lying below. Straw brooms sweep the kernels and chaff into piles where they are lifted into the air in shovelfuls. Chaff flits away in the breeze, softly glittering in the warm sun. Again and again the simplest of methods filters fruit from refuse, then wooden rakes spread the piles into long rectangular beds a centimeter deep, occupying a third of the highway's width. A line of rocks wards off the now unwelcome traffic squeezing through the narrow lane remaining. And there lie the result of a month's labor basking in the afternoon sun while the laborers seek the tree-lined shade.

Third-world people utilize the roadways for more than the purpose of transportation. It seems such an oddity to a Westerner, but this is a perfect and ingenious saving of labor. I crackle a few husks beneath my tires and feel a bit like a contributor. The Volkswagen Santanas squeeze toward the shoulders, trying to keep at least two tires on pavement. The evasive tactic is futile. Streaming stalks cling to their undercarriages like the bristles of a brush.

Nearing Linfen, the day's destination, hunger overtakes me and I stop for *miantiao* and a *pijiu*, a bowl of noodles and bottle of beer. Just five yuan. I think about the work still ahead of the peasants. The grain to be gathered up again then milled. Two small stone disks and then a mule or a human drives one stone's chiseled surface across the stationary surface of another, circling, circling, grinding the seed fed between to a powder. And from the powder, my *miantiao* or the steamed bread called *mantou*, a staple of northern China.

The day ends in Linfen where a bathtub awaits, and a laundry service for my exhausted and coal-sodden clothing supply. In the evening, after a rest, I leave the hotel for a walk. The town is alive with night food markets, streetside karaoke, and something unique to Linfen: streetside teahouses where the locals recline on lawn chairs ostensibly to sip tea from the small tea sets at their tables. Like the coffee served by the better street cafés of the West, tea is only an excuse to gather and jabber, to watch the world parade by, to pass the time and to be seen. I hope this catches on and spreads through China because nowhere else have I found anything like it. I have sorely missed such places to linger for a while and watch the grand parade. All the night needs is a coronet...or a *suona*, the Chinese equivalent.

Patrick Jennings was conceived on a Mediterranean beach, delivered on an RCAF air base in West Germany, and raised in the USA. Always, and only, a Canadian, he was not so much born to travel as born traveling. In 1994, he traded in Microsoft stock options and headed for the far corners of the earth for a five-year sojourn. He now lives in Vancouver and spends his time as a travel photographer, writer, and playwright.

TIM WARD

Buddha's Sex Change?

In the time of Deng, you could see the evolving
shape of modern China.

I ARRIVED IN CHINA WITH THE INTENTIONS OF VISITING THE
Four Holy Mountains of Buddhism. Once the largest Buddhist nation on earth, China had been converted by revolution to the
communist ideal of heaven on earth, foretold as inevitable by the
great prophet Karl Marx. It seemed ironic that foreign philosophy
from neighboring India had been so thoroughly supplanted by a
foreign philosophy from the neighboring Soviet Union. During
the Cultural Revolution, Buddhist temples had been desecrated,
sacred texts burned, and monks and scholars humiliated, expelled,
and forced to do menial labor as punishment for their counter-
revolutionary crimes. A few remote temples had survived, while
others were being restored under Deng Xiaoping's new freedom-
of-religion policy. I wanted to discover how the Buddha's message
had come to flourish so richly in ancient China—and whether or
not it would survive in the Glorious People's Republic.

The first Holy Mountain of my pilgrimage was Putuo Shan, a
tiny island off the coast of Shanghai in the East China Sea. On the
ferry ride to the island I met two Hangzhou businessmen, Han and
Li. They wore shapeless gray suits with woolen vests and imita-
tion-leather coats. Both smoked cigarettes furiously. Li's thumb

and forefinger had turned yellow from tobacco, and his teeth were brown. Han was several years younger, in his early twenties, with a wide, innocent face. Both had come to the island for a three-day holiday, which was their year's vacation. They talked the receptionist at the island's main temple-hotel into letting me share a four-bed dormitory room with them. After three weeks in China, this was my first night outside a tourist hotel. Usually, Chinese hotel clerks insisted that foreigners stay in the most expensive private rooms for about twenty-five dollars a night. It was a struggle as I traveled from Hong Kong into Canton [now called Guangzhou], north to Hangzhou, and then east to the port city of Ningbo, to figure out how to get into the three-dollar dormitory rooms that hotels had but seldom offered to foreigners. The clerks would flatly deny such rooms existed, with the all-purpose word *meiyou*, which meant either "there aren't any" or "I can't be bothered with you," depending on the context. If I persisted, they would tell me to go across town to another hotel, which, when I arrived, would then deny it had dorms and send me back to the place I'd just left. It was a relief not to have to haggle, for once, for a cheap, cold room with a concrete floor, tin wash basins, and a thermos of hot water for washing and for making tea. The communal toilets at the end of the hall consisted of a long tiled trench, partitioned into stalls, that one had to straddle to use. Every now and then a sudden gush of water would flush the length of the trench, sluicing it clean. I quickly learned to use the front of the trench, where I was spared the view of other people's feces flowing past beneath my feet.

Since my new comrades had only a day and a half left before the long trip back to their work units, they wanted to tour the whole island at once. At the hotel desk, I'd picked up a brochure that announced: "And now, like a resplendent pearl embedded in the East China Sea, Mount Putuo with its hills and seas, magnificent temples and splendid historic relics, is attracting more and more tourists at home and abroad." We soon discovered that most of the historical relics were in the process of being rebuilt, having been razed during the Cultural Revolution. It appeared that the reconstruction had been done to accommodate the heavy domestic tourist trade. Our dormitory had been built inside a large monastic complex. A shrine room nearby had been restored as a gift shop; another held an art museum. Up the central peak of Putuo, another temple had become a fancy government resort for Communist Party members only. Although the weather was so cold that we had to keep our hands in our pockets, the temples and mountain walks were jam-packed with Chinese visitors, most of them in large tour groups. They inspected the sites briefly, had their picture taken, then shuffled along.

Climbing up one of the main pilgrimage routes, we passed several large boulders with rectangular gouges up to several inches deep in their sides. Inside or next to some of the gouges, giant Chinese characters had been carved into the rocks, the strokes freshly painted red and black. My pamphlet explained that wise Buddhist sayings had been carved in the rocks centuries ago. But these cuts seemed quite fresh. I queried my companions about the writing and the gouges, and caught the words "Cultural Revolution" in Li's response, but could make no sense of it.

> This Countrie may bee said to excell in these particulers: Antiquity, largenesse, Ritchnesse, healthynesse, Plentifullnesse. For Arts and manner of governmentt I thinck noe Kingdome in the world Comparable to it, Considered alltogether.
>
> —Paul Mundy, *Travels in Europe and Asia* (1637)

From the summit we could see the green islands of the Zhoushan archipelago dotting the gray sea. Ocean traffic snaked in and out between them: small fishing boats, tankers, freighters, navy cruisers, weathered junks with great ribbed canvas sails. Gazing down onto the far side of the island, I noticed a large fenced-off naval base with a submarine and four warships moored at the pier, which the tourist brochure had neglected to mention. By the end of the afternoon we had toured four temples, hiked two pilgrims' routes, and feasted on the island's delicacy, salted crab. Our final destination for the day was the island's largest monastery at the far side of Thousand Pace Beach. This historic relic was in the process of being rebuilt from the paving stones up. Piles of lumber lay inside the main courtyard, where three separate work crews labored. The yellow-tiled roofs glinted, newly glazed. The painted beams and wall frescoes shone with fresh shellac. Even the red mouth of the fat laughing Buddha in the first shrine room looked as if a fresh coat of lipstick had been applied that day. I'd been so accustomed to associating Buddhist temples with dust, must, and decrepitude that the spanking new temple struck me as a spiritual Disneyland. Bored monks sold admission tickets and guarded the temple statues. The restaurant and souvenir shop buzzed with brisk business. Half a dozen photographers took group shots of Chinese holiday-makers posing on the temple steps beside great urns of burning incense.

The tourists, all clad in their Mao caps and unisex suits of navy or gray, swarmed through the monastery buildings. Some posed on the great twin lions that guarded the entrance to one shrine. They gazed, chattered, and pointed at the great gilded statues of Buddha, three stories high, and the garish plaster statues of Chinese bodhisattvas that lined the walls like a gallery of saints. In the main temple hall, kneeling cushions had been set out for pilgrims. I'd watched monks and a few old Chinese do ritual triple bows to the statues on these cushions, but young tourists grew strangely skittish before them. A few would drop down, do a quick bob, then jump up again, laughing over-loudly with their friends. Flirting with religion, the opiate of the masses, seemed to have the same appeal as experimenting with illicit drugs. The young people seemed pulled to the great golden images, yet they also looked confused and embarrassed, glancing around to see who might have caught them in the act.

In the center of the main courtyard, a craggy-limbed ornamental pine had been recently transplanted to a tiny bed of earth in the concrete floor. Barbed wire was strung around the lower limbs and trunk to discourage tourists from using it as a photography prop. A sign in bright red characters was nailed to the tree. I imagined it read: "Keep off or get shot," or something similarly subtle. It seemed to convey the real message behind the government's new approach to freedom of religion. The reconstructed temples were meant to be a peep show into the past, not places for touching or handling. A relic, after all, is something dead, embalmed, and preferably on display behind barbed wire.

Those in power had learned something from the Cultural Revolution: destroying temples builds resistance. A textile worker I had befriended in the port of Ningbo on my way to Putuo told me the people had lost faith in Communism when political struggle began to take precedence over food and family. At that time, people learned to revise their public lives almost on a daily basis in order to stay politically correct. The worker told me that many Chinese secretly turned to Buddhism or even Christianity to give them hope, since heaven on earth seemed so greatly postponed. Perhaps it was to counter this growing addiction to religion that Deng Xiaoping's government had legalized the drug. Encouraging Chinese to sightsee holy places as if they were cultural amusement parks, to have their pictures taken beside the Buddhas and have tour guides obscure the sacred with a blanket of information—this exorcises faith far more effectively than gutting temples and torturing believers.

Li and Han insisted we get our picture taken together. A young photographer strode across to meet us the moment we looked his way. He had broad shoulders and a handsome tanned complexion. Rough-looking, like a country peasant, his eyes were surprisingly sharp and intelligent behind his battered plastic spectacles.

"How do you do? I hope you are having a pleasant time on Mount Putuo," he said to me with a trace of a British accent.

His name was Zhou. He was a medical student from Shanghai, working as a photographer to make money during the school break. He handed around cigarettes, which Han and Li accepted with broad smiles. As an ardent admirer of American literature, Zhou said he was delighted to make my acquaintance. He invited me to eat lunch with him the following evening. I gladly accepted.

"Say cheese," said Zhou, and took our picture.

The next afternoon I shook hands goodbye with Han and Li and was left alone in my dormitory cell. A morning drizzle had turned to cold sleet, so I stayed indoors with all my warm clothes on and practiced Chinese calligraphy with a brush and black ink I had bought at the temple gift shop. Zhou arrived with several textbooks under his arm: Marxist interpretations of English literature. He told me he had already completed a degree in English, but had gone on to study medicine at his mother's insistence. Professors of English may end up in jail again, she had warned him, but doctors will always be useful.

The next term he would graduate as a radiologist, but outside of class, Zhou studied English, played the piano, worked on his photography, and listened to European classical music. He said he hoped one day to visit the West and eventually translate works of American literature into Chinese.

"How does your mother feel about that?" I asked.

"Well, her father was an English translator of books, and a businessman. That's one of the reasons our family was sent to the countryside during the Glorious Cultural Revolution. We had a hard time for many years. So maybe she's proud of me and maybe she's afraid. I tell her, yes, I can be a radiologist now. But I don't want to. I want to be a translator for the good of my health. You see, radiologists get a lot of exposure to X-rays…"

"Don't you have lead shields to protect you?"

"No."

We agreed that in exchange for English lessons, Zhou would instruct me in Chinese calligraphy, language, and history. He examined my primitive attempts at writing with a brush, pointing out where I had drawn the strokes in an incorrect order. He wrote out a poem for me in Grass-Style calligraphy. His blunt peasant hands, their nails bitten to the skin, moved with grace and swiftness down the page, completing each complex line without lifting his brush from the paper. A great master of the art had been Zhou's private tutor during the Cultural Revolution.

"Actually, I owe my entire education to Chairman Mao, who banished my family to the countryside," he said.

The sleet stopped. We left the temple and walked to the shore of Thousand Pace Beach, while Zhou told me the story of his life during the years of chaos. He said that at first, Mao's call to build a new China and a new culture inspired the people to work together selflessly. Intellectuals, said Mao, were arrogant and privileged. They had forgotten how peasants lived. His decision to send them to the countryside to work alongside farmers showed great wisdom, as did the decision to put working-class people in charge of hospitals, universities, and government administration. But before long, the social jumbling became less a way of educating intellectuals than of punishing them.

"Because my grandfather was a wealthy businessman, our family was sent into the countryside to starve," said Zhou. "This was a mistake. We stayed for ten years. Many times we only had one bowl of rice a day. Sometimes the men would eat rice and the women just drink the water the rice was cooked in. And at times, the rice ran out. Then we had a thin gruel of boiled oatmeal, one bowl a day. Often I would refuse to do as the soldiers ordered, even when my mother begged me. Often they beat me. If my head was shaven, I could show you scars. And yet, even though I suffered, I think Chairman Mao did a great service to my life. In the countryside, there were so many scholars around, desperate to teach. I had private tutors for calligraphy, English, tai chi, music, and many other subjects. I got the best education in China."

That evening Zhou brought over a small portable tape recorder and asked me to recite from a book of Edgar Allen Poe's poetry. He explained that memorizing recitations of English speakers was his preferred method of mastering the proper cadence and tone of the language. We then dove into Thoreau's essay on solitude, which he had been studying. I remarked that solitude was something I had yet to see in China. People slept in dormitories, and even toilet stalls had no doors.

"When I want solitude," said Zhou, "I put a Beethoven symphony on my Walkman and close my eyes. In my mind I imagine works of Western art—Michelangelo, da Vinci—and suddenly it all becomes very vivid. I no longer imagine. I see countries I have never visited, wander alone as a stranger in mountains and cities I do not know. This is all very real to me, as if it is not a dream, and I am actually traveling in a Western country. It is my dream, someday, to link these two cultures together, so we may appreciate one another."

He looked over to me, a little embarrassed. I didn't know how to tell him just how much I understood, and how strange it was to be in the company of a Renaissance man on Putuo Shan. I told him about my own quest for blank spaces on the map, and my desire to see with Eastern eyes. He smiled. That evening he invited me to live with him and his two friends from Shanghai in a peasant house across the island. I said I thought it was illegal for a tourist to stay in a private home. He said not to worry, he would manage it.

The sun returned the next day. Zhou left a message that he had to work as a photographer up on the hill with the chiseled rocks. He invited me to join him for his lunch break. In the morning I toured a quiet nunnery, off the main tourist trail. It had survived the Cultural Revolution intact. The dark weathered boards creaked with age; the gilded statues gathered dust. Only a handful of nuns still tended the place, but in its silence it seemed far more alive than any of the reconstructed temples I had visited on the holy island.

"The reason Western nations are so decadent and unrestrained is because they didn't have a long enough period of feudalism," Zhou told me as we ate cold rice out of cardboard lunch boxes on the mountain's rocky slope. "Man is naturally wild. Feudalism restrains him, makes him obedient. But for civilization to become a part of him takes a long time. The emperor passes down a morality, a virtue, wise sayings which the people can learn by heart. I could tell you hundreds of them, which as children all Chinese learn from their grandparents."

He pointed out one of the rock inscriptions, and translated some of them for me. I asked about the large gouges in the rocks next to them. It was the work of the Red Guard, he said. During the Cultural Revolution, the original inscriptions had been declared counterrevolutionary. Mao's teen fanatics had chiseled the rocks flat, eradicating all traces of religious dogma from the island. Yet even this zealous censorship had failed. Zhou had chanced to meet an old Buddhist scholar hired by the new government to carve all the inscriptions back in their original places. The old man had invited Zhou to come visit, any rainy day, and he offered to take me along.

"So is life much better under Deng Xiaoping?" I asked.

Zhou shrugged with surprising indifference. "We Chinese say, 'Under Chairman Mao, the people had no food to eat and the government killed many people. Things are different now; we have food to eat.' I could tell you about several friends of mine who have disappeared in the last few years. One, a woman artist who secretly hired a male model to pose nude. Another, a fellow student caught having sex before he was married."

"Is sex against the law?"

"Oh, the state is much more liberal now. In feudal society, unmarried people could be killed for having sex. Now, it's only a two- or three-year prison term for the man. For the girl, the punishment is becoming a woman. No one will marry her then. Actually, the government doesn't care much about sex. It just rounds up sex offenders to fill up its labor camps. Every now and then sex crackdowns in the main cities arrest thousands of young men. The state says to them, "So, you have so much extra energy to have sex? You can put that energy to work for your country.'"

> The abominable Sin of Sodomy is tolerated here, and all over China, and so is Buggery, which they use both with Beasts and Fowls, in so much that Europeans do not care to eat Duck.
>
> —Alexander Hamilton, *A New Account of the East Indies* (1727)

"No wonder China seems so puritanical," I said grimly. "At least the one-child-per-family policy is one thing that really works."

"You say so?" Zhou shot me a hard glance.

"Sure. So many places I've been in Asia, it's painful to look at the children, dressed in rags, malnourished and bony. In China the kids are so damn plump and bundled up like balls of wool."

"You know the main method of Chinese birth control?"

"The pill?"

"We have the pill, yes, but in the countryside, the peasants are still very backward. They don't like contraceptives, and they don't know how to use them. And in the cities, there are often shortages. Many of my friends ask me to smuggle birth-control pills to them. If they are single, to buy them openly is against the law. So abortion is the number-one method in China. As a student doctor, I am required to perform ten abortions every day—We have no choice." He looked down at his stubby fingers. "The first time I was frightened. When they brought in the woman, I jumped back."

"Jumped back? Why?"

"Because of the screaming. They had to drag her in, kicking and twisting, and tie her down. Now it's not so bad. You get used to it, when you do it ten times every day."

"My God, Zhou—you mean some women are forced to have abortions? That's inhuman!"

"Some? About ninety-five percent. They are treated like animals. It is our policy. Many women hide their pregnancies. But eventually they are discovered. They have broken the law, not reporting it, and so they are treated like criminals. But it's worse for unmarried women. These women are especially afraid of being caught because they have already broken the law by having sex. For them, the government has a special torture. We are forbidden to waste anesthetic on them. 'Teach them a lesson,' the state orders us. 'Then next time they will learn to push the man away.' Tell me, do you think this is an admirable policy?"

"Do many women come back?" I asked, numbly. My stomach had gone cold.

"Yes. I see many unmarried women back a second or third time, screaming and howling.... This is what it is to be a doctor in China."

The next day the sky sent bursts of icy rain onto Putuo's hills. Camera duty canceled, Zhou led me to the restored mountain temple where the old stone-carving scholar he had told me about lodged. I was surprised to find the man at a guard desk inside the main temple, minding the statues. Just because it was too wet and cold to chisel did not exempt him from a day's work. He was thin, with receding black hair and a surprisingly light, delicate handshake. He called a monk to take his place on guard duty, then brought us to his private room in the monastery, bare but for a shelf of books and many papers spread across his desk.

Zhou acted as translator. He said the old man was delighted to meet a foreign guest interested in Buddhism, and he provided a rough sketch of how the Buddhist teachings had spread across China. Sanskrit scriptures had first been carried into China by two Indian monks in A.D.

China has a one-child policy, and so each little one is prized deeply by its family. And since they are so proud of their little emperor (or empress), they love to show them off by taking them out for walks. Everywhere you go, doting grandparents are walking with their precious grandchild. I like to say hi, play with the kids a bit, admire them. The grandparents absolutely radiate with pride, and are tickled pink that I would deign to come over and honor them with my presence. Of course, the honor was mine. But because of the one-child policy, and the Chinese cultural preference for boys, newborn girls are often unwanted and abandoned. The lucky ones are found and taken to orphanages. On more than one occasion, as I was cooing at babies in the marketplace, the mother offered to sell her child to me. This is a harsh reality, but many of these babies are finding homes with Western families who adopt them.

—Nathan Waddell, "The Little Guy Peed on Me!"

65. Despite early persecution, by A.D. 500 virtually all of China had embraced the new faith. Neither Confucian ethics nor Taoist mysticism addressed the suffering of the common people as did Buddhism; through reincarnation, Buddhism offered hope for a better life beyond the present one. One sect promised believers that if they chanted the name of the Buddha Amitabha, when they died they could be reborn into his realm, the Western Paradise. The scholar admitted these teachings were nowhere to be found in original Buddhism. However, the simplicity of the practice and the desirability of the promised reward made the sect overwhelmingly popular from the tenth century up to the present. Why meditate or reincarnate for a million lifetimes, when a blissful life in paradise was just a simple prayer away?

He then told us how the island had become one of China's four holy Buddhist mountains: About a thousand years ago, a famous Japanese monk was returning to Japan with a special Buddha statue he was bringing from China to his home temple. Suddenly a thousand anchors arose from the sea, blocking his way. The monk was forced to land on the island. Amitabha came to him in a vision and told him not to return to Japan, but to establish a holy temple on the island. At that time, Putuo had only one inhabitant, an old peasant woman who lived in a one-room house. She gave it to the monk and lived in a cave. The monk returned to China. For three years he begged alms until he had collected enough money to build the temple. This original temple was all that was not damaged by the Cultural Revolution. It was called "Don't Want to Leave."

The day I moved into Zhou's farmhouse, the stormy weather turned into a typhoon. Hail, sleet, and snow kept us homebound. The house was big as a barn, a huge ancient wooden building with a tiled roof. Only a tiny portion of the interior was inhabited: four small rooms partitioned off from the rest by wooded walls covered with canvas to keep back the cold and damp. Wind blasted in through cracks in the windows. All but a few of the panes had been blocked up with loose bricks. The only heating came from a small, smoky cooking stove; the temperature stayed barely above freezing. Still, it was a home, a welcome change from the concrete dormitory. The floor consisted of rough stone squares so cold that we kept our feet up while reading or drinking tea. The house had no plumbing. The nearest toilet was a half-mile up the hill at an army barracks. In the evenings, it was too cold even to slip outside into the gale and piss against a tree. I was grateful for the chamberpot, which was kept covered with a wooden lid in the kitchen.

The woman who lived there with her two children rented half the living space to Zhou and his two friends from Shanghai. She cooked their meals, boiled water for their thermoses, and treated her boarders like honored guests, retiring from sight as soon as her services were finished. Zhou told me she was desperately poor, and had been extremely grateful for the extra money visitors brought. Her husband had been arrested for reactionary thinking at the end of the Cultural Revolution. When she was evicted from her home in town with two babies, she found shelter in the abandoned old building. As the wife of a criminal, she could not get a job anywhere on the island, nor could she get police permission to leave. As an outcast, she had done needlework in exchange for cabbages or turnips and scratched out a meager garden in the sand. Although her husband's evil deeds had long since ceased to be classified as criminal, he was not yet officially "rehabilitated." She had had no word as to when he would be released.

Zhou's companions, Bing and Shao Mei, were a young engaged couple. Bing was in medical school with Zhou and a member of Zhou's photography club. They had come to Putuo during winter break because photographers on the island could earn the equivalent of a doctor's annual wages in just a few weeks. Bing needed the money because he was getting married. Zhou was donating his earnings as a wedding gift. Shao Mei expected all the good things in life that come with a husband: a TV set, a washing machine, a ghetto blaster, a refrigerator, and an electric fan.

She was a slender young woman with mischievous feline eyes and sleek black hair that curled in slightly to frame her cheekbones. Putuo bored her to tears. Zhou told me he did not like Shao Mei's influence on his friend; Bing had been neglecting his studies since he met her. He had the tired eyes and glazed, blissful look of a man sexually surfeited. I wondered at the wisdom of having a foreigner living at the scene of a crime. Such a conspicuous guest was bound to draw attention to the place. Zhou said not to worry. Bing and Shao Mei were much safer on Putuo than they were in Shanghai.

We spent the entire day talking and drinking tea. We talked about Canada's vast, empty spaces and then argued vigorously over which country was bigger. Bing and Zhou said Chinese geographers had recently resurveyed China's total land area and found that it was much larger than previously thought. The heat of the debate kept us warmer than the stove. Finally, Bing tired of the subject.

"So tell us about the Canadian Revolution," he asked.

"The what?"

"You know," Zhou prompted, "a hundred years ago when the citizens of Canada finally succeeded in throwing off the bonds of the imperialist British conquerors and freed their native land."

I asked him where he learned this history. He told me every Chinese who studied English as a second language studied English history, including the Canadian Revolution. He became indignant at my suggestion he might have confused this with the U.S. War of Independence. I told him Canada never fought a war with Britain, and that independence occurred in gradual steps—a political evolution, not revolution—which left strong bonds of friendship and kinship between our nations. My friends looked at me incredulously.

"In fact," I continued, "most Canadians are descendants of the British and French. Canada's native people, the original Canadians who were invaded by the Europeans, have been reduced to tiny minorities."

Zhou discussed this with his friends for a while, then shrugged. "Perhaps it is so. We know there is much in our textbooks that is untrue."

It was my turn for a question. "What do you think is the biggest difference between Buddhism in China and in other countries?" I asked.

"Well, for one thing, in India, Buddha was a man. In China, she's a woman," Zhou replied.

"You're joking," I scoffed. "The Buddha is always a man."

I'd been to dozens of temples, seen scores of Buddhas. Granted, many had androgynous, Oriental faces, but most wore the traditional sash over one shoulder. Chinese women might be relatively flat-chested, but I felt certain I could tell a male nipple from a female one when I saw it.

"No, the figure you are speaking of, that's Amitabha, Buddha of the Western Heaven, or the Indian Buddha, Shakyamuni. The Buddha of China, Kuan-yin, is a woman."

In several temples I had noticed a female figure—but not seen her as a Buddha. Typically, the tableau in which she appeared was set near the back gate of a shrine room. She was the central figure of a flood, with plaster-cast monks riding various aquatic animals on either side of her. A willowy woman in long flowing robes, she rose from the waters like Venus from the sea. There was a fluid grace in her expression in each tableau, as if while rising above the turmoil of the waves, she was looking down with compassion on those trapped in the flood. Something about her reminded me of Catholic statues of Mary. I asked Zhou if this was Kuan-yin. He nodded.

"Is she historical?" I asked. "I mean, at a certain point in history, could I have met her, spoken to her, seen her riding on the waves?"

"No, she's mythical. Have you seen the sleeping Buddha in the nunnery? That's her."

"No, that one's definitely male."

Zhou suggested we settle this like good empiricists. Next morning we trudged along Thousand Pace Beach through the cold to the old nunnery to gaze at the reclining Buddha's breasts. It seemed male to me and female to Zhou, who claimed that as a doctor, he should know. To settle it, we asked an old nun. She said

it was Shakyamuni, on his death bed. The Buddha we were searching for we could find in the main temple. My jaw dropped in awe
as she led us inside the grand hall. The thirty-foot-high central idol
wore a crown on her head, which was covered with a golden
shawl. The cheeks were round, girl-like, the shoulders sloping, and
the breasts unmistakably swollen beneath a bronze flowing robe.
On either side of her, as if for contrast, sat flat-chested male
Buddhas. A monk from Thailand would have fainted at the sight
of it. To the southern-school Buddhists, among whom I had traveled for so much of the past year, the height of female potential
was to be reborn as a man in order to set foot on the Buddha's
path. A female Buddha in a temple looked as fantastic to me as
would a female Jesus on a cross.

The nun declined to answer any further questions about Kuan-
yin. She suggested to Zhou that the best person for me to speak
with was a famous old monk who lived in the large temple at the
far end of Thousand Pace Beach: the temple where I had first met
Zhou. She told us that the monk had been sent away during the
Cultural Revolution to be reeducated. Only many years later had
he been permitted to return to the island. She said he was one of
the few genuine monks left.

That evening we had a surprise visitor at our house: a police officer. I slunk into a corner of the back room, behind a divider, pre-
tending to read a book. What would happen to Bing and Shao
Mei? However, the conversation at the front door seemed friendly.
Zhou called my name. I came forward like an obedient pet, shook
hands, and forced a smile.

"Just a social visit," said Zhou. He introduced me to the island's
chief of police. "He's a friend of mine. On a previous visit to the
island, I treated his son for a broken arm. We get along well. Don't
worry. You are here because he gave his permission."

The woman who owned the rooms scurried to boil fresh water
for tea as the chief settled into a tattered chair. He apologized for
the recent bitter weather. When informed we would soon be leaving the island for Shanghai, he offered to arrange our ferry tickets
and invited us to lunch the day of our departure. He said his son

would be glad for a chance to practice his English with a foreigner. I noticed Zhou's face stiffen slightly as the conversation continued without translation.

"What is it?" I asked.

"I am sorry for this. I had thought more of his friendship," Zhou said, smiling incongruously. "And I am sorry to have to ask you this now. It seems the chief wants to buy a new Flying Pigeon bicycle. It's the top quality and can take up to six months to get one. But if he has foreign exchange certificates, he can get it right away—"

The chief wanted to change money. Foreigners in China were required to exchange their dollars for special currency called foreign exchange certificates, which they were officially required to use for all transactions in the country. Special Friendship Stores had been set up in tourist centers so that foreigners could use FECs to buy luxury goods not readily available at regular stores: everything from high-quality chocolate and imported wine to washing machines and bicycles. Not that tourists would be likely to buy major appliances. Any Chinese who had FECs could spend them in these stores. Across the country a brisk black market trading FECs for reminbi (People's Money) had developed. Tourists could get 20 to 60 percent extra for their money by trading FECs for reminbi. However, the chief was offering me an even swap. I agreed at once, and went to fetch my money belt.

"This is how China runs—on *guanxi*. Connections," Zhou said grimly after we cheerily waved the chief on his way. "Every favor a Chinese does for another is a deposit in the *guanxi* bank. To accept is to be in debt. To offer is to open an account."

"It seems a small price to pay in return for his overlooking an illegal alien and two illicit lovers in the house," I said with a shrug.

"But to collect my debt from you…. It used to be in China that *guanxi* meant the good feeling of connection between friends: that we would gladly do what we could for each other. Now it is cheap bartering and bribery. I hate it."

The sun shone blue and the winds whipped the sea with near hurricane force on the day we returned to the newly reconstructed temple in search of the old monk. Zhou instructed me to wait in the outer courtyard while he made inquiries and passed out cigarettes to the ticket clerks. Half an hour later, he and a young monk with dark circles under his eyes collected me and led the way through the main gate. We climbed a wooden stairway to a balcony running the length of one wall. The monk stopped at one of several entrances and hammered on the door.

The old monk opened it and invited us in. He looked withered but erect, with a white Mandarin beard and mustache that drooped down to his chest. His cheeks had sunken in beneath prominent cheekbones, as if at one time in his life he had been severely malnourished and had never fully recovered. His eyebrows had grown long, like those sometimes seen on old Buddhist icons, the long white hairs drooping down the sides of his face. His eyes looked surprisingly soft and kindly, and almost seemed not to belong in such an austere visage. He wore a round yellow cap that covered his shaven head and a yellow robe over his gray and blue monk's vest and leggings. His room was small, but well lit by a window with a southern exposure. A single electric bulb glowed from the ceiling. The room was bare except for a cot, two straight-backed wooden chairs, a plain wooden desk, and a bookcase. Several boxes had been shoved against one wall. The top one was open, half filled with books.

The young monk explained our request for an interview in a matter-of-fact tone that seemed devoid of the kind of reverence I had assumed was due a Buddhist master. But he was quick to notice that there were fewer chairs than people, and he strode outside to holler down into the courtyard at an adolescent monk. The old man sat on the bed. Zhou and I took chairs while the young monk stood like a guard at the door, his arms folded across his chest.

"We may speak with him for fifteen minutes about Kuan-yin," Zhou told me. "It is said that the master tires easily these days."

Through Zhou's translation, I thanked the old monk for his generosity. He smiled, showing a few long, yellow teeth. I told him briefly of my travels through various Buddhist countries, and how everywhere I had gone, the Buddha was always a man. How was it that in China a woman Buddha existed? Zhou seemed to have difficulty conveying all this to the old man. The monk seemed to falter, and for a moment I wondered if his mind had begun to fade. The chairs arrived, brought by two young novices, along with a thermos and cups for tea. After pouring our drinks, the novices bowed out, eyeing the young monk who maintained his post as sentry by the door.

Zhou repeated my questions, and this time the old monk turned to answer. He spoke slowly, a few sentences at a time, watching Zhou and me intently, as if to ensure that I comprehended every word.

"What you say is true," the master said. "Only in China did Buddha come as a woman. This is not the Buddha Shakyamuni, this is another like Shakyamuni, but not quite like Shakyamuni. This Buddha came to China from India long ago to bring dharma to the Chinese people. But when he arrived, he could see his words would be useless. The suffering was so great that the people would never hear his message. And so he changed himself into a woman, into Kuan-yin. In China, it has always been the women who suffer most. Suffer poverty. Suffer cruelty. Suffer the death of their children, the death of their sons in battle. Not born a woman, Buddha became one, so that he could speak of suffering and lead all beings to the Western Paradise."

When the young monk announced our time was up, the master said he would say a prayer to Kuan-yin to guide Zhou and me safely in our travels. The young monk led the way briskly back to the main courtyard.

> Chinese women are more likely to commit suicide than Chinese men. China accounts for more than half of the world's female suicides, which translates into a suicide rate for women that is almost five times the world average. China is the only country on earth where more women kill themselves than men.
>
> —SO'R, JO'R, & LH

He seemed agitated, and kept opening his mouth as if to speak then shutting it again. At the bottom of the stairs, he broke the silence and poured an angry-sounding speech onto Zhou. I watched my friend take the words in calmly, then turn to me.

"He says he must tell you some things about Buddhism. Correct some mistakes that the old man made. He seems very angry, angry at me. I tell him I'm not even a Buddhist, just your translator. He's no one with great authority here. No one for us or the master to fear. But maybe it would be best to listen."

We sat on a concrete ledge in the main courtyard, facing the barbed-wire-covered pine.

"This old man, he is not speaking Buddhism, just superstition," Zhou translated for the young monk. "Buddha was a man like any man, not some supernatural being who could change himself into a woman. He taught that the masses endure great suffering, and that there was a way to end this suffering. These are the ideals of socialism as well. As long as Buddhism works with the Communist Party, it performs a valuable service to society. When it degenerates into superstition, it is a danger."

"So you keep him here like just another historical relic?" I said angrily. The young monk seemed to have no more reverence for the old master than for the barbed-wired tree behind us. Correct the old man's mistakes? The arrogance of his Marxist indoctrination infuriated me. I tried to swallow my anger, but couldn't resist planting a barb of my own. "Zhou, please thank him for his opinion, and tell him sex-change operations are a common thing in Western countries. A simple medical procedure. Basic science. Tell him there's nothing in the master's story I found the least bit superstitious."

I watched the young monk's head cock sharply to the side as he heard the response, then jerk back a little as if he had discovered an extremely bad smell. He stood up abruptly without saying goodbye and strode quickly away. I watched him go with malicious satisfaction.

"I have heard of this operation before," said Zhou, a light smile on his lips as we watched the retreating monk. "I had thought it was propaganda about the decadent West. That when men and women get tired of having sex all the time with each other, they have the change, just to try something different. You say it's true?"

I nodded. "But not quite like that. Some men feel like a woman trapped in a man's body, and some women feel like a man trapped in a woman's body. The operation is a way of relieving their suffering. Do you believe me?"

"We tell each other many strange tales," he said with a grin.

Looking into the story of Kuan-yin much later, I discovered she was actually not a Buddha, but a bodhisattva—a distinction that perhaps got blurred in Zhou's translation. Her name means "Who Hears the Cry of the World." C. P. Fitzgerald's *China: A Short Cultural History* (1954) describes her as "the compassionate bodhisattva who, when about to enter into Buddhahood, turned back to listen to the cry of suffering which rose up from the earth, and vowed to postpone her own eternal deification until every living creature had been raised in the scale of existence to her own sublime elevation." According to Fitzgerald, the sex-change can be traced through sculptures from seventh to ninth centuries, as the male form gradually took on female features until he became fully feminine. In India, this figure was known, in her male form, as the bodhisattva Avalokiteśvara.

Of course: Avalokiteśvara could change himself into any form in order to relieve the suffering of those who called upon him; in fact, the standard use of "him" when referring to a bodhisattva is misleading, since according to Mahayana tradition, such beings have no gender in their true, celestial nature. Digging further into Kuan-yin's history, I found that in India the bodhisattva had a special mountain, Potala, where he dwelt. Potala was also the name given to the mountain in Tibet where his successive incarnations, the Dalai Lamas, once ruled. In China, the bodhisattva also had a sacred mountain. Its name was a Chinese pronunciation of Potala: Mount Putuo.

Winter weather had settled in for good. Putuo's tourist trade dwindled to a trickle. The photographers packed up to head home. Zhou invited me to come with them to Shanghai. I agreed, suddenly sad to leave the barn with its great curving tiled roof. It was the only real home I had stayed in in China.

"Why is so little of the house used?" I asked.

"No one wants to live here except this poor woman," Zhou replied. "You see, it used to be a temple."

I shook my head in disbelief. Zhou grabbed his flashlight and led me to one corner of the canvas wall. He pulled the drape back to reveal a wooden door, and we stepped out into the cavernous main hall. Light leaked in through the walls; rubble covered the stone floor. Icons, altars, statues—everything that sanctified a Buddhist temple had been removed, torn down, perhaps burned in a heap. The great Buddhas, including perhaps Kuan-yin, had been smashed with the hammers and pickaxes of the Red Guard. I imagined her golden face and breasts carted out in wheelbarrows and dumped back into the sea. It seemed that like a true bodhisattva, she had in this way given up her shrine so the outcast woman and her children would have a place to live.

Zhou swung the flashlight beam up into the rafters above the space that once held the main altar. Suddenly the light reflected gold. The Red Guard missed something: a huge plaque in a golden frame, streaked and worn. The paint had peeled away in places from the foot-high gilded letters, but Zhou said he could still make out the meaning. He translated:

> Help the poor, and side by side with them,
> let us cross the sea of suffering,
> until we reach paradise together.

Tim Ward is the author of Arousing the Goddess, What the Buddha Never Taught, *and* The Great Dragon's Fleas, *from which this story was excerpted. He lived and traveled for six years in Asia and is currently living with his family in Maryland, where he is president of Intermedia Communications Training Inc. He manages to keep traveling, and in 2005 will release his fourth book,* Savage Breast: Travels with My Anima Around the Mediterranean. *For more info visit www.timwardsbooks.com.*

PART FOUR

IN THE SHADOWS

EMILY HAHN

* * *

The Big Smoke

In the 1930s, an unusual American woman
developed a yen for the pipe.

THOUGH I HAD ALWAYS WANTED TO BE AN OPIUM ADDICT, I can't claim that as the reason I went to China. The opium ambition dates back to that obscure period of childhood when I wanted to be a lot of other things, too—the greatest expert on ghosts, the world's best ice skater, the champion lion tamer, you know the kind of thing, But by the time I went to China I was grown up, and all those dreams were forgotten.

My sister Helen kept saying that she would go home to California, where her husband was waiting, as soon as she'd seen Japan, but as the time for her departure drew near she grew reluctant and looked around for a good excuse to prolong the tour. As she pointed out to me, China was awfully close by and we knew that an old friend was living in Shanghai. It would be such a waste to let the chance slip. Why shouldn't we go over and take just one look, for a weekend? I was quite amenable, especially as, for my part, I didn't have to go back to America. My intention was to move on south in leisurely fashion, after Helen had gone home, and land someday in the Belgian Congo, where I planned to find a job. All this wasn't going to have to be done with speed, because I still had enough money to live on for a while. My sister accepted these plans as natural, for she knew that a man had thrown me over. Officially, as it were, I was going to the Congo to forget that my heart was broken; it was the proper thing to do in the circumstances. My attitude toward her was equally easygoing. If she didn't want to go home just yet, I felt, it was none of my business. So when she suggested China I said, "Sure, why not?"

We went. We loved Shanghai. Helen shut up her conscience for another two months, staying on and cramming in a tremendous variety of activities—parties, temples, curio shops, having dresses made to order overnight, a trip to Peiping, embassy receptions, races. I didn't try to keep up with her. It had become clear to me from the first day in China that I was going to stay forever, so I had plenty of time. Without a struggle, I shelved the Congo and hired a language teacher, and before Helen left I had found a job teaching English at a Chinese college. It was quite a while before I recollected that old ambition to be an opium smoker.

As a newcomer, I couldn't have known that a lot of the drug was being used here, there, and everywhere in town. I had no way of recognizing the smell, though it pervaded the poorer districts. I assumed that the odor, something like burning caramel or those herbal cigarettes smoked by asthmatics, was just part of the mysterious effluvia produced in Chinese cookhouses. Walking happily through side streets and alleys, pausing here and there to let a rickshaw or a cart trundle by, I would sniff and move on, unaware that someone close at hand was indulging in what the books called that vile, accursed drug. Naturally I never saw a culprit, since even in permissive Shanghai opium smoking was supposed to be illegal.

Chinese writer and social commentator Lin Yutang observed in the 1940s that the Chinese and Americans have one thing in common: they love to break the rules.

—Sean O'Reilly, "Oh Mao, Where Art Thou?"

It was through a Chinese friend, Pan Heh-ven, that I learned at last what the smell denoted. I had been at a dinner party in a restaurant with him, and had met a number of his friends who were poets and teachers. Parties at restaurants in China used to end when the last dish and the rice were cold and the guests had drunk their farewell cup of tea at a clean table. That night, though, the group still had a lot to say after that—they always did—and we stood around on the pavement outside carrying on a discussion of modern literature that had started at table. We were in that part of town called the Chinese city, across Soochow Creek, outside the boundaries of the foreign concessions. It was hot. A crumpled old paper made a scraping little sound like autumn leaves along the gutter, and the skirts of the men's long gowns stirred in the same wind. During dinner, they had spoken English out of courtesy, but now, in their excitement, they had long since switched to the Chinese language, and I stood there waiting for somebody to remember me and help me find a taxi, until Heh-ven said, "Oh, excuse us for forgetting our foreign guest. We are all going now to my house. Will you come?"

Of course I would. I'd been curious about his domestic life, which he seldom mentioned. So we all moved off and walked to the house—an old one of Victorian style, with more grounds than I was used to seeing around city houses in America. I say Victorian, but that was only from the outside, where gables and a roughcast front made it look like the kind of building I knew. Indoors was very different. It was bare, as one could see at a glance because the doors stood open between rooms—no carpets, no wallpaper, very little furniture. Such chairs and sofas and tables as stood around the bare floor seemed as impersonal as lost articles in a vacant shop. Yet the house wasn't deserted. A few people were there in the rooms—a man who lounged, as if defiantly, on the unyielding curve of a sofa, four or five children scampering and giggling in whispers, an old woman in a blue blouse and trousers of a servant, and a young woman in a plain dark dress.

This last, it appeared, was Heh-ven's wife, and at least some of the children were theirs. I was embarrassed because the whole

household gawked at me; one small boy who looked like a miniature Heh-ven said something that made the others giggle louder.
Heh-ven spoke briefly to his family and told us to follow him upstairs, where we emerged on a cozier scene. Here the rooms were
papered, and though everything still seemed stark to my Western
eyes, there was more furniture around. We trooped into a bedroom
where two hard, flat couches had been pushed together, heads
against a wall and a heap of small pillows on each. In the center of
the square expanse of white sheet that covered them was a tray that
held several unfamiliar objects—a little silver oil lamp with a shade
like an inverted glass tumbler, small boxes, and a number of other
small things I didn't recognize. I sat on a stiff, spindly chair, and the
men disposed themselves here and there in the room, very much
at home as they chattered away, picked up books and riffled
through them, and paid no attention to what was going on on the
double couch. I found the proceedings there very odd, however,
and stared in fascination.

Heh-ven had lain down on his left side, alongside the tray and
facing it. He lit the lamp. One of his friends, a plump little man
named Hua-ching, lay on his right side on the other side of the
tray, facing Heh-ven, each with head and shoulders propped on the
pillows. Heh-ven never stopped conversing, but his hands were
busy and his eyes were fixed on what he was doing—knitting, I
thought at first, wondering why nobody had ever mentioned that
this craft was practiced by Chinese men. Then I saw that what I
taken for yarn between the two needles he manipulated was actually a kind of gummy stuff, dark and thick. As he rotated the needle ends about each other, the stuff behaved like taffy in the act of
setting; it changed color, too, slowly evolving from its earlier dark
brown to tan. At a certain moment, just as it seemed about to
stiffen, he wrapped the whole wad around one needle end and
picked up a pottery object about as big around as a teacup. It
looked rather like a cup, except that it was closed across the top,
with a rimmed hole in the middle of this fixed lid. Heh-ven
plunged the wadded needle into this hole, withdrew it, leaving the

wad sticking up from the hole, and modeled the rapidly hardening stuff so that it sat on the cup like a tiny volcano. He then picked up a piece of polished bamboo that had a large hole near one end, edged with a band of chased silver. Into this he fixed the cup, put the opposite end of the bamboo into his mouth, held the cup with the tiny cone suspended above the lamp flame, and inhaled deeply. The stuff bubbled and evaporated as he did so, until nothing of it was left. A blue smoke rose from his mouth, and the air was suddenly full of that smell I had encountered in the streets of Shanghai. Truth lit up in my mind.

"You're smoking opium!" I cried. Everybody jumped, for they had forgotten I was there.

Heh-ven said, "Yes, of course I am. Haven't you ever seen it done before?

"No. I'm *so* interested."

"Would you like to try it?"

"Oh, yes."

Nobody protested, or acted shocked or anything. In fact, nobody but Hua-ching paid any attention. At Heh-ven's request, he smoked a pipe to demonstrate how it was done, then relaxed against the pillows for a few minutes. "If you get up immediately, you are dizzy," explained Hey-ven. I observed his technique carefully and, by the time I took my place on the couch, had a reasonable notion of how it was done. You sucked in as deeply as possible and held the smoke there as long as you could before exhaling. Remembering that I'd never been able to inhale cigarette smoke, I was worried that the world of the opium addict might be closed to me. In daydreams, as in night dreams, one doesn't take into account the real self and the failings of the flesh. The romantic is always being confronted by this dilemma, but that night I was spared it. When I breathed in I felt *almost* sick, but my throat didn't close, and after a moment I was fine. I couldn't dispose of the tiny volcano all in one mighty pull, as the others had done, but for a beginner I didn't do badly—not at all. Absorbed in the triumph of not coughing, I failed to take notice of the first effects, and even started to stand up, but Heh-ven told me not to. "Just stay quiet and let's talk," he suggested.

> The ability of almost any foreigner in China to afford servants for all his menial tasks gives the great mass of the Chinese the impression that he has not physical endurance of his own, but only untold riches.
> —Harry A. Franck, *Wandering in Northern China* (1923)

We all talked—about books, and books and Chinese politics. That I knew nothing about politics didn't put me off in the least. I listened with keen interest to everything the others had to say in English, and when they branched off into Chinese I didn't mind. It left me to my thoughts. I wouldn't have minded anything. The world was fascinating and benevolent as I lay there against the cushions, watching Heh-ven rolling pipes for himself. Pipes—that's what they called the little cones as well as the tube, I suppose because it is easier to say than pipefuls. Anyway, the word "pipeful" is not really accurate, either. Only once, when Hua-ching asked me how I was, did I recollect the full significance of the situation. Good heavens, I was smoking opium! It was hard to believe, especially as I didn't seem to be any different.

"I don't feel a thing," I told him. "I mean, I'm enjoying myself with all of you, of course, but I don't feel any different. Perhaps opium has no effect on me?"

Heh-ven pulled at the tiny beard he wore and smiled slightly. He said, "Look at your watch." I cried out in surprise; it was three o'clock in the morning.

"Well, there it is," Heh-ven said. "And you have stayed in one position for several hours, you know—you haven't moved your arms or your head. That's opium. We call it Ta Yen, the Big Smoke."

"But it was only one pipe I had. And look at you, you've smoked four or five, but you're still all right."

"That's opium, too," said Heh-ven cryptically.

Later that morning, in my own bed, I tried to remember if I'd had drug-sodden dreams, but as far as I could recall there hadn't been dreams at all, which was disappointing. I didn't feel any craving, either. I simply wasn't an addict. I almost decided that the whole thing was just a carefully nurtured myth. Still, I gave it another chance a few days later, and again a third time, and so on. To make a surprisingly long story short, a year of earnest endeavor went by. It's impossible now to pinpoint the moment in time when I could honestly claim to be an addict, but I do remember the evening when Heh-ven's wife, Pei-yu, said I was. I had arrived at their house about six in the evening, when most of the family was in the smoking room. It was a nice domestic scene, the children playing on the floor, Pei-yu sitting on the edge of the couch really knitting, with wool, and Heh-ven lying on the side in the familiar position, idly stocking up opium pellets to save time later, now and then rolling a wad on his second finger to test the texture. A good pellet should be of just the right color, and not too dry, but not too sticky, either. These refinements added a lot to one's pleasure. I suppose people who are fussy about their tea have the same impulse.

I was feeling awful that evening. I had a cold and I'd been up too late the night before. I was also in a tearing rage with Heh-ven. By this time, I was publishing a Chinese-English magazine at a press he owned in the Chinese city—or, rather, I was trying to publish it, and Heh-ven was maddeningly unbusinesslike about the printing. That day, I'd waited at home in vain for hours because he had faithfully promised that some proofs would be delivered before three o'clock. When I marched in on the peaceful scene in the smoking room, only a fit of sneezing prevented my delivering him a stinging scolding. At the sound of the sneezes, Pei-yu looked up at me sharply. Then *she* started scolding Heh-ven. I hadn't learned any of the Shanghai dialect—it was Mandarin I was studying—but the spirit of her speech was clear enough.

"Pei-yu says you are an addict and it's my fault," interpreted Heh-ven cheerfully.

I felt rather flattered, but my feelings about Heh-ven's lack of performance on the press made me sound surly as I replied, "Why should she say that?" I lay down in the accustomed place as I spoke, and reached for the pipe.

"Because your eyes and nose are running."

"So? Is that a symptom?" I looked at Pei-yu, who nodded hard. I inhaled a pipe and continued, "But that isn't why my nose is running. I've got the most awful cold."

"Oh yes, opium smokers always have colds." Heh-ven prepared another pipe. "When you don't get the Big Smoke, you weep. Still, in your case, I think my wife is mistaken. You are not yet an addict. Even *I* am not an addict, really—not very much addicted, though I smoke more than you. People like us, who have so much to do, are not the type to become addicted."

No, I reflected, Pei-yu was certainly exaggerating to a ridiculous degree. Of course I could do without it. I liked it, of course— I liked it. I had learned what was so pleasant about opium. Gone were the old romantic notions of wild drug orgies and heavily flavored dreams, but I didn't regret them, because the truth was much better. To lie in a quiet room talking and smoking—or, to put things in their proper order, smoking and talking—was delightfully restful and pleasant. I wasn't addicted, I told myself, but you had to have a bit of a habit to appreciate the thing. One used a good deal of time smoking, but, after all, one had a good deal of time. The nightclubs, the cocktail and dinner parties beloved of foreign residents in Shanghai would have palled on me even if I'd kept up drink for drink with my companions. Now I hardly ever bothered to go to these gatherings. Opium put me off drinking, and people who didn't smoke seemed more and more remote, whereas smokers always seemed to have tastes and ideas compatible with mine. We would read aloud to each other a good deal—poetry, mostly. Reading and music and painting were enough to keep us happy. We didn't care for eating or drinking or voluptuous pleasures.... I seem to fall into a kind of *fin-de-siècle* language when I talk about opium, probably because it was rather a *fin-de-siècle* life I led when I was smoking it, and in a social as well as literary sense. The

modern, Westernized Chinese of Shanghai frowned on smoking—
not on moral grounds but because it was considered so lamentably
old-fashioned. My friends, in their traditional long gowns, were
deliberately, self-consciously reactionary, and opium was a part of
this attitude, whereas modern people preferred to stun themselves
with whiskey or brandy. Opium was decadent. Opium was for
grandfathers.

We used to read Cocteau's book on opium and discuss it. Hua-
ching loved the drawings that represent the feelings of a man
under cure, in which the pipe grows progressively larger and the
man smaller. Then the pipe proliferates—his limbs turn into
pipes—until a last he is built up completely of pipes. During such
talks, Heh-ven sometimes spoke of himself frankly as an addict
but at other times he still said he wasn't. I never knew what sort
of statement he was going to make on the subject. "My asthma
caused it, you know," he said once. "My father is asthmatic, so he
smokes. I, too, am asthmatic, and so is Pei-yu. Now and then,
when hers is very bad, she will take a pipe, because it is a good
medicine for that disease."

One day, after he had been even more contradictory than was
his custom, I drew up a table of the smoker's creed:

1. I will never be an addict.

2. I can't become addicted. I am one of those people who take
   it or let it alone.

3. I'm not badly addicted.

4. It's a matter of will power, and I can stop any time.

Any time. Time. That was something that had lost its grip on
me. It was amazing how watches carried their rate of running,
sometimes galloping, at other times standing still. To keep up with
my job, I had to look at my watch often; it had a trick of running
away when I didn't notice, causing me to forget dates or arrive at
appointments incredibly late. I appeared sleepy. I know this from
what outsiders told me about myself—"You need sleep," they
would say—but I never *felt* sleepy, exactly; inside, my mind was

unusually clear, and I could spend a whole night talking without feeling the need of rest. This was because I was an addict. I admitted it now, and was pleased that I could feel detached. We opium smokers, I reflected, *are* detached, and that is one of our advantages. We aren't troubled with unpleasant emotions. The alcoholic indulges in great bouts of weeping sentiment, but the smoker doesn't. You never find a smoker blubbering and blabbing his secrets to the opium seller. We are proud and reserved. Other people might think us drowsy and dull; we know better. The first reaction to a good long pull at the pipe is a stimulating one. I would be full of ideas, and as I lay there I would make plans for all sorts of activity. Drowsiness of a sort came on later, but even then, inside my head, behind my drooping eyes, my mind seethed with exciting thoughts.

Still, I couldn't ignore the disadvantages. If I had, I would have been unworthy of the adjective "detached." Being an addict was awfully inconvenient. I couldn't stay away from my opium tray, or Heh-ven's, without beginning to feel homesick. I would think of the lamp in the shaded room, the coziness, the peace and comfort with great longing. Then my nose would start to run and I was afraid somebody from outside would have the sense to understand what was the matter with me. When I say afraid, that is what I mean—for some reason, there was dread in the idea of being spotted. This was strange. True, smoking was against the law in Shanghai, but only mild penalties were likely to have been visited on me. Still, I was afraid. I think it may have been a physical symptom, like the running nose.

All of these little points we discussed at great length, lying around the tray. Hua-ching had a theory that addiction lay not so much in the smoking itself as in the time pattern one got used to. "If you vary your smoking every day, you have far less strong a habit," he assured us earnestly. "The great mistake is to do it at the same hour day after day. I'm careful to vary my smoking times. You see, it's all in the head."

Jan, a Polish friend who sometimes joined us, disputed this. "It's the drug itself," he said. "If it's all in the head, why do I feel it in my body?" The argument tailed off in a welter of definitions. A smoker loves semantics. However, I resolved one day to test myself and see who was master, opium or me, and I accepted an invitation to spend the weekend on a houseboat upriver with an English group. In the country, among foreigners, it would be impossible to get opium.

Well, it wasn't as bad as I'd expected. I was bored, and I couldn't keep my mind on the bridge they insisted that I play, but then I never can. I had a awful cold, and didn't sleep much. My stomach was upset and my legs hurt. Still, it wasn't so bad. I didn't want to lie down and scream—it could be borne. On the way home, my cold got rapidly worse—but why not? People do catch cold. The only really bad thing was the terror I felt of being lost, astray, naked, shivering in a world that seemed imminently brutal.... Half an hour after I got back, I was at Heh-ven's, the cronies listening to my blow-by-blow report, expressing, according to their characters, admiration, skepticism, or envy. I was glad that none of them failed to understand my impulse to flee the habit. Every one of them, it seemed, had had such moments, but not everyone was as stubborn as I.

"You could have given her pills," said Hua-ching reproachfully to Heh-ven. I asked what he meant, and he said that addicts who had to leave the orbit of the lamp for a while usually took along little pellets of opium to swallow when things got bad. A pellet wasn't the same thing as smoking, but it alleviated some of the discomfort.

Heh-ven said, "I didn't give them on purpose. She wanted to see what it was like, and the pills would have spoiled the full effect. Besides, they are somewhat poisonous. Still, if she wants them, next time she can have them."

Snuggling luxuriously on a pillow, I said, "There won't be a next time."

Some weeks later, I got sick. I must have smoked too much. In a relatively mild case of overindulgence, one merely gets nightmares, but this wasn't mild. I vomited on the way home

from Heh-ven's, and went on doing it when I got in, until the
houseboy called the doctor. This doctor was an American who
had worked for years in the community, but I didn't know him
well. Of course, I had no intention of telling him what might be
wrong, and I was silent as he felt my pulse and looked at my
tongue and took my temperature. Finally, he delivered judgment.
"Jaundice. Haven't you noticed that you're yellow?"

"No."

"Well, you are—yellow as an orange," he said. "How many pipes
do you smoke a day?"

I was startled, but if he could play it calm, so could I. "Oh, ten,
eleven, something like that," I said airily, and he nodded and
wrote out a prescription, and left. No lecture, no phone call to
the police, nothing. I ought to have appreciated his forbearance,
but I was angry, and said to Heh-ven the next day, "He doesn't
know as much as he thinks he does. People don't count pipes—
one man's pipe might make two of another's." The truth was that
I resented the doctor's having stuck his foot in the door of my ex-
clusive domain.

All in all, if I'd been asked how I was faring I would have said
I was getting on fine. I had no desire to change the way I was living. Except for the doctor, foreign outsiders didn't seem to guess
about me; they must have thought I looked sallow, and certainly
they would have put me down as absentminded, but nobody
guessed. The Chinese, of course, were different, because they'd
seen it all before. I annoyed one or two people, but I managed to
pass, especially when the war between China and Japan flared up
just outside the foreign-occupied part of the city. Shells fell all
around our little island of safety, and sometimes missed their
mark and bounced inside it. It is no wonder that the American
doctor didn't take any steps about me—he had a lot of other
things to occupy his mind. The war didn't bother me too much.
I soon got used to the idea of it. Opium went up in price—that
was all that mattered.

But the war cut me off definitely from the old world, and so,
little by little, I stopped caring who knew or who didn't know.

People who came calling, even when they weren't smokers, were shown straight into the room where I smoked. I now behaved very much like Heh-ven; there was even an oily smudge on my left forefinger, like the one on his, that wouldn't easily wash off. It came from tasting the opium pellets as they cooled. Heh-ven, amused by the smudge, used to call the attention of friends to it. "Look," he would say, "have you ever before seen a white girl with that mark on her finger?"

Emily Hahn (1905-1997) was the author of fifty-two books, as well as hundreds of articles and short stories for The New Yorker *from 1929 to 1996. Born in St. Louis, Missouri, she became the first woman to earn a degree in mining engineering at the University of Wisconsin. She did gradu-ate work at both Columbia and Oxford before leaving for Shanghai. Her wartime affair with Charles Boxer, Britain's chief spy in pre-World War II Hong Kong, evolved into a loving and unconventional marriage that lasted fifty-two years and produced two daughters. This story was excerpted from her memoir,* No Hurry to Get Home.

"Don't Be Richard Gere!"

A traveler wrangles for permission to visit Tibet,
and a teacher gives stern political advice.

"DON'T DAWDLE. WE WILL BE LATE TO FETCH MY DAUGHTER," said Mr. Chen in his perfect, properly enunciated English. Mr. Chen, a fellow teacher at the high school in southeastern China where I was teaching English, was also my boss and de facto handler—the responsibility of dealing with the school's only resident *waigouren* (foreigner) fell to him as head of the English department. I am sure that this wasn't a task that he enjoyed, much less wanted. However, I had worked hard to build up *guanxi* (connections) with Mr. Chen—teaching extra classes, judging English competitions, opening an English Corner on Saturday afternoon—and over the school year we had established a pleasant, if not friendly, relationship.

When Mr. Chen discovered that I planned to go to Tibet during the school's two-month summer holiday, he immediately frowned on the idea. "Why do you want to go there?" he asked. "There is nothing to see there. Better to go to Xi'an. Shanghai. Or Suzhou. Better opportunities for picture taking."

And less of a chance that I might somehow get into trouble and cause problems for him and for the school, I thought to myself. I patiently explained that I had already visited Guangzhou and

Beijing and now wanted to see something different. Mr. Chen shook his head but remained silent, a temporary setback but not a total defeat.

The next week Mr. Chen approached me with a smile plastered across his face. "I am coming with you. We will go to Tibet. The two of us. Together. In Tibet." I remained calm, although I wanted to scream out that this was definitely a bad idea. I had taken day trips with Mr. Chen and the rest of the school's faculty to the "scenic spots" of our city—and the day had consisted of driving around in the school's mini-bus, stopping for a five-minute photo session in front of important monuments, and then eating a three-hour banquet lunch before returning home to our apartments again. This wasn't exactly what I had in mind for my journey to Tibet.

But I knew better than to say an outright "no." I forced a smile on my lips and said cheerfully, "That will be great." I clapped Mr. Chen on the back as I began to explain our trip to Tibet to him. Of course, we would be backpacking. As he well knew, we would have to cut costs as much as possible because of our low teacher's salaries. That meant that we would be staying in dormitories as much as possible. We wouldn't have to worry about any flights or flight reservations since we would be traveling overland the whole way. I also mentioned that I planned to make an overland trip from Lhasa to Nepal, by truck. It was going to be a real adventure for the two of us. Together. In Tibet.

I watched Mr. Chen's face for any sign of dampened enthusiasm as I piled on the details of our trip to Tibet, but he only frowned slightly. A week later, though, he told me that unfortunately his wife already had another obligation for his family during the summer holiday. Regrettably, he would not be able to accompany me to Tibet after all.

However, he would help me sort out the necessary paperwork for the trip. Specifically, I needed an exit stamp and a new PRC visa in order to return to China from Nepal. So, that is how I found myself on the back of Mr. Chen's scooter, wearing his daughter's pink safety helmet, clinging like a koala to Mr. Chen's back, as we darted through the afternoon traffic on our way to the Foreign Affairs Office, rushing to get there before going to pick up his daughter at her elementary school.

We entered the squat gray building and I looked up at the sign in large simplified characters above the double doors. Below the Chinese, in small type, the words "Alien Registration Building" were written in red and white English letters.

Mr. Chen motioned for me to sit down as he approached a stern middle-aged woman sitting at a desk behind the counter. The woman looked to be anywhere from forty to sixty and she wore a green uniform. A gray sweater underneath her uniform jacket added an extra layer of bulk. Her shoes—black pumps with ankle-high panty hose—made a clicking sound as she walked over from her desk to the counter. Mr. Chen first spoke to her in Putonghua (Mandarin), but after a few sentences he switched to the local dialect. I followed as best I could, but only really knew what was going on when Mr. Chen pointed at me and shrugged his shoulders. I heard the word "*xizang*" a lot, and what sounded to be Nepal, and then a big laugh from Mr. Chen. The woman nodded but never broke a smile. She

In my compartment on the train to Chengdu, there was an old man with a fur hat who sat holding a cup of tea and gazing out the window, a young father and mother with two children, and a third man who was studying English. The man studying English had several textbooks with him, but he was more interested in teaching me Chinese poetry than in practicing English. We got into an argument over the third line of one of the poems I had memorized: the man was leaving out the third line, my favorite: "monkeys cry on both banks of the river without stopping." He recited the poem leaving the line out, and we argued about it until the man in the fur hat by the window put an end to our dispute. "She's right," he snapped.

—Jennifer Walden, "The Road to Sichuan"

looked through my passport and then over at me. Finally, after a few minutes, she quietly called me over. Mr. Chen giggled, forced and unnatural, and said in a high-pitched voice, "Come over here. Quickly! She wants to speak to you."

I approached with a smile and was met with the stern face of a bureaucrat of the People's Republic of China. She looked at me for a while and then began to speak in a low but shrill voice. Her Putonghua was clear and perfectly enunciated. Mr. Chen translated with a seldom seen seriousness in his eyes. He didn't smile. "She says that you know that Tibet is part of China. That is history." I nodded at the woman and she continued. "You plan to go to Tibet. That is fine. But some foreign friends like to make trouble there." I nodded again. "You are a teacher in our city. When you are in Tibet, you represent our city. You represent our school." I nodded at Mr. Chen and the woman. I didn't dare break a smile. I didn't even want to breathe. The woman's voice rose. "You must promise not to make trouble in Tibet." The woman stared at me. I tried to fix my most sincere look on my face. "Of course," I said. "I won't make any trouble in Tibet." The woman stared me for another ten seconds. I wasn't sure if she expected me to make the promise again, so I just remained quiet. Finally, she handed my passport to me. I glanced inside as casually as possible and I saw that I had the proper exit stamp as well as a visa for my return from Nepal. We left amidst a flurry of "*xie xie*" and forced smiles. The woman nodded and took a sip from the covered cup on the counter in front of her.

As we walked to Mr. Chen's scooter, I smiled at him and rolled my eyes, as if trying to say that the woman had been a bit overboard about the seriousness of traveling to Tibet. Mr. Chen stopped in front of the scooter. "What she said is true. You represent our city and our school." And you, too, I thought. If I get into trouble, it will probably fall on your shoulders.

He looked at me—hard—harder than he had ever looked at me before. This wasn't the smiling, laughing, cuddly handler of the foreigner anymore. This wasn't the normal scolding and fatherly advice that Mr. Chen often gave me, "Don't ride your bicycle so fast!" "Do not be late for our meeting with the principal." "Don't eat food from the street vendors!" This was different—this was the look he used on the other Chinese teachers in the English Department, the look that he used on naughty students in class. He looked at me—hard—and we weren't equals or colleagues or fellow teachers or even friends anymore.

Mr. Chen spoke slowly and clearly. "I speak English. I am an English teacher. So, I know about Western culture. I know about your views and opinions in the West. But I do not buy the Western idea of Tibet. Tibet is a part of China. That is clear." I nodded but didn't say anything. Mr. Chen spoke again, suddenly, "I know all about your Western ideas. Other Chinese people do not. That official does not. But I have seen the films." Perhaps he noticed the confused look on my face. "I know about Richard Gere. Bu-lai-de Pi-te. And Hay-lu-sun Fo-de." I recognized Richard Gere, but could only guess that he meant Brad Pitt and Harrison Ford—he must have used the Chinese names for the last two. Mr. Chen continued, shaking a finger in my face. "That Richard Gere! He is crazy for Tibet! He is in love with the Dalai Lama. Buying him cars! Flying him to America! And always making trouble about Tibet!" He shook his head, a look of sorrow or disgust or both spread across his face. He looked at me, right in the eyes, "When you go to Tibet, don't be a Richard Gere." I just looked at him. He spoke again, louder. "Don't be Richard Gere!"

I didn't know what to say, so I said, "I won't be Richard Gere. I promise, when I go to Tibet, I won't be Richard Gere."

And in the few seconds of silence that followed, I watched Mr. Chen size me up—actually look me up and down as he evaluated what I had just said. I watched him gauge my honesty, my sincerity, and the chances of me going to Tibet and "making trouble."

Then, suddenly, he grunted and nodded for me to get on his motor scooter. "Let us go to fetch my daughter. Don't dawdle." And that was it—Mr. Chen had done all that he could for me, he had properly warned me about Tibet and had covered his ass the best that he could. He had spoken to me in language that he thought I would understand—the language of film and popular

Western culture. He had given me a specific example of what not to do in Tibet, an example that I, as a Westerner, could not fail to comprehend. Now, in Tibet, I would be on my own. I was no longer his responsibility. He handed me the pink safety helmet.

We went to fetch his daughter. And I left one month later and traveled overland to Tibet, with thoughts of Richard Gere, my high school in southeastern China, and Mr. Chen occasionally drifting into my head as I watched mountains roll out across the Tibetan plateau.

Ted Pigott is a writer based in Taipei, Taiwan. He has traveled extensively throughout Asia over the last ten years. He currently lives in Taipai, Taiwan.

Disposable Pandas

*How can you care for the natural world
if you don't revere human life?*

THIS MORNING I WATCHED A WATER OX BATHE IN A SMALL
river. He had wandered away from the others who were being
yoked and slid down a muddy bank to wallow in cool water. It was
an unusual sight in China: an animal at its own leisure, enjoying
life. Soon enough, the farmer came for him, willow whip in hand,
and led him back into service: pulling a wooden plow across un-
planted, flooded rice fields.

Mr. Tong was driving me to the Wolong Panda Preserve in the
mountains northwest of Chengdu. Though I had come to China
to climb Buddhist mountains, I also wanted to see where and how
the animals lived, if their culture had survived. Seven hundred and
twenty-five years ago, Marco Polo wrote, "On leaving Ch'eng-tu-
fu the traveler rides for five days through plain and valley, passing
villages and hamlets in plenty. The people here live on the yield
of the earth. The country is infested with lions, bears, and other
wild beasts."

The name *Chengdu* (*Cheng-t'u*) means "official road," alluding
to the distant posts where poet-scholars were once stationed while
in public service. Now the narrow alleyways of its outskirts were
lined with peasants called *manglie* ("blind drifters"), day laborers

who had migrated to the cities between harvests to look for work. Their hoes, machetes, and hand tools were neatly rolled in bits of canvas and tucked inside threshing baskets. Their share of Deng's "glorious wealth" was a meager wage of ten to fifteen yuan a day.

When Mao walked through Chengdu on the Long March in the 1940s, he made a promise to liberate workers from dire poverty, starvation, the feudal practices of landlords, penury, and unfair taxation, galvanizing the peasants into a prodigious political force. What began as a humanitarian ideal turned into government rule by brutal coercion. Utopian dreams were crushed by censoriousness and intimidation; relief from penury through land reform was given over to a collectivization of farmland so immense and thoroughgoing that the peasants were eventually stripped of everything, even something to eat. The resulting famine that gripped China from 1958 to 1961 brought about 30 million deaths. Though poverty initially had been eliminated by Mao, he grew too fond of his weapons of harassment, lawlessness, betrayal, and execution; unlike Hitler and Stalin, Mao hid while these weapons were being used.

Mao called himself *heshang dasan*—an outlaw. "I am a graduate from the University of Outlaws," he declared. *Outlaw* became a euphemism for tyrant, sycophant, and treacherous despot. He read avidly about the lives of the cruelest emperors, thinking himself to be messianic, a chosen ruler. *Heshang dasan* was an apt description. He hated state ritual and protocol, and lived and ruled beyond the law, replacing state and social conventions with customs of his own. He traveled around his country frequently, talking to local leaders face-to-face. This way, no one could know what he said to them, no one could usurp or counteract his power.

Everything he did conspired to make the political elite as well as the masses directly dependent on him and him alone. His most famous speech was called "On the Correct Handling of Contradictions among the People"—which meant being sent into exile or killed.

Original and eccentric, Mao's style was perhaps better suited to the absurdist stage of choreographer Pina Bausch than to the theatre of global politics. He was demanding, paranoid, lascivious, delusional, and impenitent. A recluse, he met foreign dignitaries in his bathrobe. He refused to wash, saying, "I bathe myself inside the bodies of women." He was an insomniac and insisted on having his personal doctor with him at all times, so that if he couldn't sleep, he had a reliable companion to chat with, usually in the middle of the night. His sexual appetite was such that he insisted on having his bed carried with him at all times for frequent sexual forays. He spent most of his days swimming and lying in bed. When times were bad, he rode around in his private railway carriage with the shades drawn down.

> The Chinaman from early youth
> Is by his wise preceptors taught
> To have no dealings with the Truth,
> In fact romancing is his "forte."
> In juggling words he takes the prize,
> By the sheer beauty of his lies.
>
> —Harry Graham,
> *China—Verse and Worse* (1905)

The Chinese people didn't know the details of Mao's private life until recently, but the lucky ones, the wily ones, did learn how to survive: by keeping a low profile; expecting betrayals from everyone and giving all their time, concern, and loyalty to the Chairman and no one else. Despite the revelations about his private life, Mao is still guardedly revered: "He had the highest ideals, but no moral backbone from which to act," a friend of mine said. "He had humble beginnings and he got lost in all his power. It was like an orchard for a starving man. Too much fruit. He ate until he was sick and then he spread that sickness everywhere."

Mao died in 1976. When Deng Xiaoping was returned to power in 1978, he declared: "To get rich is glorious." Though Deng's reforms freed the people from Mao's tyranny, there are new hardships and uncertainties. Since Tiananmen Square, people only want to make money, because money equals freedom. They aren't sure of what will happen next. For the time being, party bosses rule; corruption involving complicity between the communist government and the Chinese mafia is common knowledge. It's the only way to get ahead. After all, China is still a dictatorship and the people have few democratic rights: no free speech, no free press, no freedom of assembly or travel, and no court of justice to represent them. "But those are Western ideas," Mr. Tong said, smiling wryly.

We passed more groups of peasants waiting by the side of the road to get hired. Of the 100 million peasants coming to cities to look for work, 40 million are unemployed. My translator said, "Sometimes bad things happen to them. They are beaten or not paid. Most people just want to make enough money to feed themselves no matter how they have to do it. Who comes into power next is a subject of great concern. If it reverts to the way it was before, while the Chairman was in power, there's going to be trouble."

But when I asked what kind of trouble, Mr. Tong and the translator shrugged. Later, someone else suggested there might be civil war between the provincial armies and rebels. "We don't need democracy; we need something like a society that is part Confucian, part Taoist, a code of conduct for the people that arises from Chinese ideals."

We stopped at a Taoist temple on the outskirts of Chengdu. Priests walked the temple grounds in gray Mandarin tunics over black trousers. Their long hair was pulled up and held in place by a chopstick and cupped by a black pillbox hat with a hole for the topknot. The monks were lackluster, sour-faced, and rude. One temple and courtyard gave onto another and another until, in the main hall, I stood before three statues of Lao Tzu riding a tiger, riding a cloud, and riding a crane. Slouched in a chair in a dark corner, a monk sat with his feet propped up, pressing a small radio to his ear.

Taoism and Buddhism managed to coexist happily for thousands of years, but neither had survived Mao or the daily catechism of confession and betrayal he imposed. Buddhism was silenced but, according to my friend Raoul, "Taoism got trashed." Once, Taoism had been a source of Chinese reverence for mountains and a wild spirited textbook for living. Now, the urban temples looked like tawdry museums, theme parks for the occult. Mr. Tong had wisely stayed in the car to read his book.

It is well known to all who have taken any pains in studying the Chinese temper and character that obstinancy—obstinancy like that of mules—is one of its foremost features. And it is also known, by a multiplied experience, that the very greatest importance attaches in Chinese estimate to the initial movement. Once having conceded a point, you need not hope to recover your lost ground.

—Thomas de Quincey,
The Chinese Question in 1857

As we left the outer edges of Chengdu for Wolong we passed into the realm of intensive human labor: men hauling cement bridge parts, a woman pushing a bicycle with two hundred pounds of grain, humans hauling humans in rickshaws, horses pulling carts laden with lumber and bricks. Farther along, farmsteads' shaped terraces glistened with night soil and water, and phalanxes of women planted seedling rice. Here and there an apartment complex shot up on the plain, demarking what would someday be a new city. At one, stonemasons walked a shaky bamboo scaffold above the entry gate with a fanciful name taken from an American sitcom. The inner sanctum held a tipped-over statue of the "goddess of democracy"—a crude replica of the Statue of Liberty used in the 1989 Tiananmen Square demonstrations.

The film I had seen about China's bear farms was shown on British television. Filmed in Chengdu, sometimes using hidden cameras, it showed Asiatic black bears whose gallbladders had been implanted with permanent catheters. From these, bile was collected and sold as medicine. There were at least ten thousand bears kept on such farms. The bears were incarcerated in tiny cages and often kept in the courtyard of local houses or apartment buildings.

A close-up showed one bear's catheter site: it was full of pus and pained the trapped bear to move at all.

Another scene showed a filthy cement pit at the bottom of a three-story building where bears were kept. For a price, the public could taunt the animals by throwing food down to them from the balconies, an urban amusement park of sorts in this all-for-profit China. I wondered if the panda, the international symbol of animal preservation, would be in better shape.

Outside the city and its sprawling, linked towns, we passed a series of big ponds. In one, an old man sat unmoving on a bamboo stool in the water, holding a fishing pole, his blue pantaloons rolled up to his knees, and a conical hat shading his face. All around him, young people were throwing nets into the water and grabbing at tiny fish. A pole-pushed sampan floated by soundlessly. On the road, a young woman wearing a white dress with lace ruffles and red high heels stepped into a bicycle rickshaw and disappeared. Near the mountains a district of sawmills lined the wide highway and government trucks carried immense logs. Could there still be virgin forests somewhere in western China? Was any habitat for the panda and other animals being preserved?

Père Armand David was a French missionary who had lived in an isolated valley in these mountains. A self-made naturalist, he recorded the first sighting of a panda in his 1875 diary:"From one year's end to another, one hears the hatchet and the axe cutting the most beautiful trees. The destruction of these primitive forests, of which there are only fragments in all of China, progresses with unfortunate speed. They will never be replaced. With the great trees will disappear a multitude of shrubs and other plants which cannot survive except in their shade; also all animals, small and large, which need the forest in order to live and perpetuate their species."

Mr. Tong headed north and west up a narrow river valley where Teddy Roosevelt and his brother Kermit had come to shoot big game in the late 1800s. Not long after Père Armand saw his first panda, Teddy and Kermit shot one and brought it back to the states. The mountains where the Roosevelts had roamed were now lined with kilns. On the side of the road men and women pounded white rock with sledgehammers, throwing broken hunks into the fires to make lime.

An explosion of dynamite rocked our car. Upstream, a coal mine spewed smoke and dust into a wild river and the vertiginous slopes were bare. Below, tea, rice, and rapeseed were grown, and on midriver islands there were truck farms: cabbages, onions, peas, and beans, but no large trees.

Deforestation had been going on in China since before the Middle Ages. By the fourteenth century, central China was denuded. During Mao's Great Leap Forward from 1957 to 1958, millions of trees were cut down to make charcoal for backyard steel furnaces where pots and pans and Buddhist icons were melted down. This was Mao's strategy to make China a self-sufficient modern nation. Later, the metal was thrown away because it was not strong enough. Women were encouraged to have children and the population increased by 450 million. Schools were closed down. Crops were left to die in the fields while both children and adults attended to their revolutionary activities. The wildlife population was decimated for food, and all arable land was plowed and planted in grain—wheat in the north, rice in the south—crops that were later neglected.

> The Walker Report, commissioned by the U.S. Congress decades ago, estimated that as many as forty million people may have died in China during the various cycles of chaos engendered by Mao.
>
> —Sean O'Reilly, "Oh Mao, Where Art Thou?"

Starvation was so extreme that people ate weeds and sawdust. Grass soup was the soup du jour. Yet Mao saw nothing of it. When his train went through towns and villages where hunger was extreme, his comrades pulled the shades so he wouldn't see, because if he did, they were afraid they would be blamed for the disaster and executed. "I remember, even the worms were hungry. They came up out of the ground and ate everything in the fields and then we all starved," a friend who lived through that era told me.

We followed the Pitiao River up a narrow canyon into the Qionglai Mountains, where the pavement stopped and a one-lane track threaded through fallen boulders. The water ran fast and clear and the canyon's narrow verge offered us tantalizing glimpses of high, cloud-ridden peaks ahead. More than once we had to stop as landslides were cleared away. This was the ecozone between the Tibetan plateau and the Sichuan basin, and all this had once been forest: prime habitat for bears, golden monkeys, takin, white-lipped deer, and snow leopards. Even the trees that had been replanted had not been cared for and the regrowth was thick brush, difficult for bears and deer to travel through.

Nature reserves were established in China in 1958, and the first panda reserve in 1963. But their management ended abruptly during the Cultural Revolution and didn't start up again until 1976, when a census of surviving pandas was taken. In the six mountain areas where pandas were known to live, only 1,100 animals were counted. At Wolong, where we were headed, only eighty survived.

How we treat our animals is a mirror of how we think of ourselves. How could one expect a leader who humiliated and enslaved his followers to treat animals well?

Mr. Tong coolly navigated the bumpy Wolong road through herds of goats tended by young boys. He laughed as he told how the year before, a boulder had fallen onto the hood of his truck, then bounced into the middle of the road, stopping all traffic for days. He referred to pandas as *daxiongmao*—"bear cats"—and said he had lived near here while in cadre school, but never saw a bear.

Pandas are small, shy, slow moving and rather fragile. They are only fifteen centimeters long when they're born and weigh from 60 to 130 grams. Their dens are usually rock caves or hollow trees, and they don't breed until they are five years old or more, with estrus lasting only one week per year. Of the seven species of bamboo in Wolong, pandas eat the leaves and young stems of only two: umbrella and arrow. The 1983 flowering and subsequent die-off of arrow bamboo helped decimate their population.

At a bend in the river we turned into the Hetauping Research Center. It consisted of a group of low, flat-roofed cement buildings huddled on the banks of the Pitiao River. We entered through heavy gates, walked over a bridge, and came into the compound. Three young men dressed in sports jackets, jeans, and tennis shoes approached us. I asked if they were biologists. They said no, they were guides. Were there any English-speaking biologists around? They said the Canadian biologist who had been there for four years had left the week before. Now there were no scientists to talk to. But if I wanted, I could look around anyway.

The pandas were held in dirty, cement stalls with stalks of bamboo piled in the corners. Some had small outdoor enclosures but these seemed little used. I looked into the first cage. The panda, a small male, was slouched in the corner, his head hung down low, the bamboo untouched. "He's not eating. Not feel good," the young attendant said without interest, a cigarette hanging from his dry lips. In the next enclosure a female lay on her stomach with her paws over her masked face. "When will they be turned back out into the wild?" I asked. The young man shrugged. "These pandas are here because they are

> R enowned biologist George Schaller writes in *The Last Panda* that the ultimate responsibility for saving the panda in its natural home lies with China. The rest of the world can help, of course, but ony China can implement the measures needed to protect the animal. The situation is grave, he reports, and "if we fail to make the correct choices now, the last pandas will disappear, leaving us with the nostalgia of a failed epic, an indictment of civilization as destroyer. We cannot recover a lost world."
>
> —SO'R, JO'R, & LH

sick." And indeed, they looked sick, but probably from incarceration, not illness.

The eminent biologist and writer, George Schaller, came to Wolong in 1980 to help do fieldwork among the bears. His book, *The Last Panda*, tells of his struggles working and living in a society that values both humans and animals as commodities and where the land's carrying capacity had long been overfull. During Schaller's stay, he railed against the unnecessary capture and long detention of the bears. Now, walking around the compound, it was easy to see that these animals were sacrificial: above their cages were the names of donors to the Research Center. "Donated by Ruby Fielding, lover of wildlife," one of the plaques said. Her "adopted" panda stared at me listlessly, a hostage for raising money. Who knows how the monthly donations were spent?

As I quickly passed by the rest of the cages, I could not help returning to Mao's thoughts on using the atomic bomb. His "paper tiger theory" argued that China could afford to lose millions of people in a nuclear war. What difference did it make, since there were so many? he had said.

In the shop, there were t-shirts, mugs, and postcards for sale. When it became clear that I had no intention of adopting an animal, the attendant lost interest and rejoined his friends who appeared to be employed there, but had nothing to do. Finally, I could not bring myself to look into the eyes of another caged bear, and we departed.

Sick at heart, I wandered the mountains north of town all the next day. We had been staying in a hotel built for foreigners visiting the preserve, but the building had never been finished. Breakfast and dinner were taken in the former hotel complex, but the stench from dirt and grime made it impossible to eat. Walking up the hill to the Land Cruiser after an early breakfast, we ran into the administrators of the preserve. They had just taken their first Western ballroom dancing class the night before. Excited by their new skill, they practiced dancing in the passageway between offices: the tango, the foxtrot, and the waltz. It was six in the morning.

A map of the area, hand-drawn by a British biologist years be-fore, was posted on the bulletin board. It showed a small temple in the mountains nearby. When I asked the dancers if they knew of it, they shrugged and twirled. We drove up the mountain road and stopped to ask a group of men. Finally one of the workers stepped forward, unafraid to speak. He explained that there was an old Tibetan lama up in the hills beyond the fields. The villagers were building a temple there. He gave us the lama's name and pointed to the mountain. "He's at home now because he's sick. He will talk to you."

On foot we followed a rushing stream up a steep slope between mud-brick houses with flat roofs and terraced gardens of vegeta-bles and rice. Two young women in pink angora sweaters and vel-vet stretch pants hoed weeds between rows of tomatoes. In another field the older women wore long, homespun blue dresses and white turbans on their heads.

This northwest corner of Sichuan Province on the border of the Tibet Autonomous Region is home to the ancient Qiang mi-nority, a large Tibetan borderland group that had once lived in the northern provinces of Qinghai, Shaanxi, and Gansu. At the end of the Tang dynasty, around 900 A.D., they were defeated in a war over agricultural land and slowly migrated south to the mountains around the Wolong Preserve.

To get from one field to the next we walked the paths between plots, jumping irrigation ditches, then skirted through the yards of villagers' houses. No one seemed to mind our intrusion. In these inner sanctums, bamboo fences enclosed black pigs, guard dogs chained to posts barked as we passed, and chickens on the loose ran for cover.

A raptor had been shot and hung against a red adobe wall to dry; bundles of husked corn swung from hand-carved beams. As we continued up the mountain, a woman in the field stood, looked at us, smiled, and stooped over again, pulling weeds from between hundreds of tomato plants. Above were the high aeries where pan-das chewed on bamboo, but at this elevation we stepped on no land that had not been cultivated for thousands of years.

The lama's house—it wasn't really his, but one he shared with a young couple who took care of him—was square, with a dark, low-ceilinged entry that led to four closed doors. A young woman greeted us nervously and told us to wait while she woke the old man who had been taking his afternoon nap. Surprised to see us, she tried to look calm. I told her not to wake him, but she insisted: "He'll want to talk to you."

Above my head a false ceiling of woven bamboo held mounds of dried corn. A cat peered over the edge, then went back to sleep. The dog barked as the old lama stood in the opened doorway, stiff-backed and using a cane. Barely five feet tall and barrel-chested, his graying hair was shoved up inside an untidy turban. He wore leggings, a blue coat covered with a goatskin vest, and green tennis shoes. He stopped, looked up into our faces, and gave us a broad, nearly toothless smile.

The young woman motioned us outside into the courtyard and arranged a bench for us, but the lama preferred to sit on a stone and lean against the wall in what was left of the day's light. Lifting his face to the sun, he told me he was eighty years old and not well, though he couldn't say what was wrong with him. There had been three lamas on this mountain, but now he was the only one left and there was no one to replace him. When he was growing up in this valley there were only eighteen families here.

"In those days there was no road and bandits roamed the mountains. Everyone helped each other," he said. "Now, it's all government. Now, it's hard to survive."

I asked how he became a lama in an area so remote. "My three brothers and I were very poor. We had nothing to eat. So I went to a temple down the mountain and told the lama there I wanted to study with him."

Now all his brothers were dead and he was the only one left in the valley who could read Tibetan. During the Cultural Revolution, his temple was burned down and he hid in this house. "We lived quietly. We practiced quietly; practice was reading sutras," he said. "I also did something bad," he whispered, and a smile came over his face. He motioned to the young husband to get something from the house. A bundle wrapped in old red cloth was laid before me. Inside were Buddhist scriptures written in Tibetan on long narrow sheafs of yellowing paper held between two wooden boards. The lama untied the bundle. Wind picked up a few of the pages and swirled them across the courtyard. When I retrieved them the paper almost came apart in my hands.

"I hid these during the Cultural Revolution. In this house. If they had been found, I would have been killed," the lama said. I asked him to read one of the sutras. He straightened up and when sound came from his mouth, it wasn't speaking, but song. His wizened face was dark against the stubbled adobe wall and his voice was birdlike. A breeze picked up, the dried corncobs rattled, and the chanting blended into the wind.

We rewrapped the scriptures in the red cloth. The old lama held them between his hands and bowed until his forehead touched the wooden cover. "He sings that way every morning and evening," the young woman said. She had moved to another part of the courtyard where she busied herself drying millet in a flat basket, sifting through the grains with one hand and holding her baby with the other. The lama rolled the unlit cigarette we had given him between his fingers, then asked for a light. The wind kept blowing out the match, which amused him. Finally he inhaled deeply, coughed, and gazed up at the ridge where the new temple was being built.

"I don't understand it. The people who burned the temple down during the Cultural Revolution are the same ones rebuilding it. Why do they bother?" His eyes twinkled and we laughed. Standing to leave I looked at the high peaks behind his house. Had he ever seen any panda bears? He said no, not since he was a child, but he knew of people down in the valley who still shot and ate them.

From my rucksack, I pulled out the oranges we had bought in Chengdu and gave them to the lama. Still gazing at the peaks, he said, "All the Han Chinese live below in the valley. We Tibetans were made to live up here where the soil is no good. They thought they were punishing us, but they don't understand. Up here in the mountains, this is where the spirit lives. Who cares if things don't grow!"

He held an orange up, inspecting its pockmarked skin. "I only want sunshine for everyone," he said with a wry smile. Sun emerged from behind a bank of clouds for the first time all day. Bemused, the old lama laughed, thanked us, then shuffled back into the dark house shaking the bag of oranges as if they were tiny, portable suns by whose light he could read sutras.

Gretel Ehrlich is author of the Solace of Open Spaces, A Match to the Heart: One Woman's Story of Being Struck by Lightning, *and* Questions of Heaven: The Chinese Journeys of an American Buddhist, *from which this story was excerpted. She lives near Santa Barbara, California.*

Run for Cover

On the heels of the Red Army came more thugs.

THERE IS A CHINESE PROVERB WHICH GOES, "OF ALL THE thirty-six options available, running away is the best." The proverb always intrigued and amused me. But, mind you, when the bandits came, I began to see that it contained a layer of hidden wisdom, too.

The bandits came in the wake of the Red Army and the Red Army came very unexpectedly to our district on May 9, 1949. That afternoon, I had walked to an outlying mission station some miles away to baptize a baby. On my return journey, as I approached the bridle path, I could scarcely believe my eyes. Yes, there they were, the advance guard of the communist army marching into South China and into history. The soldiers were unchallenged, marching along casually in groups of twenty or thirty, the groups following each other at intervals of 150 yards. They sang a communist song, "*Mei Yu Chung San Tang, Mei Yu Shin Dzung Kuo,*" "No Communist Party, No New China."

I slipped across the bridle path between two detachments and, unlike Lot's wife, never looked back till I reached the church compound. They left only a token garrison in the country capital. They made no attempt to organize local government in the countryside. The result was that gangs of bandits suddenly sprang up like mushrooms after a rainy night in July, all over the district. Some of the bandits were deserters from the Nationalist Army which had fled before the advancing Reds, others were civilians who had been misled into joining a gang.

Their methods were simple. They called on people who were supposed to be well off and asked for money or other valuables. If the people pleaded poverty, as they usually did, the bandits singed their skin with burning faggots, or hung them up by their thumbs, or even held one of their children for ransom.

None of the Chinese in my village stayed home at night while the bandits were on the prowl. Each evening, Christians and non-believers alike took to the hills with as much of their goods and chattel as they could carry. At dawn, they returned to the village, because the bandits had an unwritten law that they finished their operations well before daybreak.

For the first week, I turned a deaf ear to the entreaties of the Christians that I should take to the "everlasting hills" each night with my flock. However, the realistic argument of a hard-headed merchant at length prevailed. "How much money have you in the house?"

"About five dollars," I replied. A look of terror came into his eyes.

"Do you think that bandits will believe you if you tell them that? They are convinced every foreign priest is well off and that the bishop would pay a couple of thousand dollars ransom money for your release." He spoke slowly and with great conviction.

His words jolted me—no bishop in his senses, I felt, could afford the outrageous extravagance of paying a couple of thousand dollars ransom for me. I know only too well that my bishop was in his senses round the clock so I decided that, of all the options, and there were far less than thirty-six of them, running away to the hills was the one for me.

The prospect of going on the run brought me a sense of boyish adventure. But first there was the problem of leaving my house in a proper state of preparedness for bandits. The Chinese, with 4,000 years of civilization behind them have a ritual for this eventuality.

> The Chinese people take to indifference as Englishmen take to umbrellas, because the political weather always looks a little ominous for the individual who ventures too far out alone.
> —Lin Yutang, *My Country and My People* (1936)

The approach was spelled out for me by the hard-headed merchant. "Leave the door open," he said.

"That doesn't sound very wise," I replied.

"Well," he continued, more in sorrow than in anger at my European obtuseness, "if you lock it the bandits will break it down and then you will have no door. You have a small safe there, leave it open and leave the dollars where they can easily find them. This will give the bandits a bit of 'face.' As well as that, it will keep them from getting annoyed. If they get annoyed at what they re-gard as a discourtesy, they would resort to extreme measures like burning down your house."

Burning down my house, I mused, is a bit much, but breaking down the door on top of that is the limit, even for a bandit. But my instructions were not yet complete.

"Take your own clothes out of the house," he said, "and hide them somewhere else. Then leave used garments and shoes as a gesture of goodwill for the bandits."

That evening, Mr. Dong and I were busy preparing to go on the run. We hid my clothes in so many different places that, afterwards, we forgot where some items were hidden. My predecessor had gone on leave and, to keep the bandits happy, I left out for them his best Chinese gown and his best foreign clothes—woolen cap, umbrella, and so forth. As sundown approached, I noted with sat-isfaction that we had carried out, in detail, the instructions given by the merchant. I noted with less satisfaction that Mr. Dong was getting more serious and silent as we finished our preparations. To boost his morale a bit, I ventured, "Mr. Dong, do you think we should leave a note for the bandits saying we regret we have been called to the hills on urgent business and cannot be on hand to receive them?" The gravity lifted and he laughed heartily as he replied, "No need for a note. I think the bandits will understand."

In fairness to Mr. Dong, there were good grounds for gravity. The hills to which we were fleeing were pretty well jungle, inhabited by snakes that came in different sizes and species. Other habitants were tigers who had the audacity to come down to the village from time to time and help themselves to village pigs and, of course, mosquitoes were there in droves. Mr. Dong detested tigers, while I had little time for snakes. Their bite was much worse than their bark.

We were fortunate, though, because with Mr. Dong's expert guidance, we wended our way cautiously through briars, brushwood, and brambles without encountering any of our "kindred of the wild." In about an hour, we reached a fairly bare hilltop. From our vantage point, we could see the occasional flicker from the bandits' torches in the spacious valley below. According to Mr. Dong, they were heading for a village on the other side of the valley remote from us—so we just waited wearily, beating off the ever-present mosquitoes with fans till the first flush of dawn drove the bandits from the valley. Then we returned to church and I said Mass with quite a large congregation present.

Next day, the Columban Sisters at headquarters kindly sent me a pair of dungarees. In a note, Sister Attracta, the Nursing Sister, said the ordinary snake bite would not penetrate through the hard material from which the dungarees were made. The threat from the snakes receded; I had the ultimate deterrent. So I went on the run relatively carefree till the next note from the Columban Sisters arrived a few days later. The gist of it was that if a snake were biting really well and in good form, then he could penetrate through the dungarees and I would find myself suffering from snake bite. In which case, all I had to do was simply bleed the vein between the snake bite and the heart, making sure that I had used a sterilized razor blade, then apply a tourniquet and, presumably, live happily ever afterwards.

The rigmarole about the tourniquet I heard before when we did a crash course of tropical medicine in University College, Dublin, as seminarians. But putting it into practice, with the possibility of a tiger looking over one's shoulder and the certainty of a swarm of mosquitoes ready and willing to sting a debilitating dose of malaria into one's system, was a fairly sticky problem. No longer carefree, I pondered the problem as we climbed the hills and, later that night, I got a severe dose of fatalism, compounded with fantasy. This was the night, I felt sure, a snake would bite me right through the dungarees. As we could not turn on a torch without attracting the attention of the bandits, the odds were that I could mess up the tourniquet and razor blade operation and bleed to death. Strange to say, the prospect of death did not worry me much, because I doubt if I shall ever be as well prepared again as during those hectic and sometimes hilarious days. But the dreaded snake didn't turn up that night, and neither did the bandits.

I was getting rather tired of all this waiting around, what with five or six nights in the hills and attending to people who came to the dispensary

---

When Mao Zedong's government established a cabinet Bureau of Religious Affairs in 1951, it sponsored an autonomous movement which would result in a self-supporting, self-governing, and self-propagating Catholic Church. In Nancheng our Catholics were told that "the face of the Church had to be washed"; religion was not being destroyed, merely purified by the expulsion of imperialists. Some teachers who had apostatized, under pressure, in 1949 were told in 1951 that they had no freedom to do so and that they must re-join the Church, i.e., the Autonomous Church. Religion, specifically the Catholic Church in China, "is like a bird free to fly, but only in a cage." The Catholic Patriotic Association is the cage which the Bureau of Religious Affairs has devised for the Catholic Church.

—Rev. Seumas O'Reilly, former
   Columban missionary in China

during the day, so I decided to go to a Mission Station about seven miles away and say Mass for the people and have a good sleep. Once the Reds got established, they might not allow me to go. Mr. Dong was less than enthusiastic and did not consider my idea particularly bright.

Maybe he sensed that I was running away from my problem, which I was, and that I might run into another, which I did. However, he did admit that Yang Fang village was a rather remote place, unlikely to attract bandits and that it would afford us an opportunity of catching up on our sleep. So we sent word to Li Tai Li, in whose house we usually had Mass, and toddled off on our journey under a roasting sun of a morning in June. We walked briskly for an hour and rested for a few minutes at a Catholic's house in the village of Wutien. To our consternation, we learned that Wutien had been raided by bandits the night before. The people were still scared. And talk about rumors! I don't like boasting, but I think this part of my parish must have been one of the most prolific rumor-producing belts in China. Blood-curdling, terror-inspiring, original, plausible rumors. Usually garnished with the genuine gestures the bandits used and the words they said before punishing their victims, real or imaginary.

Thus encouraged, we set off on the second leg of our journey and reached Yang Fang shortly after high noon. Li Tai Li received us cordially. We had a wash, a change, and then a nice meal. During the meal somebody mentioned that a tiger had come down from the hills the night before and carried off a calf. I was shown to my large room, one end of which was the buffalo's apartment. As it happened, he was out that afternoon and I fell into a deep overdue sleep as soon as I lay on the bamboo bed.

A few hours later, I woke to find the village humming with excitement. Reliable information had reached Yang Fang that the bandits were coming there that very night. When I got up, everybody was preparing for the hills. Blankets and clothes were folded up and put into boxes and a constant stream of basket carriers operated between the village and the hideout on the hilltop a mile away. All valuables, everything in fact which might place temptation in the way of a bandit, were either buried underground or taken to the hills. Old pigs were driven and also cattle. As pastor, I felt I should lend a willing hand, now making a flying tackle on a fleeing pig, now grabbing a chicken in flight. By nightfall, Yang Fang was deserted.

The site chosen for our bivouac commanded a good view of the village and the valley beneath but we were quite invisible from either. Li Tai Li very kindly brought out a door for me to sleep on and laid it by the side of a stream. He placed a smoldering dried plant near my head and said the smoke would keep the mosquitoes at bay. We said the Rosary in whispers, as did all the Catholics who lay on their mats along the hillside. I was just dozing off on the door when Mr. Dong called me in a frightened whisper.

"Sen Fu," he said, "I am very scared."

"What are you scared about?" I replied a little testily I fear, as his fright was very understandable.

"You remember," he continued, "the tiger who came to Yang Fang and ate the calf, it was from this hill that he came." Well, it was not the most tranquilizing bedtime thought and for a little time after that I couldn't get off to sleep but I did have the opportunity of hearing the frogs serenade in the neighboring ponds. They seem to be striking up a sprightly tune, as if piping out the bandits. Maybe they don't make music in the strict sense of the word. Maybe outside the scale, there is none. But they seemed quite melodious just then. They say the ear is not filled with hearing but the sounds of a summer night in tropical China make a good attempt. I wonder did anyone ever count them. There were old frogs, who had borne the burden of the day, with weak voices. Then the cicada with its *whank, whank, whank*, like the sound one makes when sharpening a scythe with a sound. And then cicadas in low gear who emit a kind of purring sound. And then the night bird (I am told) with a sort of whistle. All in harmony, all orchestrating with other birds in the countryside, all serenading the Creator. And so to sleep.

About two hours later, I was awakened by a whisper saying the bandits had come. I saw the faint glimmer of a torch in the foothills to the east of us. They were making for the village. When you have a door for a bedroom, it is child's play to convert it into a bedsitter. I invited Mr. Dong to come and sit beside me.

"I wonder what they will do," he said. "They are bound to be upset when they reach the village and find all the property and all the people gone."

"Yes," I said, "they are rather sensitive on points like that." Nearer and nearer came the bandits. We waited in suspense. The cry of a child, the mooing of a cow, the grunt of a pig might betray us. The shadowy figures crouched low as they approached the village.

"They are just opposite us," whispered Mr. Dong, "not two hundred yards away."

"They are past us," he explained joyously, "thanks be to God."

When the bandits discovered that the property and people of Yang Fang had disappeared without a trace, they were disappointed, and rather irritated. To show their displeasure, they broke a few benches, and continued their journey westward. Soon, I was wakened by Li Tai Li's shout "*Pan shin gung.*" A new and beautiful day had dawned. "*Pan shin gung*" means "make your confessions" and Li Tai Li was just reminding the people that confessions would be heard before Mass. The people on the hillside had already started for the village. Like the snail who carries his house on his head, I picked up my bedsitter and took my place in the procession.

In a few minutes, the Catholics were making their confessions. Before starting Mass, we noticed that quite a number of non-believers were present. They felt that they had a lot to be thankful for, but they did not know whom to thank. I told them in the homily that Eucharist literally means thanksgiving and that, united with Our Lord in the Mass, we were able to give worthy thanks to God, who had brought us safely through the "terrors of the night."

It was a moving and memorable ceremony and the Christians sang the prayers in Chinese soulfully and from the heart. It was the last Mass in Yang Fang.

Luke O'Reilly was born in County Galway in 1915 and ordained a Columban priest in 1941 at Dalgan Park, Navan. He served first in England until 1946, when he went to China with seventeen other young Columbans. The story of his work in China over the next seven years is the subject of his book, The Laughter and the Weeping: An Old China Hand Remembers, *from which this story is excerpted. He is not related to the editors of this book.*

ZHANG XIANLIANG

✦ ✦ ✦

Dying Is a Frequent Occurrence

Welcome to the hell of political correctness,
as an imprisoned writer observes the demise
of a fellow convict.

AT THAT TIME, A VERY YOUNG RIGHTIST WAS SLEEPING BESIDE me. He was only a few years older than I. He too was tall and thin, and from the outside he really looked more or less like me. The difference was that he had a very pink complexion, and broad and fleshy lips. Moreover, white spit would accumulate at the corners of his mouth. He rarely spoke. Generally, he was even more exhausted than I was, so tired that he wouldn't take the trouble to do up his belt or his shoelaces. When we were hauling dirt with the back-baskets, he would automatically move on after someone had shoveled in just one shovelful of dirt. No matter how the person packing the dirt yelled to him to come back, he wouldn't even turn his head. Dumping the dirt at the other end, he would let it slump out, then straighten his back and, like a donkey kicking its heels, kick the basket back up on his back. While doing this, his gloomy, vacant eyes would be gazing out at some distant place. Only after a long, long time would he sluggishly walk back for more. On the return route, he would seemingly be thinking, or savoring the vistas that he had just been gazing at. When it was the practice in the camp to make yourself a kind of face mask to keep off mosquitoes, he would leave it on even while he was working.

If you looked carefully, under the netting you could see that his eyes were closed.

People called him an idiot. Only I had some slight understanding that he had cordoned off his entire being, that after removing himself from the world he found he could enjoy living in a dream state. I would have liked to follow his example, but I couldn't. It required an incredibly resolute determination to cast off the world. If one had the slightest lingering desire or care, then it was impossible to achieve that state.

There was no one with whom he could really talk. He never said anything to me, even though he slept right next to me. If he happened to press against me when he turned over, he seemed to be unaware of it. When I pressed against him he didn't care in the slightest. He certainly would never say, "Please pull your legs back," or anything like that. Dinner was taken "home" and eaten there after work. Everyone would take his grass soup and, very carefully, carry it to his place on the *kang*. Each curled up on his own bedding. Spoonful by spoonful, we would each slowly savor our meal. My custom was to eat while I read an old newspaper, trying my best to extend the pleasurable experience of "eating."

> Alas! My heart is heavy,
> Mourning for my native
>   land's misfortunes.
> Nine Years now I have left
>   without returning.
> Alone I go on my lonely
>   way to the south.
> —Liu Xiang (77-6 B.C.),
>   "Saddened by Suffering,"
>   *Nine Laments*

Despite this, he managed to eat more slowly than I did. This made me terribly jealous. If there was no group meeting on a particular evening, and he had not gone to listen to reports, he could make one portion of grass soup last all the way from getting off work to going to sleep. His method was to observe each spoonful of soup very thoroughly before eating it, as though he was trying his utmost to see the former green-jade succulence that had been cooked out of the weeds in the process of making the soup. Not until he could clearly see that phantom color would he put the spoonful into his mouth. After putting it in his mouth he would lightly, gently chew that one spoonful of watery soup. Only when every part of his mouth had enjoyed its moistness would he allow the liquid to go into his stomach.

In this manner, he could make each spoonful of soup last for one hundred years.

If we had the good fortune to be issued dry rations for a meal, such as a steamed bun or rice, he would first use his spoon to divide the food into tiny portions. The steamed bun would be made into kernel-sized bits. Each small portion then seemed to become as difficult to chew as bones. Chewing bones was naturally more difficult than chewing soup—it couldn't be accomplished without several hours of valiant effort.

He only ever said one thing to me that was interesting. He said, "...like...to...eat watery things. I...don't...like...to eat dry things."

My God! The man was so hungry that the skin of his belly was practically sticking to his spine, and yet he could say that he preferred watery soup to real food.

Perhaps it was because of his high moral standing, or perhaps it was simply out of laziness, but he never "ate greens," and he never traded for food. On a rare day of rest, people rushed in and out like mad, making a market like at a county fair. But he buried his head in his stinking bedding, looking like some kind of hump-backed bird. His two thin, dry legs, sticking out at the other end, seemed exceptionally long. He still had things he could have traded. He had a leather case that appeared to be packed full, but he never once opened it. This also meant the he never changed his underwear. When we were reassigned to a different group, when we "moved house," that leather case became an encumbrance to him.

The Troop Leader would never look after this kind of idiot— he would certainly never let him put his luggage on the cart. Plus he had no friends, so there was no one to help him. With that remarkably good-looking leather case on his back, it was three steps and a gasp, two steps and a pant. He was always the last one to reach a newly assigned place.

Why had he come to do labor reform? What had his position, his background been? What kind of crime had he committed? No one in the group knew. One day when it rained, the convicts were all together in the barracks plaiting rope, and a question came up about the position of a certain constellation. This was in the context of a discussion about escaping. I suddenly heard him mutter to himself:

"In Babylonian times, astronomy was already quite developed."

Amazed, I turned to look at him, but he did not say anything else.

It was from his face that I first learned to recognize a "death mask." In addition to those characteristics that I have described above, his whole body emanated a particular stench. His face was a dark shade of red, it looked like a piece of filthy dirty cloth that had been left in the garbage heap. I didn't pay much attention at the time, thinking that this was the result of his extreme lack of hygiene. But who wasn't dirty? Was I so much cleaner than he was?

This kind of person was naturally a prime target for attack in the small group. He slept beside me, and his only benefit to me was that he served as a shield. With him near by, my faults were not so apparent.

He seemed to be an intellectual, but he did not speak at all during meetings. This species of intellectual was extremely rare in the camps, sighted about as often as a unicorn. Generally speaking, a meeting was an opportunity for intellectuals to put their special abilities on display. During these times, discussion would be especially shrill, and the criticism and attacks on others would become sharp and biting. Our few days of not working rarely fell on a Sunday. None the less, every Sunday men became like worshippers going to church—on that night it was obligatory to hold a meeting to scrutinize one's daily living.

In each small group on Sunday evening, convicts would sit cross-legged on their bunks, and, like true believers, confess their sins. They would tell of mistakes they had committed during the week, mistakes they now regretted.

Who really believes that he personally has made mistakes? It was much easier to consolidate all the sins and put them on somebody else, so that everyone could get the fireworks going in order to "help him." It was at times like this that the man who slept beside me became an ideal target.

Someone would say, "The Party wants us to establish socialism as expeditiously as possible. But this guy comes along with his 'fewer, slower, poorer, and more costly.' He intentionally sings a counter-revolutionary tune to our great Party…"

Someone else would say, "We shouldn't be deceived by what he looks like on the outside. Never saying a word and all. In fact, that's one of the most vicious tricks used by class enemies against the proletariat. The Great Leader told us from the beginning, when times are not opportune for them, class enemies will always lie down and play dead…"

"Do you know what he believes?" somebody else would laugh in a sinister way. "You don't, right?! Because he never reveals himself. Those who don't talk are

Zheng Yi, a leader of the 1989 Tiananmen Square protest, captures the ghastly end state of political correctness in his memoir, *Scarlet Memorial: Tales of Cannibalism in Modern China*:

> During the period when Guan had been incarcerated in addition to being criticized, interrogated, and beaten, she was also forced to engage in heavy manual labor. One day, after returning home from the labor site, she wrote the following line in her diary. "The golden-yellow sun is suspended above the sheltering forests, sending forth golden sunshine." This led to a new accusation.
>
> "What do you mean by the golden-yellow sun?"
>
> "The sun at dusk is golden-yellow," she responded.
>
> "Reactionary! Chairman Mao is the reddest sun. How dare you use a golden-yellow sun to allude to Chairman Mao.
>
> —SO'R, JO'R & LH

most full of hatred for the Party, for socialism. It's not that he doesn't speak because he doesn't have anything to say—if the American imperialists and the KMT counter-attacked, I guarantee he would have more to say than anyone…"

I kept the minutes of the meeting. Keeping minutes had the virtue of allowing you to say less, or nothing at all. I always wrote as slowly as possible. When the speaker finished, I would pretend that I was still writing what he had said. Minutes had to be written under the light of a lamp, though, sitting in the most visible place. One couldn't hide in the shadows, like some others, curled up into as small a presence as possible. When awkward silence descended on the meeting, the Group Leader would always remember that there was still someone, me, who hadn't spoken.

"Hey! You! Tell us what you think! You sleep beside him, after all. What kind of behavior have you noticed that isn't proper? Has he said anything counter-revolutionary?" During the last meeting, the Group Leader discovered me and indicated that I had better speak up.

I still had a degree of self-awareness, and I felt that the idea that these convicts considered themselves to be proletariat was ludicrous. I myself was humble enough to believe that I didn't dare count as proletariat, although I was also not willing to be "capitalist." Since we ourselves were not proletariat, how could he be considered our enemy? If not us, then of which class was he the enemy? It was difficult to say anything before coming to terms with my own position on all this.

None the less his way of eating was, undeniably, annoying. Every single evening his eating habits would drive me crazy. So far as I was concerned, his noiseless existence was like the loudest racket. There was no reason in the world that I should protect him—it might not be a bad thing to take this opportunity, as they say, to throw stones on him while he was down in the well. Didn't I too have to "represent" myself well, to make a good impression?

And so, after clearing my throat for a while, I said, "When he eats…well, he intentionally dawdles. It takes him half a day to finish a meal. I think there's something funny about that…some problem there."

It should be said that an unwillingness to appear foolish is probably a common ailment of all mankind. Even in exposing someone, there is a desire to show that you know something others don't know. This does not necessarily mean than one has a specific grudge. It was, therefore, with the greatest difficulty that I kept myself from revealing that sentence he had uttered: "I…like…to eat watery things, I don't…like…to eat dry things." I knew that although this had a specific meaning for him, to someone else's ears it would gain a very different significance. Specially, it would indicate that he was "viciously holding our Party's grain in contempt, using food to ridicule our Great Leader's enlightened strategy of substituting-gourds-and-greens-for-lowered-rations."

Whoever heard of a man who liked to drink watery things and didn't want to eat proper food? Except for someone who had an intestinal disease, of course.

Since my exposé carried within it a small bit of seemingly factual evidence, it aroused some of the intellectual convicts to further reflection.

"Say, that's right! When this bastard is eating, what's he really thinking?…"

"I think that when he intentionally dawdles over his food, he's brazenly saying to the Party in a silent way, 'So you give me such a small amount to eat? Well I'll show you! I'll make it look as though I'm eating a lot!'"

Someone then began to criticize him viciously in a low voice. "Right! Slowly tasting the flavor—isn't that just like a *petit bourgeois*! Still thinking he's in a high-class restaurant dining for pleasure! If we don't reform it out of people like him, who else?!"

I am not exaggerating this. You don't believe it? Even today, thirty years later, all over China you can still find this sort of person, capable of performing this kind of "deep analysis." And, regrettably, this sort of person is generally someone with an education.

The young man remained silent. No matter how you analyzed,

criticized, attacked, or "helped" him, he did not defend himself. He was eternally immersed in his own world. I have every confidence that his world was the exact opposite of the reality around him. But then, who could know?

Fortunately, the convicts criticizing him only wanted to represent themselves in a good light. They didn't necessarily want to force him into this or that position. When it was time for the meeting to break up, everyone finished his spiel, turned in to bed, and went to sleep. Unlike others who were criticized, who would express their bitter determination to reform the major faults that had been revealed, he simply pulled aside his oily bedding and crawled inside. As he did, he gave me a very indistinct but definite smile. Or was he crying? In any event, I saw one corner of his mouth give a little twitch.

The Group Leader looked over the minutes of the evening's discussion: the pages were densely filled with words. That looked fine. It would satisfy the Troop Leader.

The next day was Monday. As usual, it was not yet light when we stumbled out of bed. We immediately went to have breakfast, without rinsing our mouths or washing our faces (I abandoned such capitalist practices as face-washing between 1958 and 1976). But he, in an unprecedented display of opposition, did not get up. His head stayed buried inside the bedding.

Without him, we were not allowed to get anything to eat. Our entire group of eighteen men had to be together, lined up before the window of the kitchen, before breakfast could begin. First there would be a tally of all the men: if one were absent, the cook would not feed any of us. The fact of his absence soon became obvious, and the Group Leader ordered me to go wake him up.

"Huh! So this bastard thinks he can play dead dog? Forget it! Drag him out!"

Half awake myself, I went back to shake him. His body gave with my shove, but he still didn't make a sound. I then pulled back his bedding but when my hand connected with his body I had a strange sensation. Shocked, I cried out.

"Group Leader, he's stiff!"

As the Great Helmsman (Mao Zedong) once said, "Dying is quite a frequent occurrence." Hearing my shout, the Group Leader was not at all alarmed. He just gave a "humph!" then brought in a flashlight. (Electricity had still not reached the labor reform camp—kerosene lanterns were used for light. Each small group was issued one flashlight, which was under the control of the Group Leader.) He crawled up beside the silent man to take a look. After touching his body, he said calmly, "O.K., so we forget him. We'll go and eat first." With that, he made his bed and told the others to line up under the kitchen window.

> ———✳———
>
> E verything I did, Mao told me to do. I was his dog; when he said to bite, I bit.
> —Jiang Qing, last wife of Mao, on trial for "counter-revolution"

This Group Leader belonged to the variety of criminals called "historical counter-revolutionary elements." He had once been a company commander in the Kuomintang Army and was a graduate of the Whampoa Military Academy in its later years. I couldn't help but admire his mettle, his military discipline in turning such a blind eye to death. When the remaining seventeen men in the group lined up at the kitchen window, the Group Leader reported to the cook that one of the bastards was sick, and couldn't come for his meal. Naturally, the cook had to believe the Group Leader, and so as usual he ladled out eighteen portions of the watery soup that the dead man had liked so much. Without caring about whether they like it or not, the Group Leader split the extra portion between two criminal convicts who were particularly good workers.

The Group Leader's quiet demeanor was contagious—sixteen men silently ate the soup in their bowls. Two of them, the criminal convicts, were quite pleased with the situation. Only I was unable to make the food go down. It seemed to have become a bowl of the white spit that always settled at the corners of his mouth.

When the Group Leader came to have a look at him, I took

advantage of the light from his torch to glance at the man's face. Apart from the death mask that I had grown accustomed to seeing, I noticed with horror that long hairs had grown out overnight. His thick, heavy lips were wide open and the eyes that so loved to gaze over the scenery stared out. Under the light of the torch, he seemed to be searching in all directions, all the while shouting, "Babylon! Babylon!"

It was in that moment that the thought of escaping came to me. That twitch of the mouth that he gave me just before dying—I'll never be sure if he was contemptuous of me, reproaching me, or thanking me. How responsible was I for his death? The question plagued me, to the extent that I never again felt innocent and naïve.

After returning from my escape, I saw many more corpses—death became commonplace. Later I came to be just like the graduate of the Whampoa Military Academy, but even more brave. Once, in a heavy rain, when I had picked up my soup and was carrying it back to the barracks, so that on the way it was in danger of becoming even more watery, I ducked into an empty earthen shed nearby. I figured that I would stay out of the

---

P ublic executions take place throughout China in the run-up to National Day. I have grown up reading these death notices and have attended several executions. I once watched an army truck stop, a young man called Lu Zhongjian come out, handcuffed, and two soldiers escort him away. When he started to scream, they slung a metal wire over his mouth and tugged it back, slicing through his face. Then they kicked him to the ground and shot three bullets into his head. His legs flailed and his shoe flew into the air. A year later I married his girlfriend. I only found out they had been lovers when I discovered his death notice hidden at the back of Guoping's drawer. I wonder how many people have been executed so far in the Campaign Against Spiritual Pollution.

—Ma Jian, *Red Dust: A Path Through China*

downpour while I ate my precious meal. It turned out that the room was occupied by the convict who had just died. He was stretched out like the character for "big" on the door that had been removed for the purpose. I very politely moved one of his arms aside, asking if he could make a little room. Then I sat down beside him to finish my still-warm soup.

I had been reformed to the extent that I could share a room with any ghost, especially as I had shared a night on a sixty-centimeter-wide bunk with a stiff that grew long hairs overnight.

Oh Babylon! Babylon! My Babylon!

The author of numerous novels and collections of poetry, Zhang Xianliang is now regarded as one of China's leading writers. He was born in 1936 and spent twenty-two years in Chinese labor camps for being a "rightist." He was finally "rehabilitated" in 1979, and since then has continued to live in China. In 1993, he established a trading company in Ningxia to assist the local community in developing a market economy. Zhang Xianliang's previous works in English translation include the novels Getting Used to Dying *and* Half of Man Is Woman. *This story was excerpted from his memoir,* Grass Soup.

MIRIAM ROBERTS

In Tiananmen Square

May dark memories honor the dead.

THE PLACE WAS TIANANMEN SQUARE—THE DATE—
Saturday, June 3, 1989.

As a pleasant evening in a traditional Beijing coffeehouse drew to a close, we heard a terrific noise in the street outside. The soldiers had arrived ready to carry out orders, to clear the Square of the troublesome "Counter-Revolutionaries."

I just happened to be in Beijing waiting for my train back to Europe, after nine months of traveling in Asia. I did not expect to find myself involved in such a traumatic situation. My curiosity got the better of me and, regardless of the explosive atmosphere, I spent nearly two hours in the Square that night, leaving maybe half an hour before the shooting began.

Busloads of students advanced, ready to protect what had become their territory. I chatted to other, less angry people who all assured me there would be no violence. What unnerved me most were all the children and babies on the backs of bicycles, as their parents stood around, seemingly unconscious that catastrophe was waiting to strike. The first sign of violence I saw was a student marching triumphantly, soldier's hat on his head, the number plate of a tank proudly held up in his hand, as others gathered around him for news.

Feeling uneasy, I began to cycle home. Buses and all traffic had come to a halt. Instead the streets were full of army vehicles with punctured tires. Soldiers and students chatted pleasantly with each other, standing on the vehicles. Near my hotel in Yongdingmen, maybe two miles to the south of the Square, at least twenty tanks were held up under a bridge. As I took photos, strangely enough, I was waved off threateningly, not by the soldiers—but by the students. I went to bed and slept, oblivious of what was happening all around me.

The next morning we had no news, but everyone was full of stories. Someone had heard the BBC news, could it possibly be true? Regardless of the danger, my first instinct was to go out and see for myself just what was happening. With some friends from the hotel, I cycled down to town, stopping in horror to take pictures of roads covered in brick and glass, shattered and crushed buses, still burning tanks and jeeps.

Nearer to town it was worse. Outside a destroyed shop, the date had been marked heavily in black letters, this date soon to become history. Bullet scars could be seen everywhere, and I was shocked to see blood on some lampposts. People gathered in large groups heatedly discussing what had happened, and any new piece of information that came their way.

We approached the south side of the Square, where soldiers were congregated in a big green mass. I remember thinking how depressed they looked. Some leaned casually on the barricades, chatting to people outside. It was hard to believe these harmless-looking people had really committed the atrocities I was hearing about.

Taking another route, we approached from the east side, beside the Beijing Hotel, scene of heavy fighting the night before. A line of apparent greenery turned out to be another block of soldiers. Someone told me they were shooting regularly, just to keep the crowd back. Many times that day, I would drop my bicycle and run, as the crowd would turn in panic at some gunshot.

The most heartbreaking experience of that day was talking to those students who had escaped with their lives the night before and had seen people dying all around them. With tears in their eyes

━━━━━✸━━━━━

Walking across Tiananmen Square, I saw ten guys in uniform running full court. I'd finally found my game in Beijing! Two temporary hoops were set up in front of the memorial to Mao Zedong. The massive building is fenced in and guarded by People's Liberation Army sentries every few meters, and apparently they decided to get some exercise in the shadow of the Great Helmsman. I begged the guard to let me join them, promised him I was a scout for the Celtics, told him I was Michael Jordan's second cousin, but he said it would compromise national security. The PLA soldiers inside had piled their uniforms under the basket and like Superman, had their NBA outfits on underneath. Each soldier-player wore a different NBA team: Lakers, Bulls, Magic. The pounding of the ball echoed across the open square. I wondered if Mao, lying embalmed inside, would have made a good power forward, and walked off, in search of another game.

—Jeff Booth,
"Basketball in Beijing"

they pleaded with me to tell the rest of the world of their plight. "What can we do? We have nothing, no arms. We are only asking for some form of democracy." They were so angry, so defiant, so destroyed by what had happened. In those deathly quiet streets, the only sound to be heard was the tinkle of bicycle bells and the low murmur of voices. The people would break this silence by the occasional chant of defiance. Their desperate words, aimed at the soldiers so near, were their only means of revolt.

Sickened by all we had seen, we turned to go back. It was not easy to cycle with all the roads barricaded by buses and only a small space to pass between. People were often looting the burned out tanks. The worst thing was yet to come. Tied from a bridge outside the Chongwenmen Hotel, I saw the burned body of a soldier. He hung there pitifully, charred and bloody. I couldn't believe at first that it was real. I saw the feet— they were real enough. I was told he had been hung there as an example. "He killed a woman and a child, so we burned him alive." Unwilling to see the army's reaction to this, I left this sordid scene, but I would never forget it.

It was only in discussion that evening that I realized just how dangerous it had been for me to cycle around town, taking pictures. Cameras had been confiscated, people had been arrested, and soldiers were shooting like maniacs at anyone, whenever it took their fancy.

That night I lay in bed, miserably listening to the sound of gunshots. The early rumbles of a storm signalled a break in the oppressive heat. Several times in the night I was woken by the most shocking thunder I had ever heard.

As I was to leave on Wednesday, I had to go to the Russian Embassy to pick up my visa. This meant cycling along Chaoyangmen Nan Avenue, which was lined by hundreds of armed soldiers. They were so close to me. I felt, for the first time, a real sense of fear. Before this I had only felt outrage and disgust. Coming back I made a detour, and was thankful I did. From a distance I saw black smoke rising from under that bridge, and the sound of guns.

Our train was to leave early Wednesday morning. As several people from my hotel were also catching this train, we went in a group to the station on Tuesday afternoon. It seemed safer to be in numbers and to avoid being out early.

I went out of the station that evening to eat and met an elderly Chinese professor from the south. He had come to Beijing to support the students. He spoke strongly and emphatically about the recent atrocities, and his passion moved me. He even quoted Shelley to me, "If winter comes, can spring be far behind?" Later, as he said goodbye to me, he shook my hand long and hard.

Spending the day and night in Beijing station, which is very central, was itself a risk, but it appeared we made the right decision. Half an hour before the train left, soldiers opened fire just outside the station. One girl on the train told me that as she was coming in, three people just next to her were shot.

As we rode out of Beijing, we all felt the most immense sense of relief. Not only had we escaped from the most horrific situation, but we still had all our film intact, in my case, from nine months of traveling. Grateful for my safety I settled down to enjoy the Trans-Siberian trip and think over the last few weeks.

It may have been a disturbing, shocking adventure for curious travelers, those merely passing through China. But for the brave young Chinese, this was the bitter, cruel end to all their hopes and efforts, a government turning against them, unreasonably and unforgivingly. Students, supported by teachers and workers, had stood up for so long for what they believed should happen in China, they had risked their lives in hunger strikes under extreme temperatures, while insisting all along that there should be no violence in their protests.

The rest of the world must never forget what happened in Tiananmen Square, nor must they minimize the tragedy of this suppression and the murder of so many innocent people. It must not be just another "dramatic incident" flashed on our screens, received with some incredulity and outrage, then forgotten with the passing of time.

Miriam Roberts has traveled widely and has done varied volunteer work in countries such as Bangladesh, Nepal, and Costa Rica. In 1995 she began working with international students in the UK, building on her understanding and experience of different cultures. She now runs her own company—Multicultural UK (www.multiculturaluk.com) based in Cheltenham, England. Her work involves writing guides for international students and providing training in cross-cultural communication for business-people and educators.

PART FIVE

THE LAST WORD

ED READICKER-HENDERSON

Night in the Forbidden City

A night in a train station
reveals the heart of China.

I FLAT OUT REFUSE TO SPEAK CHINESE BETWEEN THREE AND five A.M. When you're traveling, you have to make certain rules and nods to your own comfort, just to keep from stretching yourself too thin in the new place.

We wash up in Xi'an, the capital of China hundreds of years farther back than the days of Genghis Khan, around two-thirty in the morning. The station is brightly lit, and even at this hour it's half full of people. All the chairs are uncomfortable molded plastic, and the floor is covered with things it's better not to think about.

They'd whisked us out of the sleeper car on the train three hours before we'd arrived—or right about the time we had started thinking about getting a little sleep. A woman half my size came into the compartment, yanked away the covers despite the fact that we were covered by them, kicked us out into the corridor as she locked the compartment door behind us, and left without comment.

You are probably not a stranger to this: the arrival in a train station when it's too late to go out, too early to get a hotel. Outside the safe lighting of the station is a city where you've never been before; you have no map, you don't speak useful parts of the language, and the guidebooks always have vague insinuations about danger lurking right outside.

Outside, it's pouring rain. The ancient city of Xi'an is nothing more than a sheet of wet. The world ends five feet outside the windows of the station, a station which has none of the grandeur you expect from one built during the glory days of communism. It's a newer station, just outside the city walls that did nothing to hold out the invading Mongols. Or hold in the locals. There are a couple ways of looking at walls.

The station itself has all the flavor of a modern airport, with low ceilings and lots of cheap tile, but the rain makes it imperative to find a place inside to hide until the taxis start their morning runs.

The Xi'an station is full of spaces that echo and clank like chains or bad heating ducts. There are people eating, sleeping, wandering with the aimlessness that you only see in people waiting to be somewhere else. There are a lot of people spitting on the white tile floor. Babies chase balls under rows of men curled into chairs like contortionists on a retreat.

Once you've watched all this for a few minutes, there is nothing at all to do in the Xi'an train station before dawn. My wife and I find a staircase to hide under, tuck ourselves out of sight, our backs against a window that is seeping from the rain outside.

We're pretty well hidden, almost invisible from the rest of the station. My wife is out like a light within two minutes.

Within ten minutes, there is a crowd of thirty people gathered around us, watching her sleep, watching me watch them.

Six years in rural Japan taught us survival mechanisms, ways of shutting out the world when you're caught by a crowd as intent on you as kids in a schoolyard would be if a UFO landed during recess. But we're pinned like butterflies on a fanatical twelve-year-old's wall. My wife, sound asleep in a way that sometimes makes me hate her, doesn't notice this. The crowd gathers around us, politely growing, about ten feet away, peering at us under the stairway risers. The people simply squat back, watching us, until one—there's always one—who speaks English allows his curiosity to win out over his shyness.

Really, they are not being rude, they are simply staring. In the West, we have some problems with this, but Asia is different. When you meet other travelers, part of the fun is telling crowd stories—the unofficial record from anybody I've talked to is 110, but he was probably lying.

We're peaking out around 40, as a few more people shuffle up to see what the crowd is all about. Not bad for pre-dawn.

The English speaker takes a half-step closer to me. He's dressed in classic rumpled Mao green, and he's down a few teeth. He's smoking, and over the next few hours, I will turn down enough cigarettes to keep a chain smoker coughing for years.

I want to ask him what he's doing in a train station at this hour, but it's not my place to ask questions; I am far from home, in their territory. I resign myself to giving an hour of English lessons—this wouldn't be the first time I've been buttonholed for some declensions—but something quite different happens.

Someone in the crowd asks a question in Chinese. I understand it perfectly, but I'm not about to go into that. The man who speaks English translates it; him, I don't understand. The odds are, he learned his language skills before the Cultural Revolution, and the bad years where speaking English could get you sent for "re-education" caused his skills to erode. He's my age, and while I was watching the *Brady Bunch*, he was skipping school to march in a nightmare of revolutions and counter-revolutions.

I don't have a clue what he's saying, but I answer, in English, the question I heard in Chinese, because it would be rude of me to answer back in Chinese after he was so kind as to make this effort for me and dredge up a language from a time when the world was quieter.

Besides, it's after three in the morning, and I'm not about to speak Chinese. I know there is no chance whatsoever that, as foggy as I'm feeling, I'll get the tones right—you sing Chinese as much as you speak it, and a word with the wrong note changes meaning—and I'll just end up confusing everybody.

They ask where we're from, what we do, how we like China. Where did we come from, where are we going? Do we own a car?

They ask if we want to change money on the black market. They ask how my wife can possibly sleep with all this noise going on, and is she comfortable enough, propped up against her pack, lying on the cold tile floor? They want to make sure, truly make sure, that we're having a good time, and they genuinely want to know that we like China. The questions are exceptionally polite, punctuated by offers of cigarettes. After more than a month of traveling in China, it's the first time I've had a real conversation with anyone. My answers are not always translated back correctly, but close enough, and, really, what are the odds I'm going to think of the right way to bridge the kind of gap caused by the fact that just my boots cost more than most of them would make that year? On the edges of a language, there's only communication, and no chance for anyone to have hurt feelings.

One of my greatest travel dreams has always been to do something highly illegal: I want to go to the Forbidden City, once home of the Chinese Emperor in Beijing, and hide in a courtyard—there are hundreds to choose from, some the size of football fields—until the place shuts down. Then, after the moon comes out, I'd walk among the palaces, owning the place the way no one has since the Son of Heaven himself. And this is the way it often is when you're in a train station at night, when you go out into the cold of a new city: the world is there just for you, its eyes open for no one else, and only if you were not tinged with unease at each dark corner, you would be as happy as it is possible to be.

This night in the Xi'an train station is just that. The world outside is cold and rainy, but inside, hunkered under the staircase, we are warm and safe; we're just people waiting together for sunrise and the world to start again.

And when it finally comes, still partially hidden by the pouring rain, I wake my wife, and while we gather our stuff up, in my best Chinese, I thank the crowd for stopping by to talk to us.

Ed Readicker-Henderson writes about sacred places and the effects of tourism; this means lots of time to study life in train stations, airports, and other places that aren't quite places.

Index

Index of Contributors

Acknowledgments

We would like to thank our families and friends for their usual forbearance while we are putting a book together. Many thanks also to Susan Brady, Krista Holmstrom, Michele Wetherbee, Stefan Gutermuth, Cynthia Lamb, Judy Johnson, Alexandria Brady, Cindy Williams, Jennica Peterson, and Christi Harrington for their support and contributions to the book.

"Running" by Peter Hessler excerpted from *River Town: Two Years on the Yangtse* by Peter Hessler. Copyright © 2001 by Peter Hessler. Reprinted by permission of HarperCollins Publishers, Inc.

"The Walls Come Tumbling Down" by Mark Stevens reprinted from the November 16, 2003 issue of *The New York Times Magazine*. Copyright © 2003 by The New York Times Company. Reprinted by permission.

"Waltz at the End of Earth" by Paula McDonald published with permission from the author. Copyright © 1995 by Paula McDonald.

"Before the Flood" by Arthur Zich originally appeared as "China's Three Gorges: Before the Flood" in the September 1997 issue of *National Geographic*. Copyright © 1997 by Arthur Zich. Reprinted by permission of the author.

"The Tao of Bicycling" by Stephanie Elizondo Griest excerpted from *Around the Bloc: My Life in Moscow, Beijing, and Havana* by Stephanie Elizondo Griest. Copyright © 2004 by Stephanie Elizondo Griest. Reprinted by permission of the author and Villard, a division of Random House, Inc.

"Into the Heart of the Middle Kingdom" by Kathleen Lee originally appeared in *Condé Nast Traveler*. Copyright © 2000 by Kathleen Lee. Reprinted by permission of the author.

"Six Lessons in Communist Travel" by Sean Presant published with permission from the author. Copyright © 2004 by Sean Presant.

Down and Out in the Middle Kingdom by J. D. Brown. Copyright © 1984, 1991 by J. D. Brown. Reprinted by permission of the author.

"China's Unknown Gobi" by Donovan Webster reprinted from the January 2002 issue of *National Geographic*. Copyright © 2002 by the National Geographic Society. Reprinted by permission.

"The Wheat Was Ripe and It Was Sunday" by Patrick Jennings published with permission from the author. Copyright © 2004 by Patrick Jennings. (www.synaptic.bc.ca)

"Buddha's Sex Change?" by Tim Ward excerpted from *The Great Dragon's Fleas* by Tim Ward. Copyright © 1993 by Tim Ward. Reprinted by permission of the author.

"The Big Smoke" by Emily Hahn excerpted from *No Hurry to Get Home* by Emily Hahn. Copyright © 1937, 1938, 1940, 1946, 1950, 1963, 1964, 1966, 1967, 1969, 1970 by Emily Hahn. Reprinted by permission of Seal Press.

"Don't Be Richard Gere!" by Ted Pigott published with permission from the author. Copyright © 2004 by Ted Pigott.

"Disposable Pandas" by Gretel Ehrlich excerpted from *Questions of Heaven* by Gretel Ehrlich. Copyright © 1997 by Gretel Ehrlich. Reprinted by permission of Beacon Press, Boston.

"Run for Cover" by Luke O'Reilly excerpted from *The Laughter and the Weeping An Old China Hand Remembers* by Luke O'Reilly. Copyright © 1991 by Luke O'Reilly. Reprinted by permission of the author.

"Dying is a Frequent Occurence" by Zhang Xianliang excerpted from *Grass Soup* by Zhang Xianliang, translated from the Chinese by Martha Avery. Copyright © 1993 by Zhang Xianliang. Translation copyright © 1994 by Martha Avery. Reprinted by permission of David R. Godine, Publisher, Inc.

"In Tiananmen Square" by Miriam Roberts published with permission from the author. Copyright © 2004 by Miriam Roberts.

"Night in the Forbidden City" by Ed Readicker-Henderson published with permission from the author. Copyright © 2004 by Ed Readicker-Henderson.

Additional Credits (Arranged alphabetically by title)

Selection from "The American Dream" by Dorothy Aksamit published with permission from the author. Copyright © 2004 by Dorothy Aksamit.

Selections from "Basketball in Beijing" by Jeff Booth published with permission from the author. Copyright © 2004 by Jeff Booth.

Selection from "A Monolinguist Abroad" by Nancy Pellegrini published with permission from the author. Copyright © 2004 by Nancy Pellegrini.

Selection from "My Chinese Family" by Daneal Charney published with permission from the author. Copyright © 2004 by Daneal Charney.

Selections from "Oh Mao, Where Art Thou?" by Sean O'Reilly published with permission from the author. Copyright © 2004 by Sean O'Reilly.

Selection from *Out to Lunch* by Paul Levy reprinted by permission of Chatto & Windus, on behalf of Paul Levy. Copyright © 1986.

Selections from *Pigs in the Toilet (And Other Discoveries on the Road from Tokyo to Paris)* by Jeff Vize published with permission from the author. Copyright © 2004 by Jeff Vize.

Selections from *Red Dust* by Ma Jian copyright © 2001 by Ma Jian. Reprinted by permission of Pantheon, a division of Random House, Inc.

Selections from "Reflections on Chinese History" by Sean O'Reilly published with permission from the author. Copyright © 2004 by Sean O'Reilly.

Selections from "The Road to Sichuan" by Jennifer Walden published with permission from the author. Copyright © 2004 by Jennifer Walden.

Selection from "A Slippery Shelf Above the World" by Tony Brasunas published with permission from the author. Copyright © 2004 by Tony Brasunas.

Selection from "The Stranger" by Stephanie Elizondo Griest excerpted from *Around the Bloc: My Life in Moscow, Beijing, and Havana* by Stephanie Elizondo Griest. Copyright © 2004 by Stephanie Elizondo Griest. Reprinted by permission of Villard, a division of Random House, Inc.

Selection from "A Teacher's Journey to China" by Katherine Lee Clark published with permission from the author. Copyright © 2004 by Katherine Lee Clark.

Selection from *Unraveling on the Old Silk Road: Hitchhiking China and Beyond* by Antonio Cammarata published with permission from the author. Copyright © 2004 by Antonio Cammarata.

Selection from "Up Against the (Great) Wall" by Katherine Walker published with permission from the author. Copyright © 2004 by Katherine Walker.

About the Editors

Sean O'Reilly is a former seminarian, stockbroker, and prison instructor who lives in Arizona with his wife Brenda and their six children. He's had a life-long interest in philosophy, theology, and travel, and his most recent travels took him on a journey through China, Indonesia, Thailand, and Ireland. He is editor-at-large and the director of special sales for Travelers' Tales, and the author of the controversial book, *How to Manage Your DICK: Redirect Sexual Energy and Discover Your More Spiritually Enlightened, Evolved Self.*

James O'Reilly, president and publisher of Travelers' Tales, was born in England and raised in San Francisco. He graduated from Dartmouth College in 1975 and wrote mystery serials before becoming a travel writer in the early 1980s. He's visited more than forty countries, along the way meditating with monks in Tibet, participating in West African voodoo rituals, living in the French Alps, and hanging out the laundry with nuns in Florence. He travels extensively with his wife, Wenda, and their three daughters. They live in Palo Alto, California, where they also publish art games and books for children at Birdcage Books (www.birdcagebooks.com).

Larry Habegger, executive editor of Travelers' Tales, has been writing about travel since 1980. He has visited almost fifty countries and six of the seven continents, traveling from the Arctic to equatorial rain forests, the Himalayas to the Dead Sea. In the early 1980s he co-authored mystery serials for the *San Francisco Examiner* with James O'Reilly, and since 1985 their syndicated column, "World Travel Watch," has appeared in newspapers in five countries and on WorldTravelWatch.com. As series editors of Travelers' Tales, they have worked on some eighty titles, winning many awards for excellence. Habegger regularly teaches the craft of travel writing at workshops and writers conferences, and he lives with his family on Telegraph Hill in San Francisco.

TRAVELERS' TALES
THE POWER OF A GOOD STORY

New Releases

THE BEST
$16.95

TRAVELERS' TALES 2004
True Stories from Around the World
Edited by James O'Reilly, Larry Habegger & Sean O'Reilly
The launch of a new annual collection presenting fresh, lively storytelling and compelling narrative to make the reader laugh, weep, and buy a plane ticket.

INDIA
$18.95
True Stories
Edited by James O'Reilly & Larry Habegger
"*Travelers' Tales India* is ravishing in the texture and variety of tales."
—*Foreign Service Journal*

A WOMAN'S EUROPE
$17.95
True Stories
Edited by Marybeth Bond
An exhilarating collection of inspirational, adventurous, and entertaining stories by women exploring the romantic continent of Europe. From the bestselling author Marybeth Bond.

WOMEN IN THE WILD
$17.95
True Stories of Adventure and Connection
Edited by Lucy McCauley
"A spiritual, moving, and totally female book to take you around the world and back." —*Mademoiselle*

CHINA
$18.95
True Stories
Edited by James O'Reilly, Larry Habegger & Sean O'Reilly
A must for any traveler to China, for anyone wanting to learn more about the Middle Kingdom, offering a breadth and depth of experience from both new and well-known authors; helps make the China experience unforgettable and transforming.

BRAZIL
$17.95
True Stories
Edited by Annette Haddad & Scott Doggett
Introduction by Alex Shoumatoff
"Only the lowest wattage dim bulb would visit Brazil without reading this book." —Tim Cahill, author of *Pass the Butterworms*

THE PENNY PINCHER'S PASSPORT TO
$14.95
LUXURY TRAVEL (2ND EDITION)
The Art of Cultivating Preferred Customer Status
By Joel L. Widzer
Completely updated and revised, this 2nd edition of the popular guide to traveling like the rich and famous without being either describes, both philosophically and in practical terms, how to obtain luxurious travel benefits by building relationships with airlines and other travel companies.

Women's Travel

A WOMAN'S EUROPE $17.95
True Stories
Edited by Marybeth Bond
An exhilarating collection of inspirational, adventurous, and entertaining stories by women exploring the romantic continent of Europe. From the bestselling author Marybeth Bond.

WOMEN IN THE WILD $17.95
True Stories of Adventure and Connection
Edited by Lucy McCauley
"A spiritual, moving, and totally female book to take you around the world and back."
— *Mademoiselle*

A WOMAN'S WORLD $18.95
True Stories of Life on the Road
Edited by Marybeth Bond
Introduction by Dervla Murphy

—— ★ ★ ★ ——
Lowell Thomas Award
—Best Travel Book

A MOTHER'S WORLD $14.95
Journeys of the Heart
Edited by Marybeth Bond & Pamela Michael
"These stories remind us that motherhood is one of the great unifying forces in the world"
— *San Francisco Examiner*

A WOMAN'S PASSION $17.95
FOR TRAVEL
More True Stories from A Woman's World
Edited by Marybeth Bond & Pamela Michael
"A diverse and gripping series of stories!"
—Arlene Blum, author of
Annapurna: A Woman's Place

Food

ADVENTURES IN WINE $17.95
True Stories of Vineyards and Vintages around the World
Edited by Thom Elkjer
Humanity, community, and brotherhood comprise the marvelous virtues of the wine world. This collection toasts the warmth and wonders of this large extended family in stories by travelers who are wine novices and experts alike.

FOOD $18.95
A Taste of the Road
Edited by Richard Sterling
Introduction by Margo True

—— ★ ★ ★ ——
Silver Medal Winner of the Lowell Thomas Award
—Best Travel Book

HER FORK IN $16.95
THE ROAD
Women Celebrate Food and Travel
Edited by Lisa Bach
A savory sampling of stories by the best writers in and out of the food and travel fields.

THE ADVENTURE $17.95
OF FOOD
True Stories of Eating Everything
Edited by Richard Sterling
"Bound to whet appetites for more than food." — *Publishers Weekly*

THE FEARLESS DINER $7.95
Travel Tips and Wisdom for Eating around the World
By Richard Sterling
Combines practical advice on foodstuffs, habits, and etiquette, with hilarious accounts of others' eating adventures.

Travel Humor

SAND IN MY BRA AND OTHER MISADVENTURES $14.95
Funny Women Write from the Road
Edited by Jennifer L. Leo
"A collection of ridiculous and sublime travel experiences."
— *San Francisco Chronicle*

HYENAS LAUGHED AT ME $14.95 AND NOW I KNOW WHY
The Best of Travel Humor and Misadventure
Edited by Sean O'Reilly, Larry Habegger, and James O'Reilly
Hilarious, outrageous and reluctant voyagers indulge us with the best misadventures around the world.

LAST TROUT IN VENICE $14.95
The Far-Flung Escapades of an Accidental Adventurer
By Doug Lansky
"Traveling with Doug Lansky might result in a considerably shortened life expectancy…but what a way to go."
— Tony Wheeler, Lonely Planet Publications

NOT SO FUNNY WHEN $12.95 IT HAPPENED
The Best of Travel Humor and Misadventure
Edited by Tim Cahill
Laugh with Bill Bryson, Dave Barry, Anne Lamott, Adair Lara, and many more.

THERE'S NO TOILET PAPER...ON THE ROAD LESS TRAVELED $12.95
The Best of Travel Humor and Misadventure
Edited by Doug Lansky

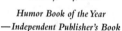

Humor Book of the Year
— *Independent Publisher's Book Award*

ForeWord Gold Medal Winner — *Humor Book of the Year*

Travelers' Tales Classics

COAST TO COAST $16.95
A Journey Across 1950s America
By Jan Morris
After reporting on the first Everest ascent in 1953, Morris spent a year journeying across the United States. In brilliant prose, Morris records with exuberance and curiosity a time of innocence in the U.S.

TRADER HORN $16.95
A Young Man's Astounding Adventures in 19th Century Equatorial Africa
By Alfred Aloysius Horn
Here is the stuff of legends—thrills and danger, wild beasts, serpents, and savages. An unforgettable and vivid portrait of a vanished Africa.

THE ROYAL ROAD $14.95 TO ROMANCE
By Richard Halliburton
"Laughing at hardships, dreaming of beauty, ardent for adventure, Halliburton has managed to sing into the pages of this glorious book his own exultant spirit of youth and freedom."
— *Chicago Post*

UNBEATEN TRACKS $14.95 IN JAPAN
By Isabella L. Bird
Isabella Bird was one of the most adventurous women travelers of the 19th century with journeys to Tibet, Canada, Korea, Turkey, Hawaii, and Japan. A fascinating read.

THE RIVERS RAN EAST $16.95
By Leonard Clark
Clark is the original Indiana Jones, telling the breathtaking story of his search for the legendary El Dorado gold in the Amazon.

Spiritual Travel

THE SPIRITUAL GIFTS OF TRAVEL $16.95
The Best of Travelers' Tales
Edited by James O'Reilly and Sean O'Reilly
Favorite stories of transformation on the road that shows the myriad ways travel indelibly alters our inner landscapes.

PILGRIMAGE $16.95
Adventures of the Spirit
Edited by Sean O'Reilly & James O'Reilly
Introduction by Phil Cousineau

ForeWord Silver Medal Winner
— Travel Book of the Year

THE ROAD WITHIN $18.95
True Stories of Transformation and the Soul
Edited by Sean O'Reilly, James O'Reilly & Tim O'Reilly

Independent Publisher's Book Award
—Best Travel Book

THE WAY OF THE WANDERER $14.95
Discover Your True Self Through Travel
By David Yeadon
Experience transformation through travel with this delightful, illustrated collection by award-winning author David Yeadon.

A WOMAN'S PATH $16.95
Women's Best Spiritual Travel Writing
Edited by Lucy McCauley, Amy G. Carlson & Jennifer Leo
"A sensitive exploration of women's lives that have been unexpectedly and spiritually touched by travel experiences.... Highly recommended."
     —Library Journal

THE ULTIMATE JOURNEY $17.95
Inspiring Stories of Living and Dying
James O'Reilly, Sean O'Reilly & Richard Sterling
"A glorious collection of writings about the ultimate adventure. A book to keep by one's bedside—and close to one's heart."
     —Philip Zaleski, editor,
     The Best Spiritual Writing series

Special Interest

THE BEST TRAVELERS' TALES 2004 $16.95
True Stories from Around the World
Edited by James O'Reilly, Larry Habegger & Sean O'Reilly
The launch of a new annual collection presenting fresh, lively storytelling and compelling narrative to make the reader laugh, weep, and buy a plane ticket.

TESTOSTERONE PLANET $17.95
True Stories from a Man's World
Edited by Sean O'Reilly, Larry Habegger & James O'Reilly
Thrills and laughter with some of today's best writers: Sebastian Junger, Tim Cahill, Bill Bryson, and Jon Krakauer.

THE GIFT OF TRAVEL $14.95
The Best of Travelers' Tales
Edited by Larry Habegger, James O'Reilly & Sean O'Reilly
"Like gourmet chefs in a French market, the editors of Travelers' Tales pick, sift, and prod their way through the weighty shelves of contemporary travel writing, creaming off the very best."
—William Dalrymple, author of *City of Djinns*

DANGER! $17.95
True Stories of Trouble and Survival
Edited by James O'Reilly, Larry Habegger & Sean O'Reilly
"Exciting...for those who enjoy living on the edge or prefer to read the survival stories of others, this is a good pick."
     —Library Journal

365 TRAVEL $14.95
A Daily Book of Journeys, Meditations, and Adventures
Edited by Lisa Bach
An illuminating collection of travel wisdom and adventures that reminds us all of the lessons we learn while on the road.

THE GIFT OF RIVERS $14.95
True Stories of Life on the Water
Edited by Pamela Michael
Introduction by Robert Hass
...a soulful compendium of wonderful stories that illuminate, educate, inspire, and delight."
—David Brower,
Chairman of Earth Island Institute

FAMILY TRAVEL $17.95
The Farther You Go, the Closer You Get
Edited by Laura Manske
"This is family travel at its finest."
—*Working Mother*

LOVE & ROMANCE $17.95
True Stories of Passion on the Road
Edited by Judith Babcock Wylie
"A wonderful book to read by a crackling fire." —*Romantic Traveling*

THE GIFT OF BIRDS $17.95
True Encounters with Avian Spirits
Edited by Larry Habegger & Amy G. Carlson
"These are all wonderful, entertaining stories offering a *bird's-eye view!* of our avian friends."
—*Booklist*

A DOG'S WORLD $12.95
True Stories of Man's Best Friend on the Road
Edited by Christine Hunsicker
Introduction by Maria Goodavage

Travel Advice

THE PENNY PINCHER'S PASSPORT TO LUXURY TRAVEL $14.95
(2ND EDITION)
The Art of Cultivating Preferred Customer Status
By Joel L. Widzer
Completely updated and revised, this 2nd edition of the popular guide to traveling like the rich and famous without being either describes, both philosophically and in practical terms, how to obtain luxurious travel benefits by building relationships with airlines and other travel companies.

SAFETY AND SECURITY $12.95
FOR WOMEN WHO TRAVEL
By Sheila Swan & Peter Laufer
"An engaging book, with plenty of first-person stories about strategies women have used while traveling to feel safe but still find their way into a culture."
—*Chicago Herald*

THE FEARLESS SHOPPER $14.95
How to Get the Best Deals on the Planet
By Kathy Borrus
"Anyone who reads *The Fearless Shopper* will come away a smarter, more responsible shopper and a more curious, culturally attuned traveler."
—Jo Mancuso, *The Shopologist*

SHITTING PRETTY $12.95
How to Stay Clean and Healthy While Traveling
By Dr. Jane Wilson-Howarth
A light-hearted book about a serious subject for millions of travelers—staying healthy on the road—written by international health expert, Dr. Jane Wilson-Howarth.

GUTSY WOMEN $12.95
More Travel Tips and Wisdom for the Road
By Marybeth Bond
Second Edition
Packed with funny, instructive, and inspiring advice for women heading out to see the world.

GUTSY MAMAS $7.95
Travel Tips and Wisdom for Mothers on the Road
By Marybeth Bond
A delightful guide for mothers traveling with their children—or without them!

Destination Titles

ALASKA $18.95
Edited by Bill Sherwonit, Andromeda Romano-Lax, & Ellen Bielawski

AMERICA $19.95
Edited by Fred Setterberg

AMERICAN SOUTHWEST $17.95
Edited by Sean O'Reilly & James O'Reilly

AUSTRALIA $17.95
Edited by Larry Habegger

BRAZIL $17.95
Edited by Annette Haddad & Scott Doggett
Introduction by Alex Shoumatoff

CENTRAL AMERICA $17.95
Edited by Larry Habegger & Natanya Pearlman

CHINA $18.95
Edited by James O'Reilly, Larry Habegger & Sean O'Reilly

CUBA $17.95
Edited by Tom Miller

FRANCE $18.95
Edited by James O'Reilly, Larry Habegger & Sean O'Reilly

GRAND CANYON $17.95
Edited by Sean O'Reilly, James O'Reilly & Larry Habegger

GREECE $18.95
Edited by Larry Habegger, Sean O'Reilly & Brian Alexander

HAWAI'I $17.95
Edited by Rick & Marcie Carroll

HONG KONG $17.95
Edited by James O'Reilly, Larry Habegger & Sean O'Reilly

INDIA $18.95
Edited by James O'Reilly & Larry Habegger

IRELAND $18.95
Edited by James O'Reilly, Larry Habegger & Sean O'Reilly

ITALY $18.95
Edited by Anne Calcagno
Introduction by Jan Morris

JAPAN $17.95
Edited by Donald W. George & Amy G. Carlson

MEXICO $17.95
Edited by James O'Reilly & Larry Habegger

NEPAL $17.95
Edited by Rajendra S. Khadka

PARIS $18.95
Edited by James O'Reilly, Larry Habegger & Sean O'Reilly

PROVENCE $16.95
Edited by James O'Reilly & Tara Austen Weaver

SAN FRANCISCO $18.95
Edited by James O'Reilly, Larry Habegger & Sean O'Reilly

SPAIN $19.95
Edited by Lucy McCauley

THAILAND $18.95
Edited by James O'Reilly & Larry Habegger

TIBET $18.95
Edited by James O'Reilly & Larry Habegger

TURKEY $18.95
Edited by James Villers Jr.

TUSCANY $16.95
Edited by James O'Reilly & Tara Austen Weaver
Introduction by Anne Calcagno

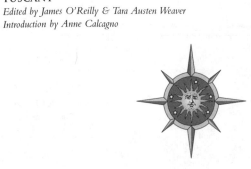

Footsteps Series

THE FIRE NEVER DIES $14.95
One Man's Raucous Romp Down the Road of Food,
Passion, and Adventure
By Richard Sterling
"Sterling's writing is like spitfire, foursquare and jazzy with
crackle...."   —*Kirkus Reviews*

ONE YEAR OFF $14.95
Leaving It All Behind for a Round-the-World Journey
with Our Children
By David Elliot Cohen
A once-in-a-lifetime adventure generously shared, from the
author/editor of *America 24/7* and *A Day in the Life of Africa*

THE WAY OF THE WANDERER $14.95
Discover Your True Self Through Travel
By David Yeadon
Experience transformation through travel with this delightful,
illustrated collection by award-winning author David Yeadon.

TAKE ME WITH YOU $24.00
A Round-the-World Journey to Invite a Stranger Home
By Brad Newsham
"Newsham is an ideal guide. His journey, at heart, is into
humanity."   —Pico Iyer, author of *The Global Soul*

KITE STRINGS OF THE SOUTHERN CROSS $14.95
A Woman's Travel Odyssey
By Laurie Gough   *ForeWord Silver Medal Winner*
Short-listed for the prestigious Thomas Cook Award, this is an   —*Travel Book of the Year*
exquisite rendering of a young woman's search for meaning.

                              ★ ✶ ★

THE SWORD OF HEAVEN $24.00
A Five Continent Odyssey to Save the World
By Mikkel Aaland
"Few books capture the soul of the road like The *Sword of
Heaven,* a sharp-edged, beautifully rendered memoir that will
inspire anyone."
      —Phil Cousineau, author of *The Art of Pilgrimage*

STORM $24.00
A Motorcycle Journey of Love, Endurance,   *ForeWord Gold Medal Winner*
and Transformation   —*Travel Book of the Year*
By Allen Noren
"Beautiful, tumultuous, deeply engaging and very satisfying.
Anyone who looks for truth in travel will find it here."   ★ ✶ ★
      —Ted Simon, author of Jupiter's Travels